HAVER-

Studies in Shinto Thought

Classics of Modern Japanese Thought and Culture

The Ways of Thinking of Eastern Peoples
Hajime Nakamura

A Study of Good
Kitaro Nishida

Climate and Culture: A Philosophical Study
Tetsuro Watsuji

Time and Eternity
Seiichi Hatano

Studies in Shinto Thought
Tsunetsugu Muraoka

The Japanese Character: A Cultural Profile
Nyozekan Hasegawa

An Inquiry into the Japanese Mind as Mirrored in Literature
Sokichi Tsuda

About our Ancestors: —The Japanese Family System
Kunio Yanagita

Japanese Spirituality
Daisetz Suzuki

A Historical Study of the Religious Development of Shinto
Genichi Kato

Studies in Shinto Thought

by
MURAOKA TSUNETSUGU

Translated
by
Delmer M. Brown
University of California, Berkeley
and
James T. Araki
University of California, Los Angeles

Greenwood Press
New York • Westport, Connecticut • London

Library of Congress Cataloging-in-Publication Data

Muraoka, Tsunetsugu, 1884-1946.
  Studies in Shinto thought.

  Selected translation of: Nihon shisōshi kenkyū.
  Reprint. Originally published: Tokyo : Japanese
National Commission for Unesco, 1964.
  Includes index.
  1. Philosophy, Japanese—History.   2. Shinto—
Doctrines—History.   I. Title.
B5241.M872513   1988   299′.5612   88-21311
ISBN 0-313-26555-0 (lib. bdg. : alk. paper)

British Library Cataloguing in Publication Data is available.

© Ministry of Education, Japan, 1964

All rights reserved. No portion of this book may be
reproduced, by any process or technique, without the
express written consent of the publisher.

Library of Congress Catalog Card Number: 88-21311
ISBN: 0-313-26555-0

First published in 1964

Reprinted in 1988 by Greenwood Press, Inc. jointly with
Yushodo Co., Ltd., Tokyo with the permission of the Ministry of
Education, Japan

Printed in the United States of America

The paper used in this book complies with the
Permanent Paper Standard issued by the National
Information Standards Organization (Z39.48-1984).

10 9 8 7 6 5 4 3 2 1

Dr. MURAOKA TSUNETSUGU (1884–1946)

Unesco, at the 9th session of its General Conference held in New Delhi in 1956, decided to launch the Major Project on Mutual Appreciation of Eastern and Western Cultural Values.

In accordance with the decision this Commission has been carrying on, since 1958, within the framework of the Project, a programme of publishing modern Japanese philosophical works translated into foreign languages.

We have so far brought out the following four books: "The Ways of Thinking of Eastern Peoples" by Hajime Nakamura; "A Study of Good" by Kitaro Nishida; "A Climate" by Tetsuro Watsuji; and "Time and Eternity" by Seiichi Hatano. The present volume is the fifth of the series.

This volume is compiled of selected articles on Shinto by the late Dr. Tsunetsugu Muraoka, which are contained in a series of his books entitled "Nihon Shisōshi Kenkyu" (Studies on the History of Japanese Thought.)

It is the hope of this Commission that this volume will prove useful to those foreign scholars and students who wish to get familiar with Japanese thought.

Our acknowledgement is due to Prof. Ichiro Ishida of Tōhoku University and his colleagues who have cooperated in the compilation of this volume and also to the translators, Dr. Delmer M. Brown and Dr. James T. Araki.

It should be noted that in the text of this volume the Japanese system of writing the family name first has been followed for Japanese names.

February, 1964

Japanese National Commission
for Unesco

Contents

Translators' Preface I
Introduction: Muraoka Tsunetsugu, the Man and his Work III

Chapter
I   Characteristic Features of Japanese Shinto:
    Japan's Uniqueness in Oriental Thought 1
II Moral Consciousness and its Development in
    Ancient Shinto 51
III Scholarly Nature of National Learning 71
IV Kamo Mabuchi and Motoori Norinaga as Thinkers 95
V   Changes in Ideas about 'the Concealed and
    the Mysterious' in Restoration Shinto 171
VI Hirata Shinto and the Ideological Control of the
    Meiji Restoration — Down to the Time of the Offi-
    cial Recognition of Religious Freedom 203
VII Separation of State and Religion in Shinto:
    Its Historical Significance 230
VIII On Methods of Research in Japanese Intellectual
    History 245

INDEX i

Translators' Preface

The decision of the Japanese National Commission for UNESCO to publish an English translation of studies by Muraoka Tsunetsugu may come as a surprise to the Western reader, for Muraoka is not well known outside Japan. But to those historians, Japanese or Western, who are concerned with the process of change in Japanese thought and belief, the choice is inescapable. Muraoka's analysis of the special characteristics of Shinto belief and morality, and especially his comparative study of the ideas and beliefs of principal participants in the Shinto revival of the pre-Meiji era, have made him Japan's most distinguished scholar of Shinto thought. Few will deny that he has deepened our understanding of the "hard core" of Japanese intellectual and religious experience.

In translating these eight Muraoka studies, our most serious difficulties stem from the author's preoccupation with that which is truly unique in Japanese Kami worship, and by his assumption that the reader would be familiar with the religious history of Japan. The text is therefore filled with words for which there is no exact English equivalent and with passages that can be understood only by the specialist. We decided not to leave untranslatable terms in Japanese, but to use the nearest equivalent — striving for consistency and placing the romanized form of the original Japanese in parentheses when the word or phrase first appeared. In cases of a particularly unique school or concept, the English equivalent was capitalized. Thus *kokugaku* and *kokutai* were rendered as National Learning and Nation Body.

In places where the author seemed to assume specialized knowledge, we attempted to supply brief explanatory notes. If he referred to a book that has been translated into English, we added a reference to the most recent translation; and we inserted birth-death dates after the names of historical figures. We also tried to show where the longer quotations could be found, but this was sometimes impossible, either because the author had not indicated the book from which the quotation was taken, or because the book had not been published or was not available in the University of California libraries. All additions by the translators, whether in the text or the notes, have been placed within brackets.

We are particularly grateful to Robert Backus for assistance in locating quotations, correcting numerous errors, and making valuable suggestions for improving the translation; and to the Center for Japanese Studies at the University of California for supporting our joint endeavor with clerical and financial assistance.

February, 1963

Delmer M. Brown
James T. Araki

Muraoka Tsunetsugu

The Man and his Work

Muraoka Tsunetsugu was born in the Asakusa district of Tokyo in 1884. He attended Kaisei Middle School in Tokyo while staying at the home of a relative, Sasaki Nobutsuna. Sasaki was a leading figure in the *Chikuhaku-kai*, a society devoted to the study and appreciation of Japanese classical literature. From this association with Sasaki, Muraoka became strongly oriented to the study of native literature and gained an abiding interest in the study of intellectual history. Upon the completion of his secondary education, he entered Waseda University where he specialized in the study of western philosophy under the guidance of Hatano Seiichi. Through this study he developed a special interest in modern western methods of research. The training Muraoka received at Waseda influenced him when, in later years, he undertook to investigate, and wrote on, problems in Japanese intellectual history. His close association with Sasaki Nobutsuna and Hatano Seiichi help to account for two fundamental aspects in Muraoka's research: the Japanese-thought content, and the western methodological approach to analysis and interpretation.

Muraoka's later academic training reveals a strong interest in religion. After graduating from Waseda University in 1906, he spent two years at the German Institute of Protestant Theology in Tokyo. This was probably a result of Professor Hatano's own interest in Christianity. The training received at the Institute is related to a later preoccupation with Shinto, and the religious aspects of National Learning (*kokugaku*), and to a tendency to use, in later years, western theological methods.

After working on the *German-Japan Post* — a German newspaper in Yokohama — between 1908 and 1914, Muraoka entered the academic profession. At first he taught western philosophy at Waseda University and English at the Japanese Military Academy. In 1919 he received a position at the Hiroshima Higher Normal School and was promoted, in the following year, to the rank of professor. In 1922, he was appointed to the Chair of Japanese Intellectual History at Tōhoku Imperial University in Sendai, where he remained until his retirement in 1946. While a professor at Tōhoku University, he often delivered lectures on problems of Japanese intellectual history at the Tokyo Imperial University and the Tokyo University of Arts and Sciences. His sudden death in 1946, soon after retirement, was a great loss for the academic community of Japan.

Muraoka's work falls into four general categories: (1) Western philosophy; (2) Christianity; (3) Japanese intellectual history and National Learning; and (4) the methodology of Japanese intellectual history. Although there is some overlapping, the main part of his work in the field of western philosophy was done prior to his appointment at Hiroshima. Some work of considerable importance, however, was published in later years. His most serious work in the field of Christianity was carried out during his early years at Tōhoku Imperial University. And his last twenty years were devoted completely to the third and fourth fields. Since his greatest achievements were in Japanese intellectual history, seven of the eight chapters in this volume are devoted to studies in that area.

During the period of Muraoka's interest in western philosophy, he translated into Japanese an English version of A. Sabatier's *Esquisse d'une philosophie de la religion d'apaès la psychologie et l'histoire* (1897), and also W. Windelband's *Geshichte der neueren Philosophie* (1878–1880). He gave a special lecture, "Studies in Heraclitus", at a conference of the Waseda Philosophical Association, and contributed an article on Greek philosophy to the *Tetsugaku daijiten* (Dictionary of Philosophy), published by Iwanami in 1919. In 1921 he lectured on Plato's idea of the state at Hiroshima Higher Normal School. Thereafter, his interests turned gradually from philosophy to religious thought — first to that of the West, and then to that of Japan.

Muraoka did not make the study of western philosophy his life work, nor did his research in this field have much effect on the world of scholarship. But it was significant for its great influence on the character of his later work.

As can be seen from Muraoka's decision to attend the German Institute of Protestant Theology — after graduation from Waseda University — he seems to have had an early and deep interest in religious matters. Both his translation of Sabatier's book, in 1907, and his writing of an article, in 1915, for the *Tetsugaku zasshi* (Journal of Philosophy) entitled "Fukko shintō ni okeru yūmei-kan no hensen" (Changes in Ideas about 'the Concealed and the Mysterious' in Restoration Shinto) show an early interest in religious questions. (The latter study is included in this volume as Chapter 5.) His study of Christianity led to an article entitled "Hirata Atsutane no shingaku ni okeru yasokyō no eikyō" (The Influence of Christianity upon the Theology of Hirata Atsutane), published in the *Geimon* (Arts and Letters) in 1920. The highpoint of his interest in Christianity seems to have come, however, during his stay in Europe between 1922 and 1924. Much of the two years abroad was spent collecting materials on Christianity. At the British Museum, for example, he transcribed a Japanese translation of a Portuguese religious tract, the *Guia do Pecador,* that had been used by the Jesuits for their missionary work in Japan during the sixteenth century. This transcription was used when the tract was published in the *Nippon koten zensho* (Collection of Ancient Japanese Classics). Muraoka also brought back with him, for the Tōhoku Imperial University, a work known as the Catalogue of Bibles in Chinese. In 1942 he contributed an article on "Gya do pekadōru kō" (Thoughts on the Guia do Pecador) to the *Shisō* (Thought). Between 1925 and 1929 he published a number of articles dealing with Christianity, and in 1926 edited and published *Kirishitan bungaku shō* (Selection from Christian Literature). Muraoka stopped publishing in the field of Christianity after he edited the Japanese version of the *Guia do Pecador* for a volume which appeared in 1929. Although he retained an interest in the subject, his subsequent writings were principally in the field of Shinto thought.

Beginning with his early connection with the *Chikuhaku-kai* Muraoka had a continuing interest in Japanese intellectual history. Even while a student at Waseda University, he became impressed by the writings of Hirata Atsutane. It was logical, then, that he should also become interested in the thought of Motoori Norinaga, Hirata's teacher. He sought out the religious element in Motoori's thought and in 1911 completed *Motoori Norinaga*. This has been regarded as one of the most valuable works in the field of Japanese intellectual history. After 1929, when he focused his efforts on the investigation of Japanese religious thought, he turned first to the Shinto thought of Hirata and other National Learning scholars of the Tokugawa period.

Prior to Muraoka's scholarship, only popular essays on National Learning — little more than briefs for a kind of conservative nationalism — had been written by others. But Muraoka undertook a thorough investigation of National Learning in the context of Japanese cultural history, paying careful attention to the reliability of documentary evidence, and to research methods. As a result of his emphasis on method and philosophical content, he defined a new field of historical inquiry designated *Nippon shisō shi* (Japanese intellectual history, or the history of Japanese thought).

His attempts to understand the entire context of problems in Shinto thought led to studies in such related fields as Bushidō, the Mito school of Learning, and Dutch Learning. He studied the scholarship of such Confucianists as Yamaga Sokō, Ogyū Sorai, Yamazaki Ansai, Arai Hakuseki and Ninomiya Sontoku. He wrote about the Dutch Learning scholar Shiba Kōkan and the British Japanologist B. H. Chamberlain. And he made detailed analyses of important Japanese classics like the *Kojiki*, the *Nihongi*, the *Kogo Shūi, the Man'yōshū*, the *Genji monogatari*, the *Makura no sōshi*, the *Gukan shō*, the *Tsurezuregusa*, and the *Jinnō shōtō ki*.

Muraoka's earlier studies of Shinto thought usually dealt with rather specific questions, and all points were fully supported by quotations from primary sources; but his later studies tended to deal with larger problems — syntheses in which he attempted to see the whole of a given intellectual development. Chapters 2, 4, and 5 of this volume — studies that were all written before 1929 — fall into the first category; while chapters 1, 3, 6, and 7 — all written after 1934 — are in the second. (The chapters are arranged in chronological order of subject.) Other articles written in the later period of interest in synthesis include: " Chūko ni okeru kyōyōkan " (The Concept of Education in the Heian Period) published in 1940 in the *Iwanami kōza: rinrigaku* (Iwanami Lecture: Ethics) and " Gekokujō to bushidō " (The Disrespect of Low-ranking People for their Superiors, and Bushidō) published in 1941 in the same series. Muraoka's ultimate objective was to write a general synthesis of the whole of Japanese intellectual history. He experimented with patterns of synthesis in his lectures at Tōhoku Imperial University and planned to write an over-all synthesis after retirement. He died before the task was taken up. After his death a committee, of which I was a member, was established to publish his notes. One of the volumes, *Nippon shisō-shi gaisetsu* (Outline of Japanese Intellectual History), published in 1962 by Sōbun-sha, indicates the direction in which he was moving.

Studies in the field of methodology, other than the one included in this volume as Chapter 8, include; (1) " Kokubungaku no chūshakuteki kenkyū ni tsuite " (On Interpretative Studies of Japanese Literature) published in 1934 in *Bungaku* (Literature); (2) " Shika to shite no Motoori Norinaga " (Motoori Norinaga as a Historian) published in 1935 in *Hompō shigaku-shi ronsō* (Collection of Studies on history of Japanese Historiography); and (3) " Nippon seishinshi hōhōron " (Methodology of the History of 'Japanese Spirit').

In general, intellectual history was considered by Muraoka to be the ideological side of cultural history, and to be a logical approach to cultural history before the history of scholarship and the history of philosophy had become defined as separate disciplines. He felt that the groundwork for a proper study of intellectual history had been laid by National Learning scholars — particularly by the work of Motoori Norinaga — and by the German philological studies of the nineteenth century, especially those of August Boeckh. In his own attempt to develop Japanese intellectual history, Muraoka endeavored to discard the normative aspects of National Learning, and to extend its historical empiricism by applying the philological methods of Boeckh.

While his achievements as a historian are important, his greatest contributions were as a pioneer in empirical research, and as the founder of *Nippon shisō-shi*, a new discipline in Japanese scholarship. In the light of more recent advances, we can detect flaws in certain of Muraoka's methods and findings, but his work will long remain important for the continuing development of this new field.

I have never had the opportunity of meeting Professor Muraoka, and was not appointed to the chair he formaly held until twelve years after his death. I have had to rely, therefore, on Dr. Isezō Umezawa and Professor Ryūkichi Harada — students of Muraoka — for assistance in writing this introduction.

Ichirō Ishida

Professor of Japanese Intellectual History
Faculty of Arts and Letters
Tōhoku University
Sendai, Japan

Chapter I

Characteristic Features of Japanese Shinto: Japan's Uniqueness in Oriental Thought[1]

Shintoism is a national religion with a long history—beginning in remote antiquity and continuing on down to the present. It has been associated with three great world religions: Confucianism, Buddhism, and Christianity; but its association with Confucianism and Buddhism has been especially close. This is why Shintoism has become a problem in Oriental thought. Shintoism has a ritualistic, as well as doctrinal and intellectual, side. The former is the subject of study in what is called "Kami history" (*Jingi shi*), and the latter is dealt with in "Shinto history" (*Shintō shi*). An investigation of the unique features of rites would probably lead to interesting problems in Orientology, especially in the field of folklore. But I will not deal with rites here, for my interests are on the side of doctrine and thought. And it seems appropriate to approach these interests in terms of Oriental thought. By way of introduction let me start, then, with a discussion of the meaning of the term "Shinto."

---

1) [First published in *Iwanami kōza*: *Tōyō shichō* (Iwanami Lectures: Oriental Thought) in May of 1936 and included in Muraoka Tsunetsugu, *Zoku Nihon shisō shi kenkyū* (Studies in Japanese Intellectual History, Continued) (Tokyo, Iwanami Shoten; 1939), 419–68.]

1. "Shinto": Definition and Connotation

Actually the word "Shinto" appears to have emerged quite late. In ancient times "Kami" was an honorific term for sacred objects having awesome potency (*iryoku*) —whether in heaven, on earth, or among men. The word "*Kamigoto*" referred to the worship of these Kami. But in no case was the word "Kami" joined with "way" to produce the word "Shinto" or Way of Kami. In those early times "way" meant no more than a road or path; and it had not yet become an abstract religious or moral term. "Shinto," originally a Chinese word, was used in Japan only after the introduction and spread of Chinese culture to distinguish the Way of Kami (Shintoism) from the Way of Buddha (Buddhism) and the Way of Confucius (Confucianism).

The three earliest examples of the use of the word "Shinto" are all found in the *Nihongi* [completed in 720 A.D.].[1] The first appears in the section dealing with the reign of Emperor Yōmei (586–587): "The Emperor believed in the Buddhist doctrine and revered Shinto." The second is in the chapter on the reign of Emperor Kōtoku (646–654): "The Emperor ... revered Buddhist doctrine and slighted Shinto, as was indicated by his cutting down the trees of the Iku-kuni-tama Shrine." And the third reference is in the same Emperor Kōtoku chapter where, in an Imperial Edict (*mikotonori*) of the fourth month of 647, we find this phrase: "I [the Sun Goddess] decree that my children, being as Kami (*kannagara*), shall rule." A footnote for this reference explains *kannagara* as follows: "[*Kannagara* means] to follow Shinto, or to possess Shinto in one's self."[2] This footnote is thought, however, to have been added at a later time; and the second reference, according to Kawamura Hidene [1723–1792] in his *Shoki*

---

1) [Translated by W. G. Aston, *Nihongi, Chronicles of Japan from the Earliest Times to A.D. 697* (London, 1896).]
2) [Aston II, 106, 195, 226.]

Shikkai (Collected Annotations on the *Nihongi*), is considered to be a critical note taken, later on, from the *Nihongi shiki*.[1] If we throw out the second and third references, the first becomes the earliest authentic use of the word "Shinto" in the *Nihongi*. And since "Shinto" does not appear at all in the *Kojiki* [completed in 712 A.D.],[2] we have no choice but to attempt to grasp its early meaning from this one example. But it must be admitted that with only one reference we cannot understand the term precisely.

In recent times the view has been expressed that the word "Shinto," in this first reference, referred to "Taoism," but this cannot be said with certainty. The Taoist term "*shen-tao*" [written with the same characters as "Shinto"] originally meant "the law of Heaven and Earth," as is indicated in the following passage under the hexagram "*kuan*" (contemplate) in the *I-ching* (Book of Changes): "When the 'divine way' (*shen-tao*) of Heaven is contemplated, the four seasons do not vary. When the sages give instruction in accordance with the 'divine way,' all under heaven submit." But it is clear that "Shinto," as used in the Emperor Yōmei chapter of the *Nihongi*, did not have this meaning. Even if "Shinto" was taken from the *Book of Changes* its connotation for the Japanese was different. Without doubt, the term in Japan referred to indigenous Kami rites and ceremonies in contradistinction to Buddhism, which had been recently introduced from the continent.

But we should also recognize that while "Shinto" was used to distinguish Kami rites and ceremonies from Buddhism and Confucianism, a somewhat theoretical or even abstract meaning—over and beyond reference to Kami ceremony—was soon added. This was an early indication of later historical developments. In the Heian Era

---

1) [Notes of lectures on the *Nihongi* given in the year 812. The original is not extant, but excerpts were included in the *Shaku Nihongi* written by Urabe Kanetaka during the Kamakura Period.]

2) [Translated by B. H. Chamberlain, *Ko-ji-ki or Records of Ancient Matters* (2nd ed., London; 1932).]

[784–1185] "Shinto" was used often in the *Shoku Nihongi* (Continuation of the *Nihongi*)[1] and the *Fusō ryakki* (Abbreviated Record of Ancient Japan). In those accounts the word referred only to Kami rites and Kami shrines. But it began to take on doctrinal meaning at the end of the Heian Era, or at the beginning of the Kamakura [1185–1333], when indigenous beliefs and practices became fused with Buddhism to take the form of Dual Shinto (*ryōbu shintō*). This doctrinal element was strengthened by the emergence of Shinto theology during and after the North-South Court Era [1336–1392], a development that culminated in the Unique Shinto (*yuitsu shintō*) of the Yoshida family and that led to the Confucian Shinto (*jugaku shintō*) of early Tokugawa [1600–1868].

In the Restoration Shinto (*fukko shintō*), also called Ancient-Learning Shinto (*kogaku shintō*), which developed in the middle of the Tokugawa Era, attempts were made to cleanse Shinto doctrine of Confucian and Buddhist ingredients. In this attempt to restore Shinto to its ancient form, the central aim was to eliminate Chinese influences. Consequently the use of "Shinto," being a word that was easily confused with the Way of Heaven (*t'ien-tao*) as expounded in the *Book of Changes,* was avoided. In its place Ancient Way (*kodō*) was used. People like Motoori Norinaga [1730–1801] explained that Ancient Way was: "The Way first created and supported by the Imperial ancestral Kami."[2] Hirata Atsutane [1776–1843] used the word "Shinto" in his *Kamōsho* (Rebuke of Error), an attack on Dazai Jun's [1680–1747] *Bendōsho* (Definition of the Way). But later on, Hirata favored the term Ancient Way. In *Zoku Shintō taii* (Outline of Vulgar Shinto) he dealt with the Buddhistic Shinto and the Confucian Shinto that had emerged after the Kamakura Era; but the book

---

1) [Translated in part by J. B. Snellen, "Shoku Nihongi Chronicles of Japan, continued A.D. 697–791 (Books I–VI)," *Transactions of the Asiatic Society of Japan,* 2nd Ser. XI (1934), 151–239 and XIV (1937), 209–278. Hereafter the *Transactions* will be cited as TASJ.]

2) [*Naobi no mitama* (The Spirit of Straightening), *Kokumin shisō sōsho* (Source Series of National Thought), X (Tokyo, 1932), 115.]

in which he advanced his own views of Shinto was entitled *Kodō taii* (Outline of the Ancient Way). His Ancient Way was nothing but ancient Shinto. In the Hirata School, this was referred to as the "original doctrine," the "true doctrine," or "the great doctrine." In ordinary official usage today a distinction is made between "Shinto" and "shrines" (*jinja*). As everyone knows, Shinto includes only the various founder-established sects developed as popular faiths after the middle of the Tokugawa Era [and *jinja* refers to the others].

The belated emergence of the word "Shinto," and the various efforts to avoid and restrict its usage, were based upon special conditions that do not force us to revise the definition presented at the beginning of this article. The meaning of Shinto as the indigenous religion of Japan — as distinguished from other religions such as Buddhism, Confucianism, and Christianity — is generally accepted in academic circles. This was the sense in which the term was used in books written by Europeans who first came to Japan. For example, the Jesuits — the first Christian missionaries — reported that the religious faith of Kami (*cami*) and Shinto (*Xinto*) existed in Japan as something distinct from Buddhism and Confucianism. Later on, in the *History of Japan* (1727), written by Engelbert Kaempfer [1651–1716] who came to Japan at the end of the seventeenth century, an outline of Japanese religion was presented. He divided it up into Shintoism, Buddhism, and Confucianism. And Shinto was defined as "the old religion of idolworship of the Japanese."

When considering Shinto as a subject of scholarly investigation, we must remember that the word refers to the popular, indigenous faith of Japan as distinct from Buddhism, Confucianism, and other religions, and that it includes not only the ancient Shinto which developed before the word "Shinto" was used, but also Ancient-Learning Shinto and Founder Shinto (*kyōso shintō*). And so we might say that Shinto is the indigenous religion of Japan, that it emerged in Japan's ancient past, and that after about the sixth century it was not only thrown into contact with Buddhism, Confucianism, Christianity and other foreign religions, but was changed and developed as a result of positive and negative influences and inspirations from these foreign faiths.

As is suggested by this definition of Shinto, the faith appeared, historically, in various forms. Let us therefore look at the subject now in different periods. The culture of our country passed through five periods — the ancient, the Nara, the Heian, the medieval, and the Tokugawa — before entering the modern period that began with the Meiji Era [1868–1912]. Each of these periods had its characteristic features, but if we look at Japanese history from the point of view of the foreign importations which have affected Japanese culture, we detect three distinct ages: the ancient age before the introduction of Confucianism, Buddhism, or any other foreign cultural influence; the classical-medieval age, after the introduction of Confucianism and Buddhism and when the influence of these was particularly strong; and finally the Tokugawa age, which was characterized by the development of Confucianism and by a parallel reaction to it. Shinto took different forms in these three ages.

In the simple ancient age, before the introduction of Confucianism and Buddhism, Shinto took a form which is designated " ancient Shinto "; and in the classical-medieval age it became " Buddho-Shinto." The latter, based on the doctrine that various Kami were "manifestations of original Buddhas " (*honji suijaku*), appeared as the Dual Shinto of Tendai, Shingon, Hokke, and other sects of Buddhism. This " manifestation of original Buddhas " doctrine emerged originally from the pantheistic thought of Buddhism. Although the doctrine was expounded for the convenience of propagation, it was also a natural outlook as far as Buddhism was concerned. Accordingly, we might well describe it as Shintoistic Buddhism rather than Buddho-Shinto. The beginnings of this Dual Shinto, or Buddho-Shinto, can be seen as early as the Nara Era; but it gradually developed after that and was established systematically during the Kamakura Era.

After Dual Shinto there gradually appeared, in the medieval period, Shinto doctrines which, although still colored by Buddhist influence, represented an independent development. In these doctrines the "manifestation of original Buddhas" idea was reversed: now Kami were considered the "original" and Buddhas the "manifestation." For the first time, lines of Shinto theology were formed. The principal ones were: (1) the Outer Shrine Shintoism (*gegū shintō*) fostered by the Outer Shrine of Ise; (2) the Shintoism of Kitabatake Chikafusa [1293–1354], whose family fell heir to the Outer Shrine theology; (3) the Shintoism of Ichijō Kaneyoshi [1402–1481]; and (4) the Unique Shintoism of Yoshida Kanetomo [1435–1511].

Ise Shintoism, or Outer Shrine Shintoism, arose in the Outer Shrine of Ise and stood in opposition to the Shintoism of Ise's Inner Shrine. It included various ideas and thoughts focused on a trinity theology by which Toyo-uke no Ō-kami of the Outer Shrine was associated with Kuni-toko-tachi no Mikoto and Ame no Mi-naka-nushi no Mikoto. Several points in this doctrine are worthy of note. Its canon, the *Gobusho* (The Five Books), is significant in the history of Shintoism, even if it was a forgery and has no factual value. The Shinto doctrines of Chikafusa emerged, in a sense, from the *Gobusho*. Even though his doctrines have many Buddhist influences, essentially they express the ancient Shinto spirit. Imbe Masamichi, the author of *Shindai kuketsu* (Oral Traditions of the Age of Kami), lived at about the time of Chikafusa. We know little of Masamichi's life, but his Shinto thought, as gleaned from this book, parallels that of Chikafusa. And among the Shinto doctrines of the medieval era, his stands out as the one least influenced by Buddhism.

In the Shinto doctrines of Ichijō Kaneyoshi, the most eminent scholar of his day and the author of *Nihongi sanso* (Commentaries on the *Nihongi*), Confucian and Buddhist ingredients were conspicuous. But Yoshida Kanetomo, the perfecter of the Yoshida Shinto that had been transmitted in the Yoshida family since its founding, worked to emancipate Shinto from its long dependence on Dual Shinto. And it was in this spirit that he coined the term Unique Shinto. Nevertheless, there were strong Buddhist strains at central points in his doctrine, and so it is classified as "medieval."

The first new form of Shintoism to appear in the Tokugawa Era was Confucian Shinto, started by Fujiwara Seika [1561–1619], Hayashi Razan [1583–1657], and other Confucian scholars of that day. These scholars destroyed the old Shinto subservience to Buddhism with a secular spirit that was directed at separating Tokugawa culture from Buddhism. In reacting against Buddhism, they took much from Confucianism.

The second form of Tokugawa Shintoism was a type of Confucian Shinto that emerged out of medieval Shintoism, and that was distinct from the thought and activities of professional Confucianists. Examples of this are found in the teachings of Watarai Nobuyoshi [1615–1690], who inherited the Outer Shrine theology, and Kikkawa Koretari [1616–1694], who was in the Unique Shinto tradition. Their schools were like Confucian Shintoism in their anti-Buddhism; and Confucian elements were quite conspicuous in their doctrines. But in their expressions of religious sentiment, and purity of belief, Watarai and Kikkawa differed sharply from the Confucianists.

The Suiga Shinto of Yamazaki Ansai [1618–1682] brought Confucian Shinto to completion, in both doctrine and belief. It was a great power in the intellectual circles of the Tokugawa Era. Since Ansai had moved into Shinto from Chu Hsi [1130–1200] learning, there was much Chu Hsi philosophy in his thinking about Shinto. His monistic theory of Heaven and man, and his concept of absolute reverence for the Emperor, stand — religiously and scholastically — at the pinnacle of Confucian Shinto.

In the meantime, antiquarian movements of the late seventeenth century appeared within Confucian Learning first with the work of Itō Jinsai [1627–1705] and Ogyū Sorai [1666–1728], and in Japanese Learning with Keichū [1640–1701] and Kada Azumamaro [1669–

1736]. The movements were associated with the study of philology, the study of ancient classics, and what was called Ancient Learning (*kogaku*). The purpose was to understand accurately the culture of ancient times by seizing the pure meaning of ancient classics through philological research, and by completely eliminating all later distortions and forced analogies. On the side of Shinto, this meant attempting to understand ancient beliefs and practices that had existed in Japan before the introduction of Buddhism and Confucianism — beliefs and practices that were free of all subsequent Buddhist and Confucian coloration. These antiquarian scholars looked for ancient Shintoism in the "Age of Kami" (*kamiyo*) books of the *Kojiki* and the *Nihongi* and in the early liturgies (*norito*).[1] The Ancient-Learning-Shinto of Motoori Norinaga, who had fallen heir to the *Man'yōshū*[2] Learning (*Man'yōgaku*) of Kamo Mabuchi [1697–1769], arose from a desire to revive ancient Shinto. From what has already been said it is probably clear that this Ancient-Learning Shinto was, academically, just the opposite of the Suiga Shinto [of Yamazaki Ansai]. Such theorizing as is seen in Suiga Shinto's monistic concept of heaven and man was consistently and rightly attacked by Motoori as unscholarly and absolutely impermissible in the light of textual interpretation. Thus Ancient-Learning Shinto was brought to completion by Motoori, who realized fully its anti-Confucian and anti-Buddhist objectives.

That which followed Ancient-Learning Shinto was Hirata Shinto. While Hirata Shinto belonged to Ancient-Learning Shinto, it was for various reasons not identical with the Motoori variety. Theologically, Hirata Shinto was further developed; and it had its own distinctive elements. The principal ones were its tendency toward monotheism

---

1) [Early liturgies have been translated in Donald L. Philippi: *Norito, A New Translation of the Ancient Japanese Ritual Prayers* (Tokyo, 1959).]
2) [The *Man'yōshū* (Myriad Leaves) is the earliest anthology of Japanese poetry, compiled in ca. 759. The bulk of the 4,500-odd poems belong to the seventh and early eighth centuries. The entire anthology has been translated by Jan L. Pierson, *The Manyōshū* (Leiden; 1929–49), 7 vols.]

and its eschatological character. It should be pointed out, too, that there were new Christian elements, which had actually come into Japan through books written by Father Matteo Ricci [1552–1610] who had propagated Christianity in China toward the end of the Ming Period [1368–1662]. From among the adherents of Hirata Shinto, the disciples of Hirata Atsutane, there emerged several notable thinkers.

In contradistinction to the Shinto touched upon above — Shinto which was connected with scholarship, with the study of the ancient classics, and with the study of Confucianism or Budhism — various Shinto sects emerged which were not grounded in scholarship but on the religious experience of individual founders. Chronologically, these "founder sects" coincided with Ancient-Learning Shinto and Hirata Shinto. But in contrast to the various Shinto movements mentioned above — movements which were initiated by intellectuals — the "founder sects" were based among the common people. The principal ones were: the Kurozumi, the Konkō, the Tenri, and the Misogi. There were also mountain sects: the Mitake, the Jikkō, and the Fusō. And quasi-Ancient-Learning Shinto sects: Jingū, Taisha, Shūsei, Taisei, Shinshū, and Shinri. These sects gradually acquired independent strength during and after the closing years of the Tokugawa Era. These are the thirteen sects that exist today and that are usually referred to as "Shinto," as distinguished from "*jinja*" (those served by persons connected with the Hirata and Motoori schools). In addition, there are various sects which are bracketed as Vulgar Shinto (*zoku shintō*). Since they too evolved after the middle of the Tokugawa Era and were directed at the common people, they can be thought of as being similar to Founder Shinto.

From what has already been said it is clear that each form of Shinto — from ancient Shinto to Founder Shinto — had its own individuality. Some sects were even opposed to, or incompatible with, others. It was natural that some should reject other sects and assert themselves. Consequently, if we were to concentrate on the individual qualities of each form of Shinto, it would be difficult, if not impossible, to identify the special characteristics of Shinto as a whole. The character of Shinto as a whole should be sought for in the characteristics that are common — regardless of individual differences — to all forms of Shinto and that distinguish Shintoism from Confucianism, Buddhism, and Christianity. Externally, various forms of Shintoism have been influenced — directly and indirectly — by Confucianism, Buddhism, and Christianity; and, internally, various changes have occurred in the individual character of those forms. But there are some common qualities which set Shinto apart from foreign religions. Of course it is natural that Shinto should have its special character. And it is my objective to clarify this special character, principally in the areas of doctrine and thought.

There are three main points that can be made about the special character of Shinto: its *kōkoku shugi* (Imperial-Country-ism); its realism; and its *meijō shugi* (brightness-prity-ism). The first is Japanese nationalism focused upon the Imperial Family. The second reveres reality, standing on reality and not disregarding reality — this is of course not to be equated with anti-idealism. The third upholds the immaculate in the sense that there is reverence for the bright and the pure. Now I would like to search for the meaning of these three characteristics by investigating their principal manifestations in the various forms of Shinto.

2. *The First Characteristic: Kōkoku shugi*

By *kōkoku shugi* it is proclaimed, first of all, that Japan is ruled by an Emperor who is descended in one line, for ages eternal, from a Kami ancestor; and that there is an identity of Emperor and state. This idea is quite unique — whether we think of Confucianism, Buddhism, or Christianity — and there is no doubt but that it is common to the various forms of Shinto.

Now in moving to a somewhat detailed treatment, I submit that a particularly important question is: to what extent is this idea rooted in ancient Shinto? More precisely, how deeply was the idea implanted in the thought of the ancient Japanese before they were subjected to Confucian and Buddhist influences? In order to answer this question we must probe the myths of the *Kojiki*. Even though the *Kojiki* was compiled in the Nara Era, as a compilation of legend to be used for reciting,[1] it includes — especially in the Age-of-Kami legends of the first book — thoughts of the ancient Japanese people. Since the Age-of-Kami legends emerged out of the consciousness of the ancients, we can see well, in the elements and composition of these legends, the earliest ideas, thoughts, and ideals of the Japanese. Of course, these Age-of-Kami legends are by no means religious or moral classics, nor are they political treatises. Consequently, religious, moral, and political matters are not dealt with clearly. Rather, the search must be conducted in shadowy paths. And yet we need not resort to fancies based on individual preferences. In order to investigate and clarify this early thought, we should consider, first of all, the structure of the *Kojiki*.

The *Kojiki* is broken up into three books. The first is devoted to the legends of the Age of Kami; and the second and third cover the period from Emperor Jimmu to Empress Suiko. Since the *Kojiki* was designed to treat the history of the state and the Imperial clan, it is logical to consider the legends of the Age of Kami as the source of this history. But, to move on, how should we view the legends of the Age of Kami?

The Age of Kami book of the *Kojiki*, according to Motoori's *Kojiki den* (Commentary on the *Kojiki*), has forty-three sections. These sections fall naturally into three groups. The first group is made up of the seventeen sections from the story about the origin of Heaven and earth to the one about the banishment of Susa-no-o no Mikoto. The second group is made up of the twelve sections from the myth about the great eight-headed serpent to the one about

---

1) [See page 52.]

the descendants of Ō-kuni-nushi no Kami. And the third group consists of the fourteen sections from the story about "the descent to earth of the Heavenly Grandson" (*tenson kōrin*) to the one about Ugaya-fukiaezu no Mikoto. These three myth groups, in terms of setting, are designated the Plain of High Heaven (*Takamagahara*) myths, the Izumo myths, and the Tsukushi myths. Each group takes place on a different stage and has its own independent lineage. The three groups must correspond to three major stages in the formation of the Age-of-Kami myths.

But the three stages are not merely an evolution of events, but rather a development of an idea. It is this idea which binds the three myth groups together; and that idea is none other than the concept of one great Kami personality: Ama-terasu Ō-mi-kami, or the Sun Goddess. According to the *Kojiki* and the *Nihongi*, the Sun Goddess has a dual nature: she is a sun Kami and, at the same time, the ancestral Kami of the Imperial Family. The duality is revealed in myths about her birth, and in her various Kami attributes. It would seem that since the sun, the greatest reality of the universe, is identified with the ancestral Kami of the most-revered Imperial Family, we have here a true reflection of the simple consciousness of the ancient Japanese. If we look at the circumstances in which the three myth-groups are united around this one great Kami personality, we will see that in the Plain-of-High-Heaven myths, stories about the Sun Goddess are central. Those that precede her birth tell of her origin, and the later ones record events that were the working out of her Kami will. The section about the rock cave of Heaven is the most glittering of these stories.

The Izumo myths are focused on Ō-kuni-nushi no Kami. But if we examine the relationship between the Plain-of-High-Heaven myths and those of Izumo, we will see that the Sun Goddess connects the two. Susa-no-o no Mikoto, the procreative Kami of the Izumo myth, is treated as the antagonist of the Sun Goddess. In the Plain of High Heaven he is a bad Kami as well as the younger brother of the Sun Goddess, suggesting that the divinity of the Sun Goddess was central to both myth groups.

In the Tsukushi myths Ni-ni-gi no Mikoto, who descended from Heaven to Takachiho Peak, is the grandson of the Sun Goddess. The relationship between the two is thus made clear.

The supreme divinity of the Sun Goddess is a historical reflection of the augustness of the Emperors who, as descendants of the divine Sun Goddess, are considered manifest Kami (*arahito-gami*). In this idea there is already the implication that the Emperors, revered as descendants of the Sun Goddess, are at the center of the state. The legend of the "birth of land" (*kuni-umi*) in the Plain-of-High-Heaven myths is an expression of this idea in an even more remarkable and very special form. This is the section about Kami cohabitation, in which two Kami, Izanagi and Izanami, give birth — as the first man-and-wife Kami — to the lands of the "eight large islands." The ancient myths of Japan include many elements that are common to other parts of the world, and therefore we cannot hastily assert that the Japanese myths are unique. But the "birth of lands" legend may be unique. There are difficulties in interpreting this legend, and possibly because of these difficulties, it has been interpreted in various ways since ancient times. The Shinto sects, mentioned above, have all understood it differently. For example, in Confucian Shinto it was regarded as a figurative representation of creation by the interaction of the two forces: *Yin* and *Yang*. In Suiga Shinto, it was explained by the principle that Heaven and man were one. By this theory, although nature and man differed, their causal principle was one and the same — nature and man were one in the sense that everything was created by the interaction of *Yin* and *Yang*. And so the Age-of-Kami book of the *Kojiki* gave rise to various interpretations — in some cases man was seen from the point of view of Heaven, and in some cases Heaven was seen from the point of view of man; and in the complexity of these interpretations lies the mystery of the myths. Thus the legend of the "birth of lands" was thought to explain Heaven from the point of view of man. On the other hand, the historical schools, represented by Arai Hakuseki [1657–1725], took it as an allegorical account of two heroes — the two Kami — who combined their armies to conquer and exploit territory. None of these interpretations is a literal reading of the *Kojiki* myths. Such ideas were not included in ancient Shinto. In terms of ancient Shinto, the legend should be interpreted literally as "mating on the couch" by the two Kami, that is, as the "creation of land" by the act of reproduction. Such a simple outlook is characteristic of antiquity.

The two Kami also gave birth to other Kami, to Kami who were the ancestors of the Japanese people. And finally after Izanami, the female Kami, went to the nether land of Yomi and after Izanagi, the male Kami, had pursued her and then cleansed himself of Yomi pollution, the Sun Goddess was born. From these myths there arose the idea that the land, the people, and the ruler — the three elements that make up the state — were all descended, by blood connection and Kami origin, from the same Kami. And the divinity of the Sun Goddess was a historical reflection of Emperors being thought of as manifest Kami. Here we see *kōkoku shugi*. The Emperor is identified in a mysterious way — as a manifest Kami — with the state. Again we see that the three myth groups of Plain of High Heaven, Izumo, and Tsukushi are united around the myth of the Sun Goddess. This is nothing but an expression of the ideal that the Japanese state was a state conceived on the principle of *kōkoku shugi* and could not be otherwise. Just how useful this ideal was, as an intellectual base for the great work of unifying the state at the time of its inception, can be clearly understood by noting the *Kojiki's* mythological structure.

Kōkoku shugi, which had its roots in ancient Shinto, was exalted differently in later forms of Shinto. In spite of the fact that Buddhism was not originally a state faith, the proponents of Buddhistic Shinto, for example, did not fail to adopt *kōkoku shugi* in the

Mahayana spirit. And although Confucianism was associated with the concept of the virtuous becoming rulers, proponents of Confucian Shinto not only violated Confucianism on this point but even effected, through Confucianism, a moralistic development of *kōkoku shugi*. In short, both Buddhistic Shinto and Confucian Shinto, insofar as they were Shinto, supported *kōkoku shugi*.

In some form or other, *kōkoku shugi* was the most important tenet in the doctrines of Ancient-Learning Shinto (which aimed at a reawakening of the spirit of ancient Shinto and a return to ancient Shinto), in quasi-Ancient-Learning Shinto, in Vulgar Shinto, and also in Founder Shinto (represented by the Kurozumi Sect and other " pure " religious faiths). Let us turn to two or three examples. First, to the Suiga Shinto of Yamazaki Ansai.

We have already noted that Suiga Shinto was the most highly Confucianized form of Shinto. Through Chu Hsi philosophy — the highest philosophy of that day — Shinto was most thoroughly theorized. Nevertheless, *kōkoku shugi* occupied a central position in Suiga thought. The proponents of Suiga Shinto, proceeding from the position that the Japanese Emperors ruled as descendants of the Sun Goddess in whom Heaven and man were one, advocated — with ardor — an absolute and unconditional reverence for the Emperor. They stated that the Japanese Emperors, in comparison with those of China, were appropriately identified as Heaven itself, not as " sons of Heaven." The Confucian Heaven, in the minds of Suiga thinkers, was the Imperial Family. In Confucianism the Ruler of Heaven (*t'ien-ti*) was above the Earthly Ruler (*ta-chün*), and the mandate of Heaven was above Imperial orders. But in Japan, said the Suiga scholars, the earthly Emperor was the Ruler of Heaven, and an Imperial order was the mandate of Heaven. Therefore, even if a Japanese Emperor was not virtuous, or did unreasonable things, the people would certainly not disobey him or become angry at him because of that — just as in time of natural disaster in China, the Chinese would not oppose or become angry at the Ruler of Heaven because of the disaster. Such absolute reverence stood at the foundations of Japanese morality.

All books on Suiga Shinto expounded this reverence, but the most representative was *Dōjō monjin on-kokoroegaki* (Instructions for Students in the Inner Palace) by Takenouchi Shikibu [1712–1767], the principal instigator of the famous Hōreki Incident of 1759.[1] The main theme of the work was that Japanese Emperors, since they were descendants of Heavenly Kami, should be accorded absolute obedience by all things born in Japan: man, plants, trees, fowl, and beasts. Such obedience was required especially of court nobles, for they served Emperors directly. For them to express anger against an Emperor in any service whatsoever was a sacrilege. Takenouchi maintained that noblemen should have the same feelings in attending Emperors as they have when attending Heavenly Kami, never resenting them in the least; and that they should take greater care of their health when serving at the Court. Just as one does not become angry at Heaven when there is a typhoon, a person at Court should not become the least bit resentful toward the Emperor, no matter what the Emperor does, since a nobleman's whole life is devoted to the service of the Emperor. Such thoughts were expressed by Takenouchi with very deep feeling. In these writings we see a notable revival and development of reverence for the Emperor as a manifest Kami, the most fundamental idea of *kōkoku shugi* as expressed in ancient Shinto. Although Ancient-Learning Shinto fiercely attacked the unscholarliness of Suiga Shinto's interpretations of the classics, it placed Suiga Shinto ahead of other sects with respect to reverence for the Emperor.

Motoori Norinaga, the perfecter of Ancient-Learning Shinto, stated that in Japan the supreme value was loyalty, in contrast to the Confucian emphasis upon filial piety. At the same time, he explained quite clearly that although the concept of the virtuous becoming

---

1) [In 1759 Takenouchi was banished from Kyoto by the military government because his teaching had stirred up subversive discussion at the Court.]

rulers, and its corollary ideas about revolution, appeared to be rational and of temporary benefit to society, this was definitely not so. On the contrary, he said, if one looks at the matter from the point of view of the distant past, he will see that the teaching of absolute reverence for the Emperor is the correct teaching, and the way of bringing happiness to the world. The *kōkoku shugi* which he espoused, from this point of view, need not be discussed, since it was stated so clearly.

Hirata Atsutane and his students added new elements and dimensions to Ancient-Learning Shinto through contact with Christianity, a world religion. Nevertheless, *kōkoku shugi* remained in force — in fact, we might say that under the influences of the day it became more pronounced than it had been in Motoori's Shinto. After Hirata, all thinkers advocated *kōkoku shugi*. All of them, like Hirata, used their knowledge of Confucianism, Buddhism, and Christianity to advance the doctrine that the Imperial Country (*kōkoku*) was central. They actually used, in reverse, the Buddho-Shinto theory of "manifestation of original Buddhas," stating that Japan was the Father Country (*sokoku*) of all countries and that, likewise, Shinto should be considered the source of all religions and the Emperor the supreme ruler of all countries.

We see a manifestation of the special character of such thought in the state socialism of Satō Nobuhiro [1769–1850]. Nobuhiro's study was in the field of agricultural administration, a kind of economics; but it was rooted in Shinto and Hirata thought. He asserted that Ame no Mi-naka-nushi no Kami was the highest sovereign Kami of the universe, that Taka-mi-musubi and Kami-musubi were Kami that manifested the virtue of creativity (*musubi*) and that by means of this creativity all creatures including man were given life and growth. And so agricultural administration, or economics, was the study and consideration of this "Way of creativity," and a carrying out of the virtue of the "Kami of creativity." Here lay the basis of his scholarship. His "method of handing down the rule" (*suitō hō*) was propounded as the way to apply these fundamental principles to society. The method, he said, required that all trade and employment be managed by the state and that all people, as workers or officials, be direct instruments of the state — permitting no private trade or employment. After completely abolishing the existing social classes of samurai, farmer, artisan and merchant, Nobuhiro would have had all people assigned to one of the following eight occupational groups: cultivators, woodmen, miners, artisans, merchants, laborers, boatmen, or fishermen; and an individual would be permitted to engage in no more than one occupation. Establishing the above three principles, he divided all administrative functions of the state among six Bureaus (*fu*): the Bureau of Basic Concerns, the Bureau of Development, the Bureau of Manufacturing, the Bureau of Finance, the Bureau of the Army, and the Bureau of the Navy. People of the eight occupations would be attached to these Bureaus, and appropriate officials appointed. Above the six Bureaus would be three Directorates (*dai*): the Grand Council Directorate, the Directorate of Religious Affairs, and the Directorate of Indoctrination. These were to be the highest administrative organs of the state. In each of the three Directorates Nobuhiro would have had three Masters (*shi*) — upper, middle, and lower — and three Officers (*kan*) — upper, middle, and lower. The highest official of all would be the Upper Master of the Directorate of Indoctrination (*kyōkadai no daishi*). The three Directorates were to be arranged on a north-south line with shrines to the west. The shrines would be dedicated to the following Kami: Ame no Mi-naka-nushi, flanked by the two Kami of creativity, Taka-mi-musubi and Kami-musubi; Izanagi and Izanami to the south of the above; and, to the south of these, the Sun Goddess and Susa-no-o. The Upper Master of the Directorate of Religious Affairs would conduct rites and ceremonies at these shrines every morning. Nobuhiro's plan called for the establishment of a university (*daigakkō*), located to the east of the Directorates, where all administrative orders and Imperial Edicts would be issued. The university would have a Discussion Hall (*gijidō*) attached to it where the

Emperor and officials would gather and discuss administration. Here the above-mentioned Kami were to be worshipped, and a lecture platform was to be set up — a platform from which lectures would be given every day by the Upper Master of the Directorate of Education and Indoctrination. This lecture platform would be made as splendidly as possible, and music would be played as the Upper Master entered and left the Hall. The Upper Master would teach, in behalf of the "Supreme Creator," the Great Way of Creativity. At the side of the lecture platform would be placed the "Jeweled Seat"; and here the Emperor would sit and listen to the lectures. Such an "economic" policy can be understood as the implementation of Satō's *kōkoku shugi*.[1]

In his *Udai kondō hisaku* (Secret Policy for Merging the Universe), Satō Nobuhiro urged that the Imperial capital be moved to Edo, that the three Directorates and six Bureaus be set up there, that the entire country be divided into eight administrative districts, that a district office be established in each district, and that the country be administered in accordance with the "method of handing down the rule." Further, he wrote that Japan was the Father Country of all nations and that the Emperor was the supreme ruler of rulers. From this point of view he maintained that his "state socialism," with Japan at the center, should be put into effect throughout the world, and the universe thereby united.

With Nobuhiro *kōkoku shugi* became, more clearly than with others, a kind of imperialism. But it should be noted that this was not simply militant jingoism. It was an economic policy based upon the concept of "the Way of the creativity" in ancient Shinto and was moreover another manifestation of *kōkoku shugi* as the essence of Shinto.

---

1) [Cf. Satō Nobuhiro's *Suitō hiroku* (Secret Record of the Methods of Handing Down the Rule) and *Udai kondō hisaku* in *Nihon keizai taiten* (Great Economic Dictionary of Japan), XVIII (Tokyo, 1929).]

CHARACTERISTIC FEATURES OF JAPANESE SHINTO

The theory of the "teachings of the true Lord of Heaven" (*shintenshu kyō*), propounded by Watanabe Ikarimaro [1837–1915], has elements that differ from the teachings of Nobuhiro. Watanabe, who became a disciple of Hirata Shinto after Hirata Atsutane's death, was a scholar of the generation after Nobuhiro. He studied Christianity, but reacted against it. Advocating, and attempting to institutionalize, a monotheism centered in Ame no Mi-naka-nushi no Kami, he wrote *Shinkyō setsugen* (Origin of the True Teaching) and *Ame no Mi-naka-nushi kō* (Study of Ame no Mi-naka-nushi no Kami). Ikarimaro's "teaching of the true Lord of Heaven" included the doctrine that the supreme god of the universe referred to in Christianity was none other than the Japanese Ame no Mi-naka-nushi no Kami, and that the Christian god was false. Thus he tabbed Christianity a "teaching of the false Lord of Heaven." Proof that the Japanese god was the true god, Ikarimaro said, lay in the fact that the Imperial Family was descended from Heavenly Kami (*tenjin*). From this point of view he even dared to liken the Christian concept of "the son of God" with the Japanese idea of "the Heavenly Grandson." Clearly we can see *kōkoku shugi* here. Probably there were more elements of Christian theology in Ikarimaro thought than in that of any other member of the Hirata School. Nevertheless, the basis of what he taught was still *kōkoku shugi*. It is even possible to say that he studied Christianity in order to develop *kōkoku shugi*.

In Founder Shinto, also, we find that *kōkoku shugi* was advocated most strongly in such sects as the Kurozumi (which stated that it was bad for any person who had been born in the Kami Country (*shinkoku*) not to honor the Kami) and the Konkō (which declared that it was wrong for a person who had been born in the Kami Country not to recognize the blessings of the Kami and the Emperor).

3. *The Second Characteristic of Shinto: Realism*

The second characteristic of Shintoism as a whole is its realism. By realism I mean that thinking which affirms and values the real.

Even when propounding ideals, such thought is based on the real, not veering toward that which is simply imagined, but emphasizing the putting of things into practice. This characteristic, like the first characteristic, *kōkoku shugi,* penetrates all forms and phases of Shinto. In this case, too, let us look first at the matter from the point of view of its origins in ancient Shinto. We will deal with two aspects: the human outlook and the world outlook.

By the human outlook I mean the outlook on life and death, on what is auspicious and inauspicious, and on what is good and evil. First, let us consider the outlook on life and death. In the consciousness of the Japanese people of antiquity there was a confrontation between the visible and the concealed worlds. The concealed which became visible was said to be "manifest" (*aru*), and the visible which became concealed was said to have "vanished" (*usu*). The process of changing, whether to the visible or the concealed, was termed "becoming" (*naru*). As a result of the action of reproduction, the emerging of things from the concealed world into the visible was "birth" (*umaru*). Conversely, when things entered the concealed world from the visible, there was "death" (*shinu*). Death, in other words, was hiding — it definitely did not mean a return to nothingness. The "concealed person" was thought of as being the opposite of the "manifest person"; and the "concealed world" was the opposite of the "manifest world." But since the "concealed person" and the "concealed world" existed as negative aspects of the "manifest person" and the "manifest world," that which was real was always fundamental.

As to what was auspicious or inauspicious, and good or evil, it was thought that the auspicious was good and the inauspicious was evil. This was essentially a simple and natural outlook, and it was conspicuous in ancient Shinto. "Good" (*yoshi*) was that which was fortunate, exalted, delightful, or excellent. "Bad" (*ashi*) was the opposite. Eventually good and evil, in a moral sense, were incorporated into this view; and that which was auspiciously associated with the birth and growth of all things was good and that which, on the other hand, was inauspicious was evil. Good Kami and bad Kami had such a relationship to birth and growth.

According to the world-outlook aspect of realism, as distinct from the human outlook, the "great eight islands" or the "central country of the reed plains" was considered a unique world. It was a glorious, peaceful country referred to as the "beautiful grain country" and the "luxuriant reed plain." And this country was created by the "birth of the land" (*kuniumi*) of the two ancestral Kami of the Imperial Family. It was a good country that was to be ruled by the descendants of the Sun Goddess in one unbroken line for ages eternal.

On the other hand, three transcendent worlds were thought of: the Plain of High Heaven, Yomi, and the Yonder World (*tokoyo*). Regardless of the changes that took place in later ages in the meaning of these three transcendent worlds, in ancient Shinto all three had a "real world" quality. Certainly the ancients did not consider them as having a higher value than the "great eight islands" without a "real world" quality. The Yonder World carried the meaning of the "distant country". Yomi was the hated, polluted place where souls went after death. It was no more than a concealed world invisible to the real world. Neither the Yonder World nor Yomi had any value apart from the real world. The Plain of High Heaven had the most ideal quality; and yet it was thought of as a "better real world," and in terms of the real. And so in the ancient world outlook it should be noted that thinking was grounded in the real.

This tendency of the ancients to see things in terms of the real — noted in their human as well as in their world outlook — is seen also in their Kami outlook, something of very great importance in ancient Shinto thought. The ancient people of Japan considered anything which manifested awesome potency to be a Kami. No distinction was made between Kami that were good or bad, noble or mean, strong or weak. The early Japanese thought of "myriad Kami" that were dispersed among natural objects and human beings. But it is significant that the Kami of "manifest being" were more fundamental than Kami of "concealed being," and that auspicious Kami were more fundamental than the inauspicious. This realism did not exist simply as an idea. It was more like a primitive philosophy that permeated myths of the *Kojiki*. And so here we can properly use the term "realism."

By explaining, with some supplementary remarks, what was meant by Motoori Norinaga's idea of "the mutual generation of good and evil fortune" (*kikkyō sōsei*), we can clarify this characteristic of realism in Shinto thought. As pointed out already, the ancients thought that there was a polarity in which auspicious activity accounted for birth and growth, and inauspicious activity hindered birth and growth. While the auspicious Kami of birth and growth were dominant, there were also inauspicious Kami that hindered birth and growth. The Kami of the latter variety were called "bending Kami" (*magatsubi no Kami*). But there were also "straightening Kami" (*naobi no Kami*) that changed the inauspicious to the auspicious. This co-existence of the auspicious and the inauspicious, with an eventual return to the auspicious through "straightening," was identified by Motoori as "the mutual generation of good and evil fortune." This is seen in particular myths, as well as in the underlying spirit, of the Age-of-Kami books of the *Kojiki* and the *Nihongi*. As for its appearance in particular myths, let us take an example from the Plain-of-High-Heaven myths. Here the formation of the world through the procreation of all things by the two Kami represents the attainment of the aim of creativity (*musubi*), or the operation of good fortune. But when the auspicious reaches its extreme, the female Kami dies as a result of giving birth to the Kami of fire and proceeds to Yomi. This represents a change from the auspicious to the inauspicious. And when the male Kami pursued the female Kami to Yomi and came into contact with the pollution there, the inauspicious reached its extreme. But when the male Kami returned from Yomi, and bathed at Ahakihara (at the Tachibana no Odo of

Hyūga in Tsukushi), good fortune was restored. The culmination of this good fortune was the birth of the highest Kami, the Sun Goddess, and her becoming the sovereign of the Plain of High Heaven. Ill-fortune for the Sun Goddess came with her being annoyed by the wild actions of Susa-no-o, and reached the ultimate when she hid in the "rock cave of Heaven." When she emerged from the cave, good fortune was restored. Such relationships between good and bad fortune, depicted allegorically in the Plain of High Heaven myths, appear also in the Izumo and Tsukushi myths.

Not only do we see such relationships between good and evil fortune in particular myths but if we look at the Age of Kami books as a whole, we notice that the Plain of High Heaven myths represent good fortune and that, by contrast, those of Izumo represent the bad. Finally in "the mutual generation of good and bad fortune" we see that good fortune also prevails in the Tsukushi myths that follow.

Such can be termed a very simple dialectical way of thinking. At its base was the idea that if there was good fortune in the world, there was also the bad. Bad fortune existed for the sake of the good: it was an instrument for the creation of a new good. Thus the world ultimate was good fortune. Bad fortune was not, in the final analysis, the ultimate, but existed for the good; and good fortune had a positive existence. This was a kind of optimistic philosophy. The consideration of this world as the best of all possible worlds was, of course, a complete affirmation of reality. In various ideas realism, as described above, was manifested in general outline and in fundamental principle. Here we can see the realism of ancient Shinto.

Although realism was rooted in ancient Shinto, its manifestation in later phases of Shinto development can be seen first in Buddhistic Shinto. Buddhism is "world-weary" and, in a sense, other-worldly. Nevertheless, it is a notable fact that in Japan Mahayana Buddhism developed as a state religion. This is also true of the various forms of Buddho Shinto which arose within Buddhism. Buddhistic Shinto, because of its Buddhistic qualities, may have even intensified the realism described above. Certainly realism was not rejected. It is thought that the realism of Shinto contributed to the development of Buddhism in Japan as a state religion — at least it was not a minor factor. This would apply to both Dual Shinto and Ise Shinto; but the most striking manifestation of ancient-Shinto realism is seen in the *Jinnō shōtōki* (Record of the True Lineage of the Sacred Emperors),[1] written by Kitabatake Chikafusa [1293–1354]. The thoughts of Chikafusa are defined most clearly when contrasted with the pessimistic and world-weary historical view expressed in the *Gukanshō* (Summary of My Humble Views)[2] written by Jien [1155–1225]. The historical view of the *Gukanshō* emerged out of the Final Age (*mappō*) thought which dominated the hearts and minds of the Japanese people after the closing years of the Heian Era. Consequently, Jien attempted a pessimistic interpretation of Japanese history that was based upon the idea of the four ages (*kō* or *kalpa*): the "formative" (*jō*), the "existing" (*jū*), the "destructive" (*e*), and the "empty" (*kū*). He recognized a limitary significance in the concept of the "hundred kings" (*hyaku-ō*), or the "successive kings of the multitude," which had been current in China and in Japan since ancient times; and he asserted that the present age was the last. He said: "I do not know about the Age of Kami, but I am told that with the age of man there will be one hundred kings after the reign of Emperor Jimmu. Only a few reigns remain. We are already in the reign of the eighty-fourth ruler .... "[3] Jien concluded that since Japan had already had eighty-four of the allotted one hundred rulers, after sixteen more this world would come to an end. But clearly the position of *Jinnō shōtōki* was the exact opposite. In making a frontal attack on the *Gukanshō* interpretation, Chikafusa

---

1) [Translated by Hermann Bohner in: *Jinnō Shōtōki, Buch von der Wahren Gott-Kaiser-Herrschafts-Linie* (Tokyo, 1935).]
2) [Partially translated by J. Rahder in: "Miscellany of Personal Views of an Ignorant Fool (Guk(w)anshō)," *Acta Orientalia* 15 (1936), 173–230.]
3) [*Gukanshō*, kan 3, in *Dai Nihon bunko* Ser. 2, VI (Tokyo, 1935), 246.]

wrote: " It has been stated that there will be one hundred kings. This is not the hundred of ten times ten, but an unlimited hundred." And he also stated: " Much more, the Three Imperial Regalia (*sanshu no shinki*) exist in the world. That which has no limit is the Imperial throne which inherits our country generation after generation."[1) He maintained that history was infinite, that the history of Japan was the realization of the Sun Goddess's mandate in which she said that the country would exist as long as there was a Heaven and earth and so would evolve forever. The long history of the vicissitudes of Imperial authority was ultimately the realization of the Sun Goddess's mandate. Anything like Final-Age thought was of course condemned: " Though man may forget the past, Heaven will not lose the Way. I doubt whether we can say that Heaven does not operate in accordance with just principles.... Evil will be destroyed before long, and even the disturbed world will be put right. This is the enduring principle of past and present."[2) In essence he proclaimed the view that righteousness always triumphs. For him " just principle " and " right " were nothing less than the rationale of the true lineage of divine Emperors. In such a view of the world and of history, there is really a re-realization of the optimistic ancient-Shinto idea of " the mutual generation of good and evil fortune." What was simply " good fortune " in old Shinto now became " right." And in contrasting this view with that of the *Gukanshō*, we see very vividly the special character of the realism of the *Jinnō shōtōki*.[3)

---

1) [*Jinnō shōtōki, kan* 1, in *ibid.*, 27.]
2) [*Kan* 6, *ibid.*, 143.]
3) Concerning these sharply contrasting historical and world views of the *Gukanshō* and the *Jinnō shōtōki*, I have recounted here what I have already stated in my article "Gukanshō kō" (Study of the *Gukanshō*). But a different interpretation has been presented recently by Fukushima Masao in a study entitled "*Gukanshō yori Jinnō shōtōki made: kokutai jikaku no nagare o ronzu*" (From the *Gukanshō* to the *Jinnō shōtōki*: A Thesis on the Flow of the Awareness of *kokutai*), published in the May (1935) issue of the *Kyōiku Kagaku*. Fukushima's position is that the *Gukanshō* does not necessarily present a world-weary and degenerative view of history, but is an antecedent to the thought of the *Jinnō shōtōki*. Unfortunately, I cannot agree with his thesis; but as another sort of interpretation it is quite interesting, and I refer it to the reader.

Confucian Shinto (*jukyō shintō*) and Ancient-Learning Shinto of the Tokugawa Era, all had realism as their special characteristic. Of these, I will discuss Ancient-Learning Shinto. In the Shinto of Motoori Norinaga, who perfected Ancient-Learning Shinto, an attempt was made to revive ancient Shinto through philological study of the *Kojiki*. As a matter of faith that rested on the foundations of the Pure Land Sect (*jōdō shū*) of Buddhism (the religion of Motoori's home), Motoori's idea of " the mutual generation of good and evil fortune," and his optimism based upon this idea — together with a realism that penetrated his optimism — were expressed very clearly and naturally in every aspect of his view of life and the world, like a calm surface that suggests depth. In various ideas and interests of Motoori there is a realism that takes the form of accepting the present age, avoiding radical reform, and rejecting restraints on the naturalness of human life and feeling: in his Ancient Way theory, developed in his *Tamaboko hyakushu* (One Hundred Poems on the Way) and his *Tamakushige* (Jeweled Comb Box); in his various ideas about the society of his own day, touched upon in his *Hihon tamakushige* (Secret Book of the Jeweled Comb Box) where he expounded his political policy that was based upon his Ancient Way theory; in his morality of humanism and naturalness, seen in the literary theories of the *Tama no ogushi* (Small Jeweled Comb) and *Isonokami sazamegoto* (Whispered Words of the Past); and in his views which affirm economic needs, candidly described in his *Tama katsuma* (Jeweled Bamboo Basket). From this position of affirming realism, Motoori attacked the other-worldly tendencies of Buddhism, the false good-behavior of Confucianism, and the Enlightenment (*satori*) of the Zen sects. In Motoori we can see a very wise realist who looked at life in terms of the eternal aspects of history.

The Shinto of Hirata Atsutane, who claimed to be the true academic heir of Motoori, is a continuation of Ancient-Learning Shinto. But there is a great difference. Hirata Shinto was a product of the theological development of Ancient-Learning Shinto. The difference consisted principally in the addition of teachings about the next life, the result of an eschatological development. This, together with other views about a superior creative Kami, clearly proves a Christian influence. With Hirata and his followers, Ancient-Learning Shinto developed an other-worldly tendency; and we find such statements as: the next life is more important than this, which is temporary; and the next life, as the world of souls of the dead, is the fundamental world. Nevertheless, a very prominent feature of their Shinto was that they enhanced that side of Shinto known as "the state religion of ancestral Kami." It was similar, at this point, to the *kōkoku shugi* incorporated into the "true Lord of Heaven" teachings of Watanabe Ikarimaro, touched upon above. Presumably the realism of original Shinto, and also of Ancient-Learning Shinto, was maintained as before. The special attention given to Confucianism and the rise of ancestor worship in Shinto were notable developments in Hirata Shinto. With the special development of Shinto as a state religion of ancestral Kami, we see that, along with its *kōkoku shugi*, there was a strong manifestation of realism.

In other forms of Shinto as well — particularly in Founder Shinto which developed as popular faiths, and in Vulgar Shinto which was akin to Founder Shinto — realism appeared, sometimes as a hedonistic and sometimes as a secular tendency, often accompanied by vulgarities. Liveliness, brightness, and gaiety were common to all forms of Shinto, in both ceremony and practice; and these qualities were products of the realism that had permeated Shinto since antiquity.

4. *The Third Characteristic Feature: Meijō shugi*

Meijō shugi, the third characteristic feature of Shintoism, refers to the reverence for brightness and purity in all matter and thought. Here, too, roots are found in ancient Shinto. We can understand this by noting those ancient-Shinto views of good and evil that appear in the Age-of-Kami books of the *Kojiki* and the *Nihongi*, and in the ancient liturgies, and by noting goodness and badness — discussed above — as good and bad fortune. It has already been pointed out that good was identified with that which was auspicious, and bad with that which was inauspicious. If we now ask how badness and goodness were conceived in ancient Shinto, in what was later called a "moral sense", the answer is that badness was pollution and goodness was purity. This was a very simple stage of moralistic conception — at that time the word "*tsumi*" (abomination) was identified with pollution (*kegare*). In the frequent appearances of the word "*tsumi*" in the Emperor Chūai chapter of the *Kojiki*, and in the Great Purification liturgy (*ōharae no kotoba*), the meaning is roughly the same. According to these references, such *tsumi* as defiling one's mother was something which today would be classified as a moral "sin." But natural disasters such as "disasters from birds on high" (*takatsutori no wazawai*) or "disasters from Kami on high" (*takatsukami no wazawai*) — as well as various physical disfigurements like albinism and skin growths — were also thought of as *tsumi*. Thus *tsumi* was pollution to the senses. On the opposite side of such simple thinking there existed, along with the taboo of pollution, a reverence for that which was pure and bright.

Purification (*harai*) was a means of removing *tsumi*. This was a ritual by which the body was purified and pollution expelled. The ceremony goes back to Izanagi's self-purification at Ahakihara in Tsukushi after returning from Yomi where he came into contact with pollution. It is recorded in the *Kojiki* that as a result of Izanagi's act of purification three august Kami, including the Sun Goddess, were born. Thus the aim of exorcism was to attain purity from pollution: the spirit of the act is identified with *meijō shugi*.

Just how purity is obtained from pollution, as a result of the ceremony, becomes clear when we observe the process of expunging *tsumi* in the Great Purification liturgy. When exorcism is performed, the Kami of the various river shoals and the Kami of the ocean depths cooperate in carrying the pollution from the river to the sea and, finally, to the distant ocean depths. Then the Kami of the ocean depths swallow the pollution and blow it away to the "root country" (*ne no kuni*) or "bottom country" (*soko no kuni*). Thus the pollution is chased back to Yomi from whence it came, and the *tsumi* of man is thereby completely removed — man is purified. Here, along with reverence for purity, we see manifested the thought that persons born in this world are originally pure and that the pollution of *tsumi* belongs to Yomi. In the final analysis, pollution has only a negative existence. Needless to say, this is a very simple outlook, both as a view of evil and as moral thought. But imbedded within it is the important idea of reverence for purity in all things. This idea was developed psychologically and was identified with a motivistic, not a utilitarian, point of view. We can find notable examples of this in the Imperial Edict (*senmyō*) recorded in the *Shoku Nihongi*. Of course there is variety in the sixty-two Imperial Edicts, beginning with the one issued on the occasion of the enthronement of Emperor Temmu [in 697] and ending with the one issued by Emperor Kwammu in 789; but these are unique Japanese documents that are, in general, rich in moralistic, political and legal thought. The most frequent and notable ideas appearing in these ancient Imperial Edicts are: "the pure heart" (*kiyoki kokoro*); "the bright heart" (*akaki kokoro*); and "the pure and bright heart" (*kiyoki akaki kokoro*). In the concatenation and simplification used in the following phrases we see the development of moralistic content:

" a bright, pure, and *honest and sincere heart*";
" a pure, bright, *upright and honest heart*";
" not with an *evil heart*, but with a pure, bright heart";
" not with an *obsequious, deceitful* heart, but in loyalty, with candid sincerity";
" in accord with the principle [of proper relations between] ruler and minister, with a *faithful, pure heart*";
" a brightly *faithful* heart";
" a *faithfully* bright and pure heart";

"brightly pure heart *without a double heart*";

"pure, bright heart; *upright and honest words.*"

These are quite commonplace terms that are seen in almost all of the ancient Imperial Edicts, and that signify, in each case, a sense of loyalty on the part of the minister and subject to the Imperial court. The roots of such a moralistic development can undoubtedly be found on the reverse side of the *tsumi* concept dealt with above; but the particularly important thing to be noted here is a sort of ceremony, existing in ancient Shinto, called the *ukei*. An *ukei* was a vow to a Kami. There was always the expectation of an effect, and the expectation arose out of the conviction that the purity and brightness of one's heart was of primary importance. In the legends recorded in the *Kojiki* it is written that when Susa-no-o visited the Sun Goddess in the Plain of High Heaven, and when the Sun Goddess became worried that Susa-no-o did not have a "beautiful heart," Susa-no-o swore that his own heart was pure and bright, declaring that if his heart was pure and bright, he would be able to produce a female Kami. And he produced a female Kami, thereby proving the purity and brightness of his heart. This is one example of an *ukei*.

Ideas with a moralistic content, already expressed in the Imperial Edicts, become more prominent when we come to other forms of Shinto, particularly medieval Shinto. Being associated at this later time with the Buddhist concept of purity (*shōjō*), and taking the form of "correctness and uprightness" (*seichoku*), moralistic ideas came to dominate people's thoughts. In general the idea of "correctness and uprightness" became especially important, it seems to me, after the beginning of the military age. We have evidence of this in various documents of the Kamakura Era. For example, in the sixth volume of the *Shasekishū* (Collection of Sand and Stone), [an anthology of Buddhist stories compiled in 1283], we find the following subtitles: "The Incident of the Correct and Upright Woman"; "The Incident of the Correct and Upright Commoner"; and "The Incident of the Correct and Upright Man Who Acquires Treasures." There is this passage: "If one is correct and upright, the Kami will dwell in one's head; and if one is faithful and honest *(teiren)*, the Buddha will illuminate his heart." And later on in the work we find the famous passage from the "Revelations of The Three Shrines"[1] attributed to Prince Shōtoku: "Although intrigue produces immediate gain, eventually it brings the punishment of Buddhas and Kami. Although correctness and uprightness do not bring temporary advantage, they will certainly have the sympathy of the sun and moon."[2] The sixth injunction of the *Jikkinshō* (Summary of the Ten Injunctions) — a typical didactic volume of that period [dated 1252], is entitled: "One Must Preserve Loyalty and Uprightness." Then, equating compassion with plainness and uprightness *(shitsuchoku)*, the volume cites these words from the Vimalakîrti Sutra *(yuima kyō)*: "Plainness and uprightness are of the Pure Land." And by way of amplification these words are added: "The Great Bodhisattva Hachiman vowed graciously to dwell in the heads of those who are correct and upright and, reassuringly for us, joined to the vow this poem:

Though much I see	Arikitsutsu
as I tramp back and forth,	Kitsutsu miredomo
Shall I ever forget	Isagiyoki
the heart of a man	Hito no kokoro o
Who is innocent and pure!	Ware wasureme ya.

And so, for realizing one's hopes for this life and the next, nothing is more important than an upright heart."[3] Moreover, the *Jikkinshō* defines uprightness as:

Not disputing by denying what you have said, not acting as if you know what is unknown, not going back on your word, not

---

1) [The Three Shrines were Ise, Hachiman, and Kasuga.]
2) [*Shasekekishū, Dai Nihon fūkyō sōsho*, (Tokyo, 1917), II, 328 and 331.f
3) [*Jikkinshō, Shintei zōho kokushi taikei* (Tokyo, 1932), XVIII, 101-2.]

being envious nor carrying either sorrow or joy too far, and in general holding uprightness to be your first virtue so as not to have an angry heart. It is like the sun and the moon, which do not dim their light because of a particle; and like an enlightened king, who does not bend the law for an individual. It is absence of duplicity, not varying your attitude with the person and the situation, and equability of mind, not drawing intimates to you or keeping outsiders away. Such a person is wise, honest, and upright (*renchoku*).[1]

The author of the *Jikkinshō* did not interpret the term "correct and upright" as merely the absence of falseness, or the opposite of scheming. The term had a broader and deeper meaning. He urged its importance as a principle of morality. From various references we know that the popular proverb "The Kami dwells in the head of the correct and upright" originated during this period.

But the above references are generally associated with Buddhistic Shinto. In this concept of "the correct and upright" there is of course a Buddhist influence. It can be said, however, that the stress on these ideas of honesty and uprightness, and correctness and uprightness, was a spiritual phenomenon that seems to have appeared for the first time in the period of military government in the Kamakura Era. It was definitely a spirit that pervaded the *Jōei shikimoku* (Jōei [1232–1233] Code),[2] instituted by the Kamakura Shogunate. But in these ideas of correctness and uprightness the original Shinto concept of the bright and pure heart was operative; and the Buddhist idea of purity was added. Outer Shrine Shinto emerged from developments at the Ise Shrine, a shrine which honored the Sun Goddess whose Kami Body (*shintai*) was a "bright mirror." At the

---

1) [*Ibid.*, 94–5.]
2) [Translated by John Carey Hall in "Japanese Feudal Laws: The Institutes of Judicature, being a translation of 'Go Seibai Shikimoku,' The Magisterial Code of the Hōjō Power-Holders (1232)," TASJ 34 (1906), 1–44.]

heart of the Shinto theology of the Outer Shrine a spiritual *meijō shugi* existed in diverse forms. At about this time the aphorisms known as " the revelations of the Three Shrines " emerged; and *meijō shugi* was really their main theme. The revelation which was reputed to be from the Sun Goddess ran: " Although intrigue produces immediate gain, it will certainly bring the punishment of the Kami. Although correctness and uprightness do not bring temporary advantage, they will eventually have the sympathy of the sun and the moon." (I have already noted that these words appeared in the *Shasekishū* as the words of Prince Shōtoku.) The second aphorism, which took the form of a revelation of the Great Boddhisatva Hachiman, was: " I will not accept things from men with defiled hearts, even though I may have to eat pills of iron. I will not approach the places of persons with polluted hearts, even though I may have to sit in coppery flames." And finally the third aphorism, in the form of a revelation of the Great Illustrious Kami (*daimyōjin*) of Kasuga Shrine, was: " I will not approach the house of a person with perverted views, even though it may have been surrounded by a Sacred Rope (*shime*) for a thousand days. But I will visit the room of a compassionate person, even though he may be in deep mourning for the death of a father or mother [and therefore subjected to death defilement]." Throughout these aphorisms the strongest emphasis, when a Kami faces man, is upon the heart. The offerings of defiled persons whose hearts are not pure are not to be received even though the Kami has to eat pills of iron or sit in coppery flames. Religious rites are secondary to purity of heart, for the Kami will not go to the house of a person who holds perverted views, even though the house may have been encircled by a Sacred Rope for a thousand days, and thus made ritually pure. On the other hand, the deity will go to the house of a person who has compassion in his heart, even if his house has been defiled by the death of a father or mother. And so it would appear that a man must strive, most of all, for correctness and uprightness of heart. Such a correct and upright heart may not bring temporary advantages, but in the end it will elicit the sympathy of the sun and moon. On the other hand, it is stated that even though a person might obtain immediate gain from getting involved in various sorts of intrigue, eventually he is sure to be punished by the Kami. Of course the coloration and admixture of Buddhist thought are prominent in these aphorisms, particularly in the case of the revelation of the Great Illustrious Kami of Kasuga Shrine. Nevertheless, it is clear that the original *meijō shugi* of Shinto is here deepened and developed.

We have a more theoretical exposition of this *meijō shugi*, or ethical thought about what is correct and upright, in the work of Kitabatake Chikafusa, particularly in his *Jinnō shōtōki*. As Chikafusa received his Shinto theology from Ise Shinto, he was indebted to it for moral teachings of *meijō shugi* that were focused upon concepts of correctness and uprightness. However, the teachings of Chikafusa went far beyond Outer Shrine Shinto in theoretical development, especially in ideas about morality. This was because, although not a few Buddhist elements were incorporated into Chikafusa's Shinto theology, his exposition was essentially a manifestation of ancient Shinto and, for that day, was the richest in originality. That which is most significant in the *Jinnō shōtōki*, in this respect, is Chikafusa's theory about the Hachiman Shrine, found in the section on Emperor Ōjin, and his discussion of the Imperial Regalia, in the earlier section on the descent of the Heavenly Grandson. In developing his theory about the Hachiman Shrine, he cites a revelation which is ascribed, in Outer Shrine Shinto, to Yamato-hime no Mikoto: " Man is the ' Kami stuff ' (*jinmotsu*) of the world. Do not violate the ' heart Kami ' (*shinjin*). For invoking the benevolence of Kami, prayer (*kitō*) is the most efficacious. For protection by the mysterious (*mei*), correctness and uprightness are of basic importance." Another revelation was: " Although the sun and moon revolve about the four continents and shine in the six directions, they will also shine on the head of the correct and the upright." And still another was:

" Fast and prepare yourself purely and fairly with a bright, red heart and not a dirty, black heart. Serve the Great Kami by treating left as left and right as right, without shifting things on the right to the left — without letting anything go awry — and without going back to the left or around to the right. For origins should be treated as origins, and the basic should be treated as basic."[1] To Chikafusa, truly the way of correctness and uprightness meant that no Japanese, born as he was in "Kami Country," (*shinkoku*), could live under the sun and the moon for a single day if he strayed from these virtues. It was a way which brooked not a moment's deviation. In explaining the origin of this way, Chikafusa wrote:

Its origin is in not harboring anything in the heart. On the other hand, one should not reside in nothingness, for there are Heaven and earth, and lord and vassal. The requital for good and evil comes back like reflected light or an echo. May we not say that the true way of correctness consists in meeting the world by discarding one's own desires and placing the benefit of others first, and in avoiding delusion by keeping oneself lucid and clear in any situation, just as a mirror reflects objects?[2]

This is a simple explanation, but its implications are profound. It extends the idea of correctness and uprightness to fairness (*kōsei*) and unselfishness (*mushi*). Moreover, this idea is expressed through the simile of a bright mirror, which — we must admit — renders its meaning as a moral principle with remarkable clarity. This is the first instance of Chikafusa's use of that simile. Furthermore, as Chikafusa saw it, this way of correctness was identified with the heart of the Sun Goddess and the heart of the Great Bodhisatva Hachiman (*Hachiman Daibosatsu*) — Kami that were enshrined at two different ancestral shrines (*sōbyō*). The idea that the heart of the Sun Goddess consisted solely of correctness and uprightness originated with

---

1) [*Jinnō shōtōki, Dai Nihon bunko*, Ser. 2, VI, 44.]
2) [*Ibid.*, 45.]

her sun-Kami divinity, and was due also to her transmission of the "sacred mirror" (*shinkyō*) [as her Kami Body]. As for Hachiman, there was the revelation from him that he would manifest himself in "the eight correct ways." These were: "correct views" (*shōken*, Sanskrit: *samyak-dṛṣti*), "correct thinking" (*shōshii, samyak-samkalpa*), "correct speech" (*shōgo, samyak-vâc*), "correct activity" (*shōgō, samyak-karmânta*), "correct life" (*shōmyō, samyak-âjîva*), "correct devotion" (*shōshōjin, samyak-vyâyâma*), "correct conception" (*shōnen, samyak-smṛti*), and "correct way" (*shōdō, samyak-samâdhi*). Of course these are Buddhist ideas, but in the last analysis they are included in correctness and uprightness. Chikafusa held that they must have been the reason for the original resolve of the Buddhas to come forth in the world, as well as for their manifestations as Kami. In his theories about Hachiman, it is clear that he was a follower of Dual Shinto. Nevertheless, his concept of the Sun Goddess and the Imperial Regalia indicates that the principal points of his Shinto were quite different. He said that the Sun Goddess was the essence of correctness and uprightness; and he did not advance any thesis about her being a manifestation of Buddha. Instead he expounded on her "bright virtue" on the grounds of her divinity as a sun Kami, just as she was described in the Age-of-Kami books of the *Kojiki* and the *Nihongi*; and at the same time he spoke of her venerable nature as the Imperial ancestral Kami. With regard to the relationship of Shintoism to Buddhism and Confucianism — a relationship in which he thought Shinto should be considered the source — he wrote: "As to the propagation of this Way, we must say that it depends on the strength that comes from the dissemination of both the Buddhist and Confucian scriptures. It is like catching a fish: although it is caught in a single mesh of the net, it is hard to catch it without the strength of all the meshes together. The Confucian Classics have been propagated since the reign of Emperor Ōjin, and Buddhism since the time of Prince Shōtoku. Since both of these personages existed in the sanctity of incarnation (*gonge*), they received the 'august heart' of the Sun Goddess, and have thus been able to propagate the Japanese Way far and deep."[1] As shown here, Chikafusa regarded the Sun Goddess as a unique divinity of Japan, and he considered the sacredness of the incarnation of Emperor Ōjin and Prince Shōtoku to be an expression of the divine will of the Sun Goddess. With the Sun Goddess placed clearly at the center, there is in this thesis no trace whatsoever of the "manifestation of original Buddhas" doctrine.

Although the Sun Goddess was considered the ultimate source of correctness and uprightness, Chikafusa's idea of the Three Imperial Regalia also stood at the foundations of his thought. What ought to be noted in this connection is his explanation of the symbolic significance of the Three Imperial Regalia:

The Mirror harbors nothing within itself. As it reflects all phenomena without a selfish heart, there is never an instance when the forms of right and wrong, or good and evil, fail to show up. Its virtue consists in responding to these forms as they come. This is the basic source of correctness and uprightness. The virtue of the Jewel includes gentleness, peace, goodness, and obedience. These are the basic sources of compassion. The virtue of the Sword includes strength, benefit, resolution, and decisiveness. These are the basic sources of wisdom. Unless these three qualities are combined in people, it will be truly difficult for the world to be put right. The Kami decree is clear; its words are concise and its meaning broad. Moreover, it is expressed in the Imperial Regalia. What a wonderful fact this is! Of the Three Imperial Regalia the Mirror is the most important: it is worshipped as the true Kami Body of the ancestral shrine [of the Emperors]. The Mirror gives form to light. Since its "heart nature" is bright, it embodies compassion, resoluteness, and decisiveness. And since it is an accurate

---

1) [*Jinnō shōtōki, Dai Nihon Bunko*, Ser. 2, VI, 22.]

reproduction of the august image, it must certainly contain the profound august heart![1]

The term "Kami decree" in the above quotation refers to the decree issued by the Sun Goddess to keep the Mirror and look upon it as if it were herself. It was given to her grandson, Ni-ni-gi no Mikoto, when he descended from Heaven, together with the mandate to rule the world, which included the promise that rule by his descendants would endure eternally with Heaven and earth.[2]

We note here a "basic virtue" theory that is distinctive in the history of ethics. Many examples of "basic virtue" theory are to be seen in both the Orient and the Occident, but those that are pertinent here are Buddhist and Confucian, since they had some bearing on the ideas of Chikafusa. The first to be considered is the theory of knowledge, benevolence, and courage expounded originally in the *Chung-yung* (Doctrine of the Mean) in which these three qualities are explained as factors in the realization of the ethics of the five relationships: lord and vassal, father and son, husband and wife, elder and younger brother, comrade and friend. Knowledge was the virtue of understanding the ethics of these relationships. Benevolence was embodied in them; and courage strengthened them. That which enabled a person to carry out these virtues was oneness, that is, purity and single-mindedness or sincerity; and sincerity existed within the three virtues, not apart from them. Until now it has been thought that Chikafusa's view of the Three Imperial Regalia was identified with this theory of knowledge, benevolence and courage; but to my mind this is a careless, erroneous generalization that arose after Chikafusa's day, particularly in Confucian speculation during the Tokugawa Era. The three original virtues of the *Jinnō shōtōki* are definitely not an exposition of the doctrine of knowledge, benevolence, and courage developed in the *Doctrine of the Mean*.

---

1) [*Jinnō shōtōki, Dai Nihon bunko,* Ser. 2, VI, 21.]
2) [This resumé has been amplified in translation for grater clarity.]

Probably of greater relevance is the doctrine of the three virtues that appears in the *Shu-ching* (Book of History). In the sixth division of the Great Plan in the " Books of Chou," the three virtues are identified as: correctness and uprightness, mastery through strength, and mastery through gentleness. These three virtues are quite similar to those referred to in the writings of Chikafusa, but in the *Book of History* they are propounded as a means of administering the country and of cultivating the person, as we can see from this quotation: " In peace and tranquility be correct and upright. In violence and rebellion use strength. In harmony and submission use gentleness."[1] This is certainly not identical with the theory of Chikafusa.

Rather, in contrast to the above theories taken from the Confucian classics, there is much in Buddhist doctrines which is similar to the views of Chikafusa, particularly in the doctrine of the three virtues: knowledge, decisiveness, and blessing. Chikafusa's compassion and wisdom, which he associated with the Jewel and the Sword, are both Buddhist concepts. Chikafusa's idea of wisdom, which encompassed " resolution, decisiveness, and courage," included the Buddhist virtue of decisiveness. As for the Buddhist virtue of blessing, this is the compassion of Buddha's altruism and of Buddha's salvation of living things. And wisdom, too, was not unlike [Chikafusa's] correctness and uprightness in the sense that it meant achieving true knowledge, free from delusion.

We can not deny that there were Buddhist influences on Chikafusa's theory of the three virtues, but this was certainly not imitation. Judging from what has already been said about the origin of *meijō shugi,* there should be no doubt but that an essential quality of Shinto was being activated by Buddhist thought. The conviction that the Sun Goddess — whose Kami Body was the Mirror and who was a sun Kami — was the fundamental source of correctness and uprightness

---

1) [Cf. Legge, *The Chinese Classics,* III "The Shoo King" (Hongkong, 1960), 333.]

was certainly rooted in Shinto, and definitely not derived from Buddhism. Chikafusa's doctrine, which was centered on correctness and uprightness, was without doubt based on this Shinto idea. Thus in Chikafusa's thought we see a most remarkable ethical development of a *meijō shugi* that is rooted in ancient Shinto.

With the general spread of education in the Tokugawa Era, the meaning of Shinto was further developed, even in popular education. In Heart Learning (*shingaku*) [1] and the like, Shinto — along with Buddhism and Confucianism — was a subject of instruction; and that which was given the greatest emphasis was the teaching of correctness and uprightness. It is probably correct to say that among the Heart Learning textbooks there was none that did not stress correctness and uprightness. One book of this type was the *Warongo* (Japanese Analects). It was published in 1669 by Sawada Gennai, a genealogist of the Province of Ōmi. In the section on revelations in the first volume there are more than one hundred revelations ascribed to numerous Kami. Of course these are fictitious compositions, but they are very significant expressions of thought at the beginning of the Tokugawa Era. That which is emphasized most are ideas of correctness and uprightness, and of a pure and bright heart. For example: "Just as people look at their faces in a mirror, so we should follow the commandments of our Kami with a pure and bright heart, without hiding anything." Or again: "We can not know the correctness of the image without removing the dust from the mirror." The above are revelations of the Great Illustrious Kami of Togakushi.[2] There are many such revelations, and of course into them are incorporated many ethical thoughts that are Buddhist or Confucian; but the principal emphasis is upon a pure (*kiyoi*) heart. The *Warongo* was lectured on by exponents of Heart Learning. The work was read

---

1) [Cf. Robert N. Bellah, *Tokugawa Religion, the Values of Pre-industrial Japan* (Free Press; 1957).]
2) [A Kami enshrined at Tokugawa Shrine in Nagano Prefecture.]

widely and was effective in indoctrination. The *meijō shugi* in the ethical thought of this book is something worthy of attention.[1]

In Suiga Shinto, as was pointed out in our discussion of *kōkoku shugi*, doctrines were well developed, particularly with regard to the concept of loyalty. Consequently, not only were correctness and uprightness, and sincerity, vigorously expounded, but the idea of respect (*tsutsushimi*) was stressed. *Tsutsushimi* corresponds to the Confucian term *ching*; and in Suiga Shinto it was associated with the "earthgold" (*dokon*) doctrine.[2] Here too we see an elucidation of the idea of a bright and pure heart.

The same holds for Ancient-Learning Shinto. Kamo Mabuchi got into his Ancient Way from a mastery of the *Man'yōshū* poems, and he discovered great meaning in the natural simplicity and plainness of the spirit of antiquity — a spirit that was not seen in later times. But what was especially developed in his ideas of the Ancient Way was the value of the upright or bright heart. The brightness and gaiety in the spirit of our antiquity were best captured by him. The same holds for his successor, Motoori Norinaga, who pressed Kamo's world of the *Man'yōshū* back into the world of the *Kojiki*. His *meijō shugi*, as moralistic thought, is expressed in his *Tamaboko hyakushu* (One Hundred Poems on the Way) precisely as it was in ancient Shinto. For example:

---

1) [Except for the excerpts included in the *Kokumin shisō sōsho*, IX (Tokyo, 1931), there is no modern edition of the *Warongo*. The editions of the Tokugawa Era consist of ten volumes, of which the first contains the Kami revelations.]

2) [The "earth-metal" doctrine, of which there have been several versions, is a philosophical concept in Shinto derived originally from the idea of the Five Elements (*wu-hsing*) in Chinese cosmology. The characters 土金, "earth-metal," can be read either *dokon* (in Sino-Japanese) or *tsuchikane* (in Japanese). Yamazaki Ansai, through rather specious reasoning and phonetic manipulation, interpreted *tsuchikane* as *tsuchishimaru* or "earth becomes solid"; and the latter he related both semantically and phonologically to *tsutsushimi* or respect. And on this basis, he devised his so-called "earth-metal" theory, which is an ethical theory centered in the concept of respect. See *Shinto Daijiten*, III, 17–18.]

Dare not defile	Ie mo mi mo
The home, the person, the country;	kuni mo kegasuna
For pollution is a taboo,	kegare ha shi
The gravest of evils,	kami no imimasu
In the eyes of Kami.	yuyushiki tsumi o.
How disgusting it is	Kegare o shi
To see people	tsumi to mo shirazu
Refraining from ablution, yet complacent,	misogazute
Not knowing that pollution	moda aru hito o
Is a *tsumi*.	miru ga ibuseki.

The excellence of the following poem, although not included in this particular anthology, is extolled by everyone. It, too, is a lyrical expression of the spirit of *meijō shugi*.

Should anyone want to know	Shikishima no
About the Yamato-Heart	Yamatogokoro o
Of Shikishima,	hito towaba
It is the mountain-cherry blossoms	asahi ni niou
Blowing in the morning sun.	yamazakurabana.

With Hirata Atsutane as well, there is the same attitude toward brightness and purity, and for him the views are best expressed in his *Dōmō nyūgakumon* (A Child's Introduction to Learning). This work may be described as an elementary textbook written from the point of view of the Imperial Way (*kōdō*), written in Chinese (*kambun*). It is divided into the following seven chapters: " Reverence of Kami "; " Nation Body " (*kokutai*); " Worshipping Ancestors "; " Purity and Cleanliness "; " Children "; " Eating and Drinking "; and " Reading Books." The essential points are made concisely and clearly. From the chapter on "Reverence of Kami" on through the detailed treatment of manners and ordinary behavior, this book — as an educational book in Ancient-Learning Shinto — is representative. In the fourth chapter on "Purity and Cleanliness" we read:

> Upon rising each morning, wash your hands and rinse your mouth. (Using a toothpick, eliminate totally the mouth odors. After this, wash the face and upper arms well, protecting the collar and sleeves of your clothing with a towel.) Comb your hair, and then inquire as to the health of your father and mother, and your elders. Clean the rooms and the garden with water. And, finally, when the offerings for the Kami have been prepared, worship the Kami.
>
> Eschew all that is dirty or defiled, and relish what is pure and clean. Correctness of attitude and nobleness and dignity are qualities handed down from the Age of Kami, and they are still honored. In worshipping the hallowed Kami, you must especially be more solemn and respectful.[1]

Of course this book, being intended for children, deals only with common, ordinary things. But its inclusion of a special chapter on purity and cleanness, and its stress on these as qualities derived from the Age of Kami, is another manifestation of the *meijō shugi* in Shinto. The same emphasis prevails in various sects of Founder Shinto, but I will not go into that here.

It is clear, therefore, that *meijō shugi* is a conspicuous feature of Shintoism. It is manifested, it seems to me, not only in the area of morals, but also in rites and ceremonies, as well as in the related areas of art and taste. It is to be seen, for example, in Shinto shrine architecture, which places value on freshness, and in the paintings

---

1) [*Hirata Atsutane zenshū* (Tokyo, 1911–1918), XIV.]

of the Yamato-e School, which might even be termed Shinto (as opposed to Buddhist) art.

5. *Conclusion*

In the above I have taken *kōkoku shugi* (Imperial Country-ism), realism *(genjitsu shugi)*, and *meijō shugi* (brightness-purity-ism) as three common characteristics of Shinto. By giving outstanding examples, I have explained how these characteristics emerged in ancient Shinto and how they appeared and developed in the various periods of Shinto history. Finally I should like to add a few words by way of conclusion.

These three characteristics were chosen because of their prominence — that is, they were identified inductively. I have made no attempt to analyze them deductively on theoretical foundations. Although we can not be precise about this, if we were to identify, in general, the areas where these three characteristics would be representative or paramount, we could probably say, first of all, that *meijō shugi* is an ethical characteristic of Shinto. Secondly, in view of the fact that realism makes up the underlying tone of the life-outlook and world-outlook of Shinto, it probably would not be inappropriate to say that realism is a philosophical characteristic. Finally, although it is difficult to be specific about *kōkoku shugi,* since it has an essentially broad character, it can probably be designated as a basically political characteristic.

But the several ethical, philosophical, and political attributes of these three characteristics are substantively interrelated — as if the three are fundamentally intertwined. *Kōkoku shugi,* for example, has a realistic, this-world quality in its theories that place primary importance on the state, and in an ancestor worship that is based upon the worship of Emperors as manifest Kami. Furthermore, *kōkoku shugi* affirms a realistic optimism, especially in its expectation of an endless development of an Imperial Country deriving from a Kami mandate "as eternal as Heaven and earth." Conversely, when the interrelationship is considered from the side of realism, we note an attempt to see the realization of an optimistic, this-world outlook in Japan, a country which is thought of as the principal place in world history for such a development. Finally, in its emphasis upon purity of heart, *meijō shugi* supports *kōkoku shugi* by affirming a morality of loyalty to the ruler. In its subscription to a sort of theory of the goodness of human nature — in which goodness is thought of as having a positive quality, and badness as a negative quality — *meijō shugi* is joined with an optimism that affirms reality. If we were to make a detailed comparison of the various aspects of these three characteristics of Shinto, it would probably be easy to find this kind of interdependent connection.

In the last analysis, since the three characteristics are nothing but manifestations of a single intellectual strain that lies deep within them, it is this "intellectual strain" which we may term the essence of Shinto. Although Shinto is certainly not monolithic, having appeared in different forms down through history, this strain is really basic to all that is Shinto — in other words, to all those characteristics that are common to Shinto, in contradistinction to Confucianism, Buddhism and Christianity. And "that which is Shinto" should probably be considered as forming the most important part, if not the whole, of that which is Japanese. The Japanese spirit or Japanese thought, when considered historically, undoubtedly possesses "that which is Shinto" in a fundamental way. At the same time, Shinto in this sense, but not necessarily as a religion in rivalry with others, may well have been the factor which imparted to all religions in Japan those unique features which distinguish them from their appearances in their own country or in countries other than Japan. Actually this has already been verified, time and again, in our cultural history. Notable examples are to be seen in the appearance of various Buddhist sects as state faiths, and in such nationalistic Confucian developments as seen in the Yamazaki Ansai school.

As to the Japanization of Christianity, the nature of Christian teachings certainly did not permit easy compromise. In the relationships between Christianity and Shinto, there were — from the Shinto side — the cases of Hirata Atsutane and his School, and also of Nanri Yūrin [1812–1864].[1] But these were truly exceptional. From the Christian side, on the other hand, there was historically almost no recognition of the existence of Shinto. Of course denunciations of Shinto were already included in the Christian literature written at the time Christianity was introduced into Japan, as seen in the views about Shinto expressed in *Myōtei mondō* (Dialogue between Myōshū and Yūtei).[2] It is my opinion that there must have been in some sense (to be considered later), and in some form, a Shinto influence on Christianity in Japan.

Let us consider the causal and developmental significance of that which is Shinto. As was seen when we considered each case, the characteristics of *kōkoku shugi,* realism, and *meijō shugi* all had their origin in Japanese thought, that is, in the ancient Shinto of the primitive period; and each achieved, in various ways, its development throughout a considerable length of history from the ancient period, through the medieval and Tokugawa eras, on down to modern times. But in every instance Confucianism, Buddhism, and Christianity — and in the recent period, also Western culture — were important causes, and provided motivation for these developments; they gave to the three characteristics of Shinto profundity, refinement, and rationale. In a general way the stages of Shinto development ran through the whole of history: in the ancient period its basic pattern came into existence; then various foreign faiths gave it content; and finally the content was further developed by the adoption and assimilation of elements of these foreign faiths. These "three characteristics" took

---

1) [None of his voluminous writing has been published.]
2) [Written in 1605 in the form of a dialogue between two nuns. It sets forth what is claimed to be the truth of Christianity, as opposed to the errors of Confucianism and Shinto. The first scroll, concerning the errors of Buddhism, has been lost.]

on various forms during this long history, as has been pointed out, and made Shinto itself something sharply distinct from other religions. In essence, the three characteristics of Shinto attained growth and development and were nurtured by adopting, Shintoistically, the various intellectual elements introduced from abroad, and by being acted upon by these foreign elements, and internalizing them.

While these characteristics apply generally to that which is Shinto, they also apply to "that which is Japanese." With the introduction of Confucianism and then Buddhism at the beginning of the ancient period, our culture was developed in all areas as a result of Chinese and continental influences. And in the Tokugawa Era, we came into contact with, and were stimulated by, Western culture. In the modern period it is clear that we have come to a new turning point because of the influence of Western culture. Still our culture has never been completely destroyed by submergence in pure imitation of any of the cultures imported from abroad. There is no doubt but that we were able to realize, in some form, a "Japanese culture." Because of this, our country has been able to occupy an independent and autonomous position that clearly places her among the world's nations of culture. Not only is this true for the period that can be strictly called historical, down to the end of the Tokugawa Era, but it is true also of the period since Meiji (a period during which we have been introducing Western culture) and probably it will be — in fact, it must be — true also of future cultural history, which I think will not be short, and in which the introduction of Western culture should be brought to completion. The reason why our country has been able to maintain and develop its independent position while introducing one culture after another from abroad, without being overwhelmed by them, must be that there has existed at the foundations of our national spirit something which is uniquely Japanese. That which is Japanese can probably be called "the Japanese spirit." What this spirit really is can be clarified only by looking into the history of the culture of our country and by comparing the Japanese spirit with the national spirit of various other countries of culture in the world. But this is certainly not a simple problem. Of course it is not a problem that can be resolved by merely listing what are considered to be strengths in the character of the Japanese people — strengths which must naturally be accompanied by weaknesses. Nevertheless, I do not think that it is a mistake to say that that which is "Japanese" must at least have had an important relationship to the "that which is Shinto," the subject we have been considering. If so, we can probably say that Shinto, in this sense, will have a long cultural life. If what we call "Japanese philosophy" — in contradistinction of course to Western philosophy but especially to Oriental philosophy — is to be established, it probably will result from digging deeply into that which is Japanese, or that which is Shinto; and also it will take form by giving these a theoretical base. Actually it is inconceivable that a Japanese philosophy will be established without considering, in some sense, that which is Japanese or Shinto. Anyway, if Shinto is given such a theoretical foundation, the special meaning of what is called Shinto will be further enhanced. But this lies outside the scope of the present study.

Note: For supplementary reading on various points made in this article the reader is referred to the following three articles written by me and published in the *Iwanami kōza* (Iwanami Lectures): (1) "Nihon shichō toku ni taiko no bu" (Currents of Japanese Thought, Especially Those of the Remote Past) in the *Sekai shichō* (Currents of World Thought) lectures, 1928–29; (2) "Nihon tetsugaku shi" (History of Japanese Philosophy) in the *Tetsugaku* (Philosophy) lectures, June, 1932; and (3) "Shinto no rinrigaku" (Ethics of Shinto) in the *Kyōiku kagaku* (Science of Education) lectures, December, 1932.

Chapter II

Moral Consciousness and its Development in Ancient Shinto[1]

1. *Introduction*

The *Kojiki* in particular, but also the *Nihongi* (most of it), the Shinto liturgies (*norito*),[2] the ancient provincial gazttteers (*fudoki*),[3] and the *Kogo shūi* (Gleanings from Ancient Stories)[4] may be treated as sources for intellectual history, not only of the period in which they were compiled but of earlier periods as well, provided they are under-

---

1) [First published in *Tetsugaku kenkyū* (Philosophical Studies) No. 58 in January of 1921 and included in Muraoka Tsunetsugu, *Zōtei Nihon shisō shi kenkyū* (Studies in Japanese Intellectual History, Enlarged and Revised) (Tokyo, Iwanami Shoten; 1940), 1–20.]
2) [The extant *norito* include 27 that are in volume 8 of the *Engishiki* (a compilation of laws and regulations of 927 A.D.), and a few others. They were "magic words" that were sometimes addressed to Kami and sometimes to the people. All of the *norito* included in the *Engishiki*, and five others, have been translated by Donald L. Philippi, *Norito, A New Translation of the Ancient Japanese Ritual Prayers* (Tokyo, 1959).]
3) [By an Imperial Edict of 713 A.D. each province was ordered to submit a report on its local geography, native products, local traditions, and general conditions. These reports, known as the *fudoki*, are an important source of information for Japanese life of antiquity. Many have been lost, wholly or in part; and many of the remaining ones are revisions or were written at a later date. Of special value are those of the provinces of Izumo, Harima, Bungo, Hizen and Hitachi. The first two have been translated by Sakai Atsuharu: "The Izumo-Fudoki or the Records of Customs and Land of Izumo," *Cultural Nippon* IX, 2 (1941), 141–95, 3 (1941), 4 (1941), 108–49; and "The Hitachi-Fudoki or Records of Customs and Land of Hitachi," *Cultural Nippon* VIII, 2 (1940), 145–85, 3 (1940), 109–56, 4 (1940), 137–86.]
4) [A work of written tradition compiled by the Imbe clan and submitted to the Emperor in 807 A.D., in support of the clan's claims to a more prominent position at the Court. Translated by Katō Genchi and Hoshino Hikoshirō, *Kogoshūi, Gleanings from Ancient Stories* (Tokyo, 1926).]

stood as being essentially and originally compilations of orally recited traditions that were intended to be an aid for reciters. Such a work was compiled gradually *while* the traditions were still being transmitted orally. Thus it should be possible to ascertain layers in the development of the consciousness of the ancients through an historical investigation of the formative process that is inherent in these works. In justifying the view that the above sources are on the whole works of written tradition, we can cite testimony on the origin of the *Kojiki* — the most representative work of written tradition — which is recorded in its preface. Motoori Norinaga's trustworthy historical interpretation of this preface clarifies the character of the *Kojiki* as a work of written tradition. His interpretation of 誦習 as " reciting from memory " is still valid, although it has been challenged in recent years. Those who try to understand the term as " *kundoku* " (reading Chinese characters in the Japanese fashion) are hard put to it to interpret the passage 所誦之勅語舊辭. But this passage also suggests that the *Kojiki* is a compilation of orally recited traditions that was intended to be an aid for reciters. The opposing theory which states that oral transmission could not have existed after the technique of writing had come into use seems rational enough, but it does not fit the conditions of antiquity. The reader is asked to consider the *Logios Anēr* of ancient Greece who were supposed to have had texts to help them remember oral tradition. These oral recitations by master reciters are said to have been preserved until quite late in history as an appropriate device for assuring a faithful transmission of legend. Thus, passing on the traditions orally paralleled the existence of books in which these traditions were recorded.

Assuming that the practice still existed when the *Kojiki* was being compiled, we can draw certain inferences about earlier periods. After the primitive period — before there was writing and when " high and low, old and young, all handed down traditions from mouth to mouth, and past words and deeds were not forgotten " — came the period when Chinese characters were used, the age of the above-mentioned compilations of orally recited traditions. In this later period the traditions of successive ages, beginning with those of the ancient past, were written down while they were being passed on orally and passed on orally while they were being written down. With the passing of time different versions were produced and alterations occurred; and, in the meantime, distinctions came to be made between that which was principally a chronicle and that which had the quality of pure legend — between the so-called "annals of the Emperors" (*teiki*) and the "old stories" (*kyūji*). From the contents of the *Kojiki* it is deduced that the age of oral-tradition compilations began just prior to the Suiko Era (554–628 A. D.), which marks a new age in the cultural history of antiquity. After this period of oral-tradition compilations, we enter one in which histories were compiled by the Imperial Court, when the traditional "annals of the Emperors" and "old stories" became more historicized. Naturally revisions of tradition were now quite conspicuous. Even in this later period the old custom of oral transmission persisted, continuing on into later times. If we assume that the *Kojiki* is a compilation, in the ancient manner, of "annals of the Emperors" and "old stories" and that this work was a compilation of what seems to me to be a single line of Imperial-annal and old-story descent, with relatively primitive characteristics, then it is the *Nihongi* which follows the Chinese principles of historical compilation in bringing together different lines of descent. It was natural that the compilers of the latter work, when selecting "old stories," should have done what they could to discard that which was primitive and to include that which was relatively rational — at least using the more rational for the main theme (this is suggested by the existence of a separate Age-of-Kami book). And it was also natural that they should have attempted rhetorical embellishment. The other ancient classics can also be considered in terms of these differences between the *Kojiki* and the *Nihongi*. Therefore, in discussing the development of moral consciousness in ancient and classical times, from the point of view of these considerations, it is clear that there were three distinct periods: the remote antiquity that preceded the introduction of Chinese characters, the period of oral tradition compilations, and the period of historical writing.

2. *Remote Antiquity*

Discussions about the morality of remote antiquity were carried on during the Tokugawa Era by Confucian and National Learning scholars. The Confucianists considered the period before the introduction of Confucianism as one of "chaos" when people married close relatives and observed no precedence in relations between the old and the young. Kamo Mabuchi, on the other hand, saw remote antiquity as an ideal age that was a product of naturalness and non-interference. His view, based upon the philosophy of Lao-tse and Chuang-tzu, was not unlike the "degeneration theory" which, with reference to the origin of religion, denies moral development in later times. The two diametrically opposed views both denied the existence of a moral consciousness in remote antiquity. But the Confucianists said that this led to immorality, whereas Mabuchi claimed that it led to "supra-morality." Motoori Norinaga, who was — within the limits of his scholarship about the Ancient Way — a student of Mabuchi, threw additional light on the amoral conditions of remote antiquity. Through his philological study he succeeded in reconstructing the conditions of moral consciousness that had prevailed in that early period. As a result of his work, we can see that amorality was not necessarily immorality, and that the lack of moral consciousness in antiquity was not absolute, but a primitive condition preceding development.

In the absence of definite proof to the contrary, I am inclined to think of the various mythological and religious elements incorporated into the Age of Kami stories of the *Kojiki* and the *Nihongi* — along with similar elements included in other ancient sources — as mostly products of primitive thought. Therefore, I make the beginning point of this investigation the religious consciousness of people in ancient times, or ancient Shinto thought. Among the elements that made up the content of ancient ideas about Kami — etymologically "Kami" is thought to have been identical with "superior" (*kami*) — the most powerful was the worship of the natural objects of heaven and earth (such as heavenly bodies, mountains, rivers, fields, seas, rain, and wind), but also of birds, beasts, insects, trees, wood, grass, and minerals. The next most important element was the worship of great men, heroes, or leaders. The two types were often fused. Aside from Kami that were identified with concrete objects, there were cases of a deification of the power that resided in nature or men. The creative (*musubi*) Kami [Takami-musubi and Kami-musubi] were identified with the power of growth and reproduction, "straightening Kami" with rectifying activity, "bending Kami" with the operation of misfortune, Thought-Combining Kami (Omoi-kane no Kami) with wisdom, and Strong-armed Male Kami (Ta-jikara-o no Kami) with physical strength. We see some examples of the worship of souls, a worship that is wholly unrelated to the Kami ideas mentioned above. But there were as yet no conspicuous examples in the ancient traditions of people moving beyond their fear of souls of the dead to belief in ancestral souls, although from burial customs it can be deduced that the worship of souls did exist. The Kami were conceived of as possessing awesome potency because they were "unusual," irrespective of whether they were good or bad, noble or mean, strong or weak, big or small. But there were other attributes which differentiated the nature of Kami from the nature of man. It was thought that Kami belonged to the concealed world (*yūkai*) which could not be seen by men (but which was fundamentally a material world), and that they could enter and leave the visible world (*kenkai*).

Now if, in looking at the consciousness of these ancient people, we give special attention to the relationship between man and Kami, we will note, first, that in the prayers addressed by men to Kami extremely primitive elements like curses (*noroi*), maledictions (*tokoi*) and imprecations (*kajiri*) — by which the power of Kami was invoked with a desire to inflict harm on other people — were mixed up with prayers which were appeals to Kami that good fortune be granted or evils avoided. "Curse words" (*noroigoto*) are examples of the first type of communication with Kami, and Shinto liturgies (*norito*) of the second. In both cases the repetitive phrases which express the petition have a half poetic form. Among the *noroigoto* that have come down to us, all are requests that a certain person take sick, suffer, or be short-lived; but in some cases the objective was to punish an evil doer. The *norito* that have been preserved are in the standard form of Imperial Court rites. If we examine the latter, we will see that their subject matter concerns the welfare of the Imperial Court and the people — that they contain requests for good crops, the prosperity of the reigning Emperor, and the prevention of calamities. In their primitive form, *norito* did not of course have such a public character. As a logical result of the fact that the religious feelings of the ancients had not yet moved to the point of faith (*shinrai*), the people were not content with merely reciting prayers. In order to ascertain the will of the Kami, various forms of divination were used. First of all, there were scapula divination (*kataura*), interpretations of dreams (*yumeura*), and harp divination (*kotoura*); but there were also oaths (*ukei*) which were made with the expectation of achieving desired results, and such things as immersion in boiling water (*kukadachi*), which was one way of obtaining divine judgment. The same psychology is seen in spells (*majinai*) by which, through special arrangements, mysterious powers were summoned up in an attempt to intervene — with respect to good and evil fortune — in the fate of one's self or others.

As for the intervention of Kami in the lives of men, the ancients believed in Kami exhalation (*Kami no ke*) [associated with pestilence], Kami curses (*Kami no tatari*), Kami possession (*Kamigakari*), and oracles (*takusen*). Kami exhalation and Kami curses were phenomenal manifestations of Kami anger. Kami possession occurred in response to particular requests from persons, but there were also cases of possession instituted by Kami without a human request. In most of these cases a woman or child became possessed and then, in a state of trance, passed on oracular messages. In cases where special arrangements had been made, an interpreter would wait on the one possessed and determine the will of the Kami. Finally, the principal object of a festival (*matsuri*), in the strict sense, was to appease a Kami by: arranging a festival at some time or place; inviting the Kami spirit; making offerings of clothing, food, and other objects; having music and dancing; and feasting for days and nights. The same things were done when honoring (*matsuru*) the dead, attempting thereby to bring the dead back to this world.

From the above outline we can now move on to a consideration of the question of Kami morality in the consciousness of the ancients. In the minds of these people there was a distinction between good and evil Kami. The good Kami were not specifically designated as such — they were simply not bad Kami. Most Kami were good — they manifested a power to produce life or to foster it. In other words, the good Kami displayed the fundamental nature of Kami. The bad Kami, on the other hand — like the so-called "bending Kami" (*magatsubi no Kami*), "the rough Kami" (*araburu Kami*), and the "crooked Kami" (*yokoshima no Kami*) — were those that obstructed the life-giving processes. The good life-giving Kami of the Plain of High Heaven (*Takamagahara*) line were centered around the Sun Goddess. She was a manifestation of the heliolatry of a people living in the temperate zone, and she had tolerant and merciful qualities. But there were such bad Kami as: the "bending Kami" of the Yomi (the land of the dead) line who were hindrances to life-giving power; Izanami and susa-no-o after they became the Great Kami of Yomi; the Great Kami of Izumo [Ō-na-muchi] who opposed the Kami of the Plain of High Heaven line; and the "rough Kami" that represented forces, in various local areas, opposed to the people [associated with the Kami] of the Plain of High Heaven. In the same sense, such things as pestilence and thunder claps were thought to be Kami curses. Moreover, not only were good and evil

Kami equally the object of worship, but good and evil were not necessarily absolute attributes of a Kami — if a good Kami grew angry, it became an evil Kami; and if an evil Kami quieted down, it became a good Kami. Curses and maledictions were invocations to the bad nature of Kami and most prayers were directed to the good nature of Kami.

Such a conception of good and evil in the nature of Kami was manifested, in the same way, in attitudes toward human individuals. Good (*yoshi*) meant beauty, excellence, good fortune, and nobility — goodness was identified generally with the activation of life-giving power. Bad (*ashi*) was the opposite. A good person was a noble person, not a morally good person; and a good thing was a fortunate thing, not something morally good. The Chinese term 善心 *shan-hsin* (virtuous heart) was translated into Japanese as *uruwashiki kokoro* (fine heart), and denoted an affectionate heart. In contradistinction to moralistic words, "rough" (*araburu*) was applied to Kami, "bent" (*maga*) to things, and "strange" (*keshiki*) to the human heart. These are only a few examples of the use of the word "bad" (*ashi*), but from these it can be deduced that it meant "ill-omened," "unlucky," and "inferior." In the 15th scroll of the *Man'yōshū* [compiled CA. 759] we have an early example of the original meaning of "good" and "bad":

The avenues of Nara,	Ao ni *yoshi*
Rich in *good* blue earth	Nara no ōji wa
Are *good* to walk on,	yuki *yoke* do
But this mountain path	kono yamamichi wa
I find is *bad* to walk on.	yuki *ashi* kari keri.

Thus the words "good" and "bad", in their original sense, carried this kind of sensuous or utilitarian meaning which, moreover, has not disappeared. This is true of many other words as well.

But words which illustrate the ancient view of evil and good much more concretely are "dirty" (*kitanashi*) and "bright" (*akashi*). We frequently see these words used to express the evil and good in matters of the human heart. The bad heart was a " dirty heart " which was malicious, and the pure heart was one which was not dirty — a bright heart that hid nothing. This sort of consciousness is best shown in the Great Purification liturgy in which there is a typical expression of the ancient view of evil — that is, *tsumi* was a dirty something that could be washed away by ablution and lustration (*misogi harai*). Furthermore, albinism, body growths, and disasters caused by the " birds on high " or " Kami on high " — all sensually disagreeable to people — were enumerated as *tsumi*, along with such actions as breaking down the embankments between the fields, scattering excrement, indiscriminate sexual relations, and bestiality. Thus no distinction was made between natural calamities and the evil acts of men. Because of this, perhaps, lustration was thought of as the source of all things fortunate.

Thus the ancient outlook on life and the world was essentially one of unsophisticated optimism. Nature, as a manifestation of life-giving-power, was undisguisedly good. There could be no better world than this world. There were powers that obstructed and destroyed life-giving power, but in the end they would be overcome — " straightening " (*naobi*) action would be directed against these misfortunes. Although the Great Kami of Yomi killed a thousand people every day, Izanagi gave birth to one thousand five hundred. Although the rough Kami tormented travellers in various places, at least half of them lived. As a result of such " straightening " action, life-giving power was perpetually winning. This was because good fortune was dominant. Possibly creativity (*musubi*), because of this, was a fundamental world principle. Nature was good and natural laws were moral laws. Similarly, although evil — which was against nature — merely existed negatively, goodness was by no means the norm. With respect to the ideal worlds of ancient Shinto, it was natural that Yomi — which, in view of parallels in religious history, should have been more highly developed than ideas about the Plain of High Heaven and the Yonder World — was simply thought of as " an ugly, dirty land " where everyone went after death. It was natural that there was no development of moralistic content to such thought. Feeling that the fortunes and misfortunes of this world were not necessarily the deserts of good and evil, the ancient people had absolutely no intellectual experience with projecting into the next life a separate and morally just world. The existence of [later] theories asserting the immorality or amorality of antiquity was due to this naturalism. And it is for the same reason that scholars developed views of a supra-morality in which they recognized such basically human characteristics as innocence, beauty, and strength — characteristics that were supposed to have completely disappeared in later ages.

I have attempted to explain the moral consciousness of antiquity as a primitive stage in our moral and intellectual history, and from this standpoint I probably should identify phases of development in this moral consciousness of ancient Shinto. As a matter of fact, in the above discussion — for example, in dealing with the worship of Kami and demons, and with the kinds of prayers that were addressed to them — I could not but touch upon phases of development. But the analysis of these various elements, and the clarification of the development from the simple to the more advanced, must be left to research in folk psychology. My objective has been to understand the existence, in the period of ancient Shinto, of a state of consciousness in which these various elements were intertwined. At any rate, I feel that it is proper, for the present, to set such limits to my study.

3. *Period of Oral Tradition Compilation*

The development of a more advanced stage of moral consciousness is thought to have been caused by the systemization of social conditions which took place when a state organization was perfected and, along with this, a clan (*uji*) system formed. For one thing, the increase of state power which resulted from these developments led to the establishment of relations with Korea and this international relationship further strengthened the unity of the state and increased the prestige of the Imperial Family. The various mythological elements that had existed since antiquity were now united historically around one deity, the Sun Goddess, who was called the "Imperial Ancestral Kami," so that a single Kami genealogy and a national history were formed. To the idea of "a great king who rules as a manifest Kami" was added the new ingredient of "an all-ruling Emperor" (*sumera mikoto*). It is surmised that the above-mentioned external developments were accompanied internally by a gradual refinement of moral sentiment — as is suggested, for example, by the prohibition against people accompanying their masters in death, referred to in the Emperor Suinin section of the *Nihongi*. As Confucian moral thought, which was a product of contact with Korea, gradually became a force in education, it further strengthened these growing moralistic sentiments and systematic thought and became a great force for the development of moral consciousness. A notable Confucian sentiment can be seen in the "long poem" supposed to have been composed by Waki-iratsuko, Japan's first student of Confucianism, when he saw the corpse of his elder brother, the rebel Ōyamamori no Mikoto, lying on the bank of the Uji River. Likewise, the statement that Emperor Nintoku [who probably reigned in the fifth century A. D.] was a famous "sage emperor," and also the item that these two brothers declined the throne in favor of the other,[1] show that Nara-Era Japanese wanted to see Confucian influences as early as Nintoku's time.

With the second period, which begins with the Korean affair [that is, the arrival of the first embassy from Korea],[2] we enter, as

---

1) [Emperor Nintoku, who was known as Ōsazaki before his accession, was the elder brother of Waki-iratsuko and Ōyamamori. Their father, Emperor Ōjin, designated Waki-iratsuko as his successor, thus passing over the eldest son. After Ōjin's death, Ōyamamori rebelled and was killed by Waki-iratsuko. Nevertheless, Waki-iratsuko refused to accept the throne, saying that it should go to his elder brother, Ōsazaki; and Ōsazaki declined in deference to the will of their father. After three years, during which time there was no Emperor, Waki-iratsuko ended the impasse by committing suicide; whereupon Ōsazaki ascended the throne as Emperor Nintoku.]
2) [According to the *Nihongi*, the first embassy from Korea arrived from the kingdom of Mimana in the 65th year of the reign of Sujin, who traditionally was Japan's eleventh Emperor.]

I indicated above, the period of oral-tradition compilations. By comparing variations of the following stories in the *Kojiki* and the *Nihongi*, we can detect a development of moral consciousness:

(1) In the legend about the rebellion of Prince Sahohiko and his younger sister, Empress Sahohime — recorded in the Emperor Suinin sections of the *Kojiki* and the *Nihongi*.

In the *Kojiki* version the Prince asked his sister whether she loved him (her elder brother) or the Emperor (her husband). The Empress replied that she loved her elder brother. Then the Prince revealed his rebellious designs, gave her a dagger, and made her promise to assassinate the Emperor. One night when the Emperor went to sleep with his head resting on the Empress' knee, she decided that this was the time to kill him. Three times she raised the dagger, intending to stab the Emperor in the neck. But she could not bear to do it and broke out in tears. The Emperor was awakened by her tears and told the Empress a strange dream he had had. Hearing this, the Empress confessed everything. When the Emperor sent a punitive force against the Prince, the Empress fled to join her brother. She was pregnant at the time and gave birth to a child at the encampment. The Emperor loved the Empress to the end and wanted her and the child to return. The Empress returned the child but refused to go herself and finally died with her brother.

The *Nihongi* version, however, has it that the Empress, without fathoming the intent of her brother's question, replied that she loved him. Then the Prince tried to exert influence over her by talking about the uncertain destiny of those who serve men in sensual pleasure. The Empress " trembled in her heart and did not know what to do." But knowing at the time that she could not change her brother's mind one iota, she accepted the dagger " intending eventually to dissuade him." (This last clause is thought to have been inserted later on. Even so, it is a plausible amplification of the text.) And even when the Emperor was sleeping on her knee, she had not decided on assassination. She wept, thinking vainly of her brother's plot that " this would have been the proper time." In her confession, she apologized and explained her feelings of extreme anguish and torment, being able neither to oppose the will of her brother or to forget her debt of gratitude to the Emperor. Then, when the Emperor sent a punitive force against Prince Sahohiko, the lady felt that even though she was the Empress, she could not face the prospect of presiding over the Empire after her brother's ruin. So, taking with her the infant prince that had been born by that time, she fled to her brother's army. The Emperor had the Prince's stronghold surrounded by armies and demanded the return of the Empress and the child. But the Empress said that she had fled to her brother's stronghold in hopes that her brother's crime would be forgiven on account of her and the child and that since her brother had not been forgiven, she realized that she too was guilty, and had decided to take her own life. She returned the child because she could not forget her debt of gratitude to the Emperor, and then died with her brother.

In both the *Kojiki* and the *Nihongi* it is recorded that the Empress recommended her successor to the Emperor and that he accepted her recommendation.

(2) In a story about Prince Yamato Takeru — recorded in the Emperor Keikō sections of the *Kojiki* and the *Nihongi*.

In the *Kojiki* version the Emperor became afraid of Prince Yamato Takeru because of the violent way the Prince had treated his elder brother, Prince Ōusu, who had been disrespectful toward the Emperor. The Prince had seized his brother, wrapped him up in a straw mat, and abandoned him. Consequently, the Emperor sent Prince Yamato Takeru off on an expedition against the Kumaso. When the Prince had carried out this mission, he received an order from the Emperor to undertake the conquest of the Emishi to the east. The Prince, resenting the attitude of the Emperor, called on his aunt, Princess Yamato Hime, at the Ise Shrine and complained that the Emperor wanted him to be killed. When the Prince eventually died of illness at Nobono, his wife and children came from the distant Province of Yamato and grieved deeply as they followed the trail of the Prince's soul, which had been transformed into a white bird.

But in the *Nihongi* version there is nothing about the Prince's killing his elder brother. When the Prince returned from his successful campaign against the Kumaso, the Emperor was very fond of him and rewarded him for his deeds. In the discussion about who should be sent to subjugate the Emishi in the east, the Prince recommended his elder brother. But because the elder brother was frightened and ran away, the Prince himself came forward to serve the state, being indignant with his brother and bravely not minding the trouble. In an Imperial Edict the Emperor extolled the Prince: " In form you are my child, but in reality you are a Kami man..... This land is your land and this throne is your throne." Two famous soldiers and a cook were sent along with the Prince. When the Emperor received the sad news of the Prince's death at Nobono, he was cast into such gloom that he could neither eat nor sleep. Remembering the deeds performed by the Prince ever since the conquest of the Kumaso in his youth, the Emperor lamented how he had waited, with constant anxiety for the Prince's safety, only to hear of his death.

As to these two stories — both of which belong to the period of pure legend — the first, as told in the *Kojiki,* is about a Princess who is swayed by her affection for a close relative and an Emperor who is captivated by love for his Empress. The second is about a Prince who, with respect to boldness of action and violence of emotion, is an ideal hero of antiquity, and about a father — an Emperor — who is afraid of the son. These are plain, simple stories about relationships between natural persons. But we should note the difference of tone in the later *Nihongi* treatment. In the first story we have a tragedy about a heroine who is tormented by much self-examination, and in the second a tale about a son who is loyal and an Emperor who has deep feelings of benevolence and love.

(3) In an item of a later period recorded in the Emperor Nintoku sections of the *Kojiki* and *Nihongi.*

In the *Kojiki* version the Emperor sent his younger brother, Prince Hayabusa-wake, as a go-between to seek the hand of his half-sister, Princess Metori; but the Prince fell in love with the Princess and did not report back. Finally, there was a rebellion and both the Prince and Princess were slain. Throughout this account there is a simplicity of love rivalry between natural persons — a rivalry in which the principal figure, a Princess, is always moved by her own instinctive feelings and pays for this with her life, and a rivalry in which an Emperor, who is unable to forget the Princess even though he realized the Princess did not love him, finally becomes wrathful when he hears of the plan to rebel, and has her slain.

The tenor is, however, different in the *Nihongi*. The tale becomes one of conflict over political authority, with the Prince becoming the principal figure and the Princess receding into the background. It is a conflict between this ambitious Prince and his elder brother, the Emperor, who — not wanting to destroy a relative out of personal pique — puts up with several acts of disrespect, but is compelled to have his brother slain when he hears that he has rebelled.

Moreover, in both the *Kojiki* and the *Nihongi* there is a story that the soldier who slew the Princess (his name is different in each account), stole the jewels from her hands and feet, and gave them to his wife. In the *Kojiki* it is in a separate account and merely states that the soldier was found quilty and executed. But in the *Nihongi* it is joined to the rest of the tale. The Empress, at the outset, could not bear to have the body of the Princess exposed, even though she had committed a serious crime, and so expressly prohibited the removal of her jewels. When the soldier was about to be punished for disobeying the prohibition, he was excused from the death sentence in exchange for his lands.

(4) In the love affair between Crown Prince Karu and his younger sister, Karu no Ōiratsume — recorded in the Emperor Ingyō sections of both the *Kojiki* and the *Nihongi*.

The affair was considered in both accounts to be illicit. Because of it, people turned against the Prince and finally he was attacked and captured by Prince Anaho. But the *Kojiki* places the incident after the death of the Emperor and states that when Prince Karu was captured, he alone was exiled to the Province of Iyo. Later on the Princess, unable to bear her longing for the Prince, followed him. Finally the account ends with a love suicide.

In the *Nihongi* treatment, however, the Prince — " whose handsome figure excited all who saw him " — fell in love with the " alluring " Princess. Dreading the crime of marriage between a daughter and son of the same mother, he suppressed his feelings; but because his passion was painful almost to the point of death, he finally had relations with the Princess, saying, " I will not die for nothing. Even if it is a crime, how can I bear not to have her?" Later on, when this became known, the Emperor did not punish the Prince, since he was the Crown Prince, and exiled the Princess alone to the Province of Iyo. After the Emperor's death, the Crown Prince planned to attack Prince Anaho; and when he himself was captured, he committed suicide.

The above comparison of the *Kojiki* and the *Nihongi* treatments of legend indicates that, with differences in tone and degree, some moralization — or at least some moral concern — was added in the *Nihongi*. This certainly shows that a stage of reflection had developed beyond the primitive moral consciousness. In other words, we can see here a confrontation between the ancient consciousness of natural people and an advanced consciousness that permitted criticism of earlier attitudes.

4. *Conclusions*

From one point of view such early moralistic reflection can be considered a product of the consciousness of the men who compiled the traditions in the Nara Era when the *Nihongi* was compiled — after the beginning of that period of historical writing when the original text of the *Nihongi* was written, which provided the primary evidence of such moralistic reflection. But at the same time I am positive that this reflection was a part of, and resulted from, the gradual process of development in moral consciousness which came during and after the period of oral-tradition compilation. On this point I can not agree with Motoori's view — which is an example of his going too far with his anti-Confucianism — that all the thoughts recorded in the *Nihongi* are to be regarded as contemporary Confucian imitations, merely superficial or extraneous creations. Motoori, who had clarified the "oral-tradition compilation" character of the ancient texts, certainly could not have denied that the original text of the *Nihongi* had essentially the same character. The above comparison shows that the *Kojiki* and *Nihongi* resulted from basically different situations, with some differences occurring in the plots of particular stories. It is certainly difficult to see these differences as simply the result of literary embellishment. The theory that all plot differences were artificial creations of the compilers of the *Nihongi* becomes untenable when we ask why it was that they did not resort to more thoroughgoing revision. It is certainly difficult to see any basis for the assumption that traces of, or tendencies toward, such moralization were not already present in the oral-tradition compilations that were selected as sources for the *Nihongi*. It has been pointed out that the conditions of that day were already such as to embrace forces that would arouse such moralistic reflection.

As further support for this thesis, I would like to cite another example, recorded in the *Kojiki* and the *Nihongi*, which shows this sort of moralistic development in the middle of the period of oral-tradition compilations: an item in the Emperor Kenzō sections of the *Kojiki* and *Nihongi*. Here it is said that the Emperor harbored such deep enmity toward Emperor Yūryaku, who had slain his father (Prince Ichinobe), that he ordered his elder brother (Prince Ohoke) to demolish Yūryaku's tomb. But Prince Ohoke admonished the Emperor, saying that although such action was logical in terms of personal feeling, Yūryaku — even though he was an enemy of the

Emperor's father — was the Emperor's uncle and had been, as an Emperor, the ruler of the land. The Prince pointed out that if the Emperor had the tomb demolished out of personal rancor, he would certainly be censured by the people. And it is recorded that the Emperor yielded to this reasoning. Both the *Kojiki* and the *Nihongi* are in complete agreement about these main points of the story. But the *Kojiki* states, in addition, that when Prince Ohoke received the Emperor's order, he went to the Yūryaku tomb, dug up some dirt from a place near the tomb, and had the dirt with him when he admonished the Emperor saying: if as a son you must avenge your father, preserve your self-respect by this [symbolic] act. We note here an effort to be more reasonable and charitable, and because this item is about happenings of a relatively late period, and because the traditions in both the *Kojiki* and the *Nihongi* are related to each other in such a way, I have come to believe that this tale should be regarded as evidence, firmly rooted in historical fact, of contemporary intellectual development. The substance of this tale is clearly a product of an advanced moral consciousness. Therefore, while I appreciate — from the fine work done by Motoori Norinaga and Kawamura Hidene — how much the *Nihongi* legends bear the coloration of Chinese models, I still believe in the existence of internal causes for the development of moral consciousness in antiquity, or at least in the existence of internal reasons for the fact that the *Nihongi* took on such a Chinese coloration.

Although a later development in comparison to those discussed above, such moralistic reflection is also seen in ideas about Kami. There was a trend, in other words, toward the moralization and rationalization of Kami. It was noted rather early that some Kami, besides being nature deities, became important as ancestral Kami of the state or of a clan. The idea of the sun Kami being the ancestral Kami of the Imperial clan, and of clans worshipping ancestral Kami, was conspicuous in this development. "Ancestor worship" was a result of such conceptualization of Kami as ancestral Kami. In this connection it goes without saying that the influence of Confucianism was strong. As noted earlier, however, the development of social order provided the inner cause.

Along with this development we can detect some traces of reflection about the nature of Kami. In the legend — recorded in the Emperor Ōjin section of the *Kojiki* — about the rivalry between two brothers, Akiyama no Shitabi-otoko and Haruyama no Kasumi-otoko, for the hand of Izushi-otome, the mother criticizes the elder brother for not abiding by the terms of a wager. She says: " As long as I am alive let us make sure to imitate the Kami. It must be because he imitates mortal men that he does not pay his wager." Recognizing the veracity of the Kami in contrast to the falseness of men, she is declaring that one should take the Kami as an example. In the Emperor Nintoku section of the *Nihongi*, we have the story of Koromo no Ko " saving his life " by throwing gourds into a river and determining, by the fact that they did not sink, that the river Kami who demanded the sacrifice of a human life was a false Kami. Among the ancient legends included in the *Hitachi fudoki* we have the tale of a certain Matachi, of the Yahazu clan, who slew a serpent Kami which was obstructing his work of clearing the land. Declaring " What Heavenly or terrestrial Kami defies me?," he proceeded to kill various creatures, fish, and pests without fear or hesitation. In the *Izumo fudoki* we are told of an incident, said to have happened during the reign of Emperor Temmu, in which Katari no Omi Imaro stood on the Hime Cape and appealed to the multitude of Heavenly and earthly Kami, the 399 shrines of the Province, and the Kami of the sea, to avenge the death of his daughter who had been killed by a sea-monster: " If there is really a divine power, then let him kill the sea-monster. Then I will know that there are Kami spirits." Finally, he killed the monster. Again in one of the poems of the *Man'yōshū*, there is a vow that expresses the poet's deep feeling: " Only if the Kami of Heaven and earth are unjust will I die without meeting you, for whom I long."

In all of the above we have ancient thought that expects and demands a rational Kami nature. We also have numerous examples of reflection about the harm that comes from simple superstition and ancient religious rites. There is, first of all, the reference in the Great Purification liturgy to the *tsumi* of witchcraft. Also in the Empress Kōgyoku section of the *Nihongi* we have a description of how Kadono Kawakatsu put an end to a certain superstition about the Kami of the Yonder World (*tokoyo*). And in the Emperor Kōtoku section of the *Nihongi* there is a reference to an Imperial Edict abolishing old customs — including a prohibition against accompanying one's superior in death, and one against crude customs associated with exorcism.

My study now comes to the third period: the period of historical writing. But to attempt an over-all view of the age of historical writing from the Great Reform [of 645] to the Nara Era — considering the evidence of moral consciousness and attempting to clarify the historical significance of the kind of reflection discussed above — does not fall within the scope of this study, which is limited to the moral history of remote antiquity and the period of oral-tradition compilations.

November 20. 1920.

Notes:
(1) The origins of the *Kojiki* are discussed in Satō Seijitsu's "Kojiki kō" (A Study of the *Kojiki*), *Kokin bungaku* I (February, 1900). Satō's views coincide with my own.
(2) For a comparison of the *Kojiki* and *Nihongi* references to Yamato Takeru no Mikoto, see Shigeno Yasunobu's "Yamato Takeru no Mikoto no koto ni tsuki shika no kokoroe" (The Views of Historians about the Activities of Yamato Takeru no Mikoto), *Shigakkai zasshi* XI (October, 1890). I wish to cite this as a study made from a point of view different from mine.

Chapter III

Scholarly Nature of National Learning[1)]

1

Seldom has there been as much discussion of National Learning as there is today. This is a gratifying result of a mounting academic interest in Japan's unique ideology. However, in considering this development, I cannot but fear that the interest is often not accompanied by a full understanding of either the idea of "philology" — which has been equated with National Learning — or the scholarly nature of National Learning. Therefore, I should like to submit my views on these matters.

National Learning (*kokugaku*) is of course to be differentiated from Provincial Schools (*kokugaku*), a term which referred to local schools in contradistinction to the university (*daigaku*) in the capital. National Learning, an academic term which became popular sometime after the Meiji Restoration, was coined around the middle of the Tokugawa Era, a period that took its distinctive character from developments in various fields of the cultural history of Japan. Not all scholars necessarily like to use the term, but probably no one would take exception to the view that the scholarship of the so-called "four great men of National Learning" is representative of National Learning. And when referring to the four great men, the scholarship of Motoori will surely be acknowledged as the most representative of National Learning.

In placing Motoori in such a position we naturally should consider the scholarship of Keichū [1640–1701]; and inevitably we will

---
1) [First published in *Bungaku* (Literature) in December of 1939 and included in *Zōtei Nihon shisō shi kenkyū* (Studies in the History of Japanese Thought, Enlarged and Revised) (Tokyo, Iwanami Shoten; 1940), 88–113.]

insist that Keichū occupy an important position among the great men of National Learning. This point will be clarified in the following discussion, but suffice it to say here that the epithet, "the four great men," was coined by the followers of Hirata Atsutane in the last years of the Tokugawa Era and the early years of Meiji, an anti-Buddhist period. Therefore, although Hirata — in the historical treatment of National Learning which he wrote in his *Tamadasuki* (The Jeweled Sash) — praised Keichū's scholarly achievements, Keichū was not ranked with Kada Azumamaro and his three successors, probably because he had been a Buddhist priest. Without saying any more about Keichū for the moment, and assuming it is appropriate, in any case, that the scholarship of Motoori be considered as representing National Learning, let us try to understand just what kind of scholarship National Learning was by looking at the work of Motoori. That Motoori's scholarship represents National Learning is not only generally accepted, it makes sense historically. This will be taken up later on. In order to understand his scholarship, I think that the best and clearest approach is to consider the views which he expressed in his *Uiyamabumi* (First Tramp in the Mountains).

The *First Tramp in the Mountains* was written in the 10th month of 1798, three months after Motoori completed his masterpiece, the *Commentary on the Kojiki,* and when he was 69 years old. It was his guide to scholarship, written in response to the repeated pleas of his students. On the basis of a mature erudition, he explained his own concept of scholarship and his research methods. It was truly a crystallization of many years of scholarly experience. Here we can best understand what Motoori's scholarship, and National Learning, were like. He held that, in Japan, his work ought to be called simply "scholarship," thus making a point of rejecting the designation "Japanese learning." He did not use the term National Learning. And yet he did employ the words Imperial Country Learning (*mikunimanabi*), Imperial Learning (*kōchōgaku*), and Ancient Learning (*kogaku*).

Motoori began by explaining the essentials of what he called "Imperial Country Learning." When he came to classifying fields of study, he designated four: (1) Kami study or Way study — based on the Age of Kami books in the *Kojiki* and the *Nihongi*; (2) Antiquarian study (*yūsokugaku*) — dealing with government offices, ceremonies, and laws, together with various ancient customs, costumes, and furniture; (3) historical study — a study, first of all, of the Six National Histories and other ancient works, but also including books of later times; and (4) poetry study — comprising the composition of poetry and prose, together with the interpretation of poetic and prose works, and language study. Of the four categories he emphasized Way study as the most important. About this he wrote: "If I were asked which of these is the most important, I would say that it was 'study of the Way.' To begin with, this Way — being the Way of the Sun Goddess — is the Ancient Way by which the Emperor rules the land, the true Way for the four seas and the myriad nations. But it has been handed down only in the Imperial Country. Yet what is this Way? It is based on evidence about the Age of Kami and remote antiquity, recorded in the *Kojiki* and the *Nihongi*."

In addition to outlining the contents of Imperial Country Learning, the *First Tramp in the Mountains* deals with the scholarly nature of this Learning from other points of view. In the first place, Motoori defines Ancient Learning as follows: "It is the study by which one makes clear all things of remote antiquity, considering the origins of everything as revealed in the ancient classics, and paying no heed to the explanations given in later times." It goes without saying that the Ancient Learning referred to here is the same as Imperial Country Learning. In the second place, the identification of Imperial Country Learning with the study of the ancient Japanese classics is evident in the various study hints and research methods explained in the book. For example, it states that language study is necessary as a basic discipline, that it is very advantageous for one to devote himself to the annotation of the ancient Japanese classics, that one should not be careless in the recension and investigation of these texts, and that in the study of ancient words and poetry one should achieve familiarity with, and appreciation of, this poetry by personally composing poems in the ancient style. From the above remarks on classification and nature, and on hints about research methods, we should be able to obtain some idea of the kind of scholarship that was associated with Imperial Country Learning. But if I were asked to explain Imperial Country Learning concisely and in terms of present-day academic concepts, I would not find it at all easy to reply. The principal reason for this difficulty is that National Learning preceded academic specialization and had a mixed character. The principal elements in the mixture were: exposition-study (*setsumei-gaku*) elements and norm-study (*kihan-gaku*) elements. The existence of the two within National Learning is, it seems to me, very pronounced. They are seen, first of all, in the Way-study that was given primary emphasis by Motoori.

On the one hand, he positively rejected the philosophical theories and moralistic interpretations — devised by later Confucian and Buddhist scholars — about the Age of Kami traditions found in the *Nihongi* and the *Kojiki*. Since he regarded these as distortions of the ancient thought that preceded the introduction of Buddhism and Confucianism, he rejected (in connection with his academic objective of recreating the simplicity of ancient thought just as it had been) the philosophy and morality of such theories and interpretations. Here we have a denial of norm-study and a definite affirmation of exposition-study. This is implied when Motoori says that we should search out the ancient mind by studying the ancient books, regardless of explanations offered in later times. It was from this point of view that he, contrary to the conventional view, came to assign greater importance to the *Kojiki* than to the *Nihongi*. He preferred the simplicity of the *Kojiki* to the philosophy and morality of the *Nihongi*. This was the exposition-study quality which National Learning obviously had.

But in contradistinction to this quality, and in spite of it, there was also a norm-study quality that was manifested in the Way of the Imperial Country. It is found especially in Motoori's attempt to expound the Way of the Imperial Country through the *Nihongi* and *Kojiki,* or rather just the *Kojiki.* Motoori made this clear by saying that in the whole of National Learning — which had as its objective the investigation of the ancient mind through the ancient books — the study of the Way should definitely be stressed. This was made particularly clear in the following statement:

> If one does not aspire to scholarship, discussion is useless. But a person who has the least bit of interest in scholarship should have as much interest in exerting himself in behalf of the Way. The central purpose of scholarship is not realized in neglecting matters of the Way, or in concerning one's self merely with trivia. As to the study of the Way, since we are indeed fortunate to have been born in the Imperial Country where the true Way — superior to all others on earth or in heaven — has been transmitted, we should of course concentrate on the study of the Way of this noble Imperial Country.

It almost goes without saying that such a norm-study quality is an important aspect of National Learning.

This twofold character of National Learning can also be seen in its poetry study. Along with the exegesis and annotation of poems and prose in poetry study — and clearly a product of it — there were artistic theories and literary principles, based on the ideal of *mono no aware* (sensibility to things),[1] that provided the norm for composition. It was possible for such a relationship to develop naturally in poetry-study inasmuch as the classics dealt with were works of literature or, in other words, pure sources of artistic norms. (This

---

1) [For a discussion of the meaning of *mono no aware* see Frits Vos, *A Study of the Ise-Monogatari* ... (The Hague; 1957), I, 8–9.]

stands in contrast to searching for the Way in books of ancient tradition that were not classics.) But the norms for beauty that are here discovered and asserted were always kept independent of the Way which stood on the other side of National Learning. In the *First Tramp in the Mountains* it is written, on the one hand, that the composing of poems in the old *Man'yōshū* style was a convenient way to study the Way and, on the other hand, that the later style of the *Shin kokin shū* (New *Kokinshū*) was the pure artistic ideal. This sort of thing shows that there was a dichotomy within the norm-study side of National Learning and that National Learning was not merely "studying the Way." No matter what sort of explanation we give, we can not deny that the *Tale of Genji* is remote from the Way and that, instead, it has qualities which run counter to the Way. (This in fact is made clear in Motoori's studies.) Therefore, we certainly cannot define National Learning simply in terms of ideas about ethical norm-study, for it did have this important element of research into, and activation of, the spirit of the Nara and Heian Era through the *Tale of Genji* and other literary works of the period

2

Nowadays we often hear the view that since National Learning was characterized by national uniqueness, its scholars were impelled to reject European theoretical analysis. It goes without saying, however, that such views are based upon a bias that stems from a disregard of the universality of truth. Furthermore, such views fail to take notice of the fact that National Learning, in the light of the broad history of learning, is by no means unique to our country. I cannot forget even now how my predecessors in the study of National Learning — men who had been influenced by the new education of the Meiji Era — compared National Learning with *Philologie*, a historical study that arose in Germany somewhat later than National Learning in Japan. Nor can I forget spelling out the significance of this comparison, in concrete terms, in my book *Motoori Norinaga* (published in February of 1911). In the final analysis, philology — according to August Boeckh — aimed at " the cofinition of that which had been cognized " or " a re-creation of the consciousness of people in ancient times." In the scholarly achievements of these German philological studies — studies that had as their objects of study those ancient Greek and Roman classics which were considered to be the wellsprings of human enlightenment — there are some close parallels with National Learning in cultural and scholarly spirit, and in fields of research. In the study of ancient Japanese classics National Learning, which was of course quite independent of German philology (coming a generation earlier), made the same sort of contribution. On the side of form, German philology encompassed the study of grammar, annotation, and textual criticism. On the side of content, it encompassed — intellectually and phenomenally — the whole of culture as history, or systematic principle, in all areas: philosophy, religion, morals, literature, art, law, economics and the natural sciences. In the sense that this all-encompassing content was shaped into a single academic system, German philology was more advanced than National Learning. But it was also similar to National Learning with respect to the coexistence of exposition-study and norm-study, and to the frequent appearance of a tendency toward eclecticism. But these were natural results of the study of ancient classics.

In any case, my use of the term Japanese philology — when referring to National Learning as philology — is based upon this sort of comparison of National Learning with German philology. The use of the word " philology," in the particular sense of a special development on the formal annotative and textual-criticism side of book study, had already come into existence in Europe. A similar scholarly trend is recognized in Japan as well. In this connection some have taken the position that it is inappropriate to equate National Learning with philology; but those who have expressed such views have certainly not understood the essential nature of philology, touched upon above, nor understood that this essential nature is identical with that of National Learning. My comparison of National Learning with philology is certainly not in terms of trivial points. Both are alike in having a mixture of the study of exposition and the study of norms, and the wellsprings of these two types of study lie within the scholarly nature of both philology and National Learning. Since philology requires the use of ancient texts as the material for research, its cognition is not merely cognition, but re-cognition. This is due to its character as exposition study. But the ancient classics were also sources of human enlightenment; and since the study of the classics aims at reactivating the civilization of ancient times, philology is also a norm-study. The same two elements are in National Learning. As will be brought out in detail later in this study, the reason why National Learning as a study of ancient texts was an exposition-study is because it not only insisted on the rejection of Confucian and Buddhist ideas in its interpretation of the classics, but went on to effect this rejection; and the reason why it was a norm-study is that it asserted a distinct Way of antiquity on the basis of the classics and endeavored to establish this Way, while at the same time rejecting the Ways of Confucianism and Buddhism. Naturally this overlapping or mixed character obscured the scholarly nature of philology. For this reason philology could not but be ridiculed by philosophers for being no more than a piling-up of knowledge. National Learning, too, cannot avoid being subjected to such criticism. But this is because both belong to a stage preceding academic specialization. Both philology and National Learning are disciplines that took form in such a stage — that is, from the present-day view they are studies which belong to an earlier history.

Therefore a question about the fundamental significance of National Learning will naturally elicit answers that vary according to the point of view of the writer. He could emphasize the area having to do with textual criticism and exegesis. Or else he could stress the Way-study which deals with Shinto and morality. In any case, in order to arrive at a meaningful answer that is completely objective, one that disassociates itself from these various subjective opinions (the nature of National Learning provides ample scope for such opinions), I think it is essential that we consider the meaning and position of National Learning in the broad spectrum of Japanese cultural history. Only through such an approach can we understand the true academic character of National Learning and thus arrive at a precise appreciation of the quality of its various sides.

3

National Learning emerged out of the Ancient Learning movement which developed in the scholarly world during the Genroku Era (1688–1704). This movement was first centered in Confucianism, but spread to other fields. Within Confucianism it appeared in the Ancient-Meaning School (*kogigaku*) of Itō Jinsai [1627–1705] and the Ancient-rhetoric School (*kobunjigaku*) of Ogyū Sorai [1666–1728], which might be grouped together under the term " Chinese philology " — that is to say, they both aimed at the reactivation of ancient Chinese culture and morality through a study of the *Analects, Book of Mencius,* and the Five Classics. The Ancient-Learning movement of National Learning was set off by the Ancient Learning movement within Confucianism, and it developed under the direct and indirect influence of the latter. But it may be said that with Keichū as its founder, the scholarly nature of National Learning was given a uniqueness which distinguished it from the Ancient Learning of Confucianism.

Keichū, who had been a scholar-priest of the Shingon Sect, transferred his pure religious interest to scholarship; and he devoted himself to this pursuit with a truth-seeking attitude that was unbending. His principal fields of study were: (1) exegetical interpretation of the *Man'yōshū*; and (2) historical *kana,* or a study aimed at restoring the ancient Japanese language. His search for truth, in the context of this scholarly approach, led to the adoption of inductive and positivistic methods. At times he was objectively and scientifically thorough, and at other times he moved on to a historicism in which antiquity was to be understood only through antiquity, and the ancient books were to be understood only through the mind of antiquity. His search for the facts of antiquity on the basis of ancient texts without regard to expositions of later ages went beyond his studies of the *Man'yōshū* and his language study; and it disclosed the correct approach for obtaining a true understanding of the *Tale of Genji* and *Tale of Ise* as literary works. The academic or exposition-study quality of Keichū's scholarship made the Ancient Learning within National Learning better philology than the Ancient Learning within Confucianism. The emergence of a similar development within Confucianism was obstructed by its traditional ethical character. Thus, having Keichū as the founder, was something of singular importance for National Learning. His scholarship was in no way complicated by the training or tastes he had acquired as a Buddhist. He disassociated himself, as a scholar, from Chinese and Buddhist thought and was able to maintain an extremely objective attitude. It is a tribute to the soundness of his philology that he was able to recapture the true spirit of that poem, found in Section 6 of the *Man'yōshū*, written by Yamanoe no Okura [?660–?733] as he lay critically ill. Keichū rejected the old interpretation of the first line: "Because I am mortal, I must die" (*hito nareba munashikarubeshi*). With his corrections, the poem became:

Should a man's existence	Onoko ya mo
Have proved so meaningless	munashikarubeki
That he will not have made a name,	yorozuyo ni
That will endure	kataritsugubeki
For a myriad ages?	na wa tatezu shite.

It is rather amazing that he was able to avoid the error of seeing this poem as an exposition of the transiency of life, since he had been steeped in Buddhist teachings. He was able to avoid such distortion because of a precise language study applied to his exegesis of the *Man'yōshū* and an objective attitude which made him try to understand the original spirit of the poets. Thus it was that Keichū's scholarship first defined the quality of exposition-study for National Learning. It was certainly not right that Keichū was excluded from the so-called "four great men" who were apotheosized during the Meiji Era. This situation, moreover, was a factor in preventing a complete understanding of National Learning.

National Learning was established as a concept by Kada Azumamaro [1669-1736], who followed Keichū. Kada speaks about this in his *Sō gakkō kei* (Petition to Establish a School). Although there is some question as to whether the term National Learning was actually used in the text, we can assume the existence of the concept in both the general tenor of the work and in the use of the phrase: "state learning." In this document we see: (1) the subdivision of National Learning into Kami Way (Shinto), law, history and literature; (2) the aim of clarifying the true meaning of the ancient classics by excluding Confucian and Buddhist distortions; and (3) various explanations about methods of arriving at an understanding of the ancient mind through a clarification of ancient words and books, and about the absurdity of secrets and mysteries. We are here confronted with a distinct awareness of the scholarly nature of National Learning. But if we consider Kada's actual achievements, we will note that his new National Learning was not strong in the area of the Kami Way, the specialized learning inherited by his family. Rather he undertook the study of the poems in the *Man'yōshū,* or Man'yōshū Learning. Here he was within the tradition of Keichū's Learning. That which distinguished him from Keichū — in over-all scholarly tendency — was the norm-study quality in his work. This quality, coupled with his ethical personality, gives his scholarship another important position in the history of National Learning. The validity of the conclusion that the later National Learning was not established by Keichū alone, and that for this the work of Kada Azumamaro was necessary, cannot of course be denied.

After Kada we come to Kamo Mabuchi [1697–1769], a scholar who had studied directly under Azumamaro. Mabuchi's work on the *Man'yōshū* first gave substance to Azumamaro's concept of National Learning. Mabuchi inherited his interest in research on the *Man'yōshū* from Keichū and carried it to a greater degree of refinement. He made remarkable contributions, especially in recapturing and understanding the spirit of antiquity through the *Man'yōshū,* and in actually experiencing this spirit by composing poems in the *Man'yōshū* style. In Mabuchi we not only have the appearance of a unique personality — a man who made the above-mentioned contributions by actually being a poet-thinker as well as a scholar — but a man who left an indelible imprint of the Ancient Way (or antiquarianism) on National Learning. In what he himself referred to as the " true mind of the high and the upright," he revealed the value of that simplicity of spirit which had prevailed in ancient Japan before the introduction of Confucianism and Buddhism, and also revealed the essence of that Nation Body (*kokutai*) which, as a symbol of that remarkable simplicity of the ancient spirit, had been ruled over by an eternally unbroken line of Emperors. These were his most brilliant contributions. The Ancient Way, which he proclaimed, gave to National Learning its clearest expression of the norm-study quality. We can say that in this tendency, and as a National Learning scholar, Mabuchi more often followed Azumamaro than Keichū.

Then we come to Motoori Norinaga [1730–1801]. In the breadth of his scholarship — which encompassed the three fields of linguistics, Heian Learning (*chūkogaku*), and Nara Learning (*jōkogaku*) — and in the substance of his achievements, in the thoroughness of scholarly spirit which penetrated all of his work, and in the purity of his doctrine of the Ancient Way, Motoori certainly brought National Learning to completion. With respect also to reflection about, and consciousness of, his own scholarship, he was likewise outstanding. We can see this in what he writes in the *First Tramp in the Mountains.*

SCHOLARLY NATURE OF NATIONAL LEARNING

While it is essentially true that Motoori Learning represents National Learning, Keichū and Kamo Mabuchi, as forerunners, made this possible. The relationship between Motoori and Mabuchi is well known, but it should not be forgotten that the relations between Motoori and Keichū were even more important. Of course Motoori's relationship with Keichū was different from his relationship with Mabuchi, since Keichū was known to Motoori only through books. However, when Motoori first took to the study of the Japanese classics in his youth, it was actually through contact with the scholarship of Keichū that he had an experience that was like being awakened from the torpor of dogmatism. He frequently referred to this experience as an " eye opener." After this, he first turned to Heian Learning, which provided the foundations for his life-long scholarship. And at just this time he became acquainted with Kamo Mabuchi and received from him the edification of the Ancient Way. Then he began, and brought to completion, his study of the classics of the Nara Period, especially the *Kojiki*. And he also got into his study of language. His scholarship therefore encompassed both an exposition-study side and a norm-study side. By uniting the scholarly styles of both Keichū and Kamo Mabuchi, he gave form to National Learning. It would be a gross misinterpretation to stress that side of his scholarship which asserted the Ancient Way, his inheritance from Kamo Mabuchi, and to neglect that side of his scholarship inherited from Keichū. The scholarly experience of being awakened from the torpor of dogmatism — as a result of reading the works of Keichū — penetrated, and developed in, Motoori's life-long scholarship. The exposition-study quality that resulted therefrom was fundamental to this scholarship, and it may be said that the special character of his learning consisted in the fact that the norm-study element was also based on an exposition-study foundation.

As an example of this special character of Motoori's scholarly style, let us compare his interpretation of a passage from the Great Purification liturgy with that of other scholars, especially Kamo Mabuchi. In that part of the Great Purification liturgy dealing with "the *tsumi* (abominations) committed by people who by the grace of Heaven have been born in this land," we find the following " earthly *tsumi* " (*kuni-tsu tsumi*): " albinism, skin excrescences, the *tsumi* of violating one's mother, the *tsumi* of violating one's own child, the *tsumi* of a mother's violating her child, the *tsumi* of a child's violating its mother, and the *tsumi* of transgression with animals." This portion of the Prayer troubled the older commentators. Some referred to these *tsumi* as " the mother-and-child matters of the Five Elements (*gogyō*)," explaining the *tsumi* in terms of Confucian theories about the Five Elements. Others explained the *tsumi* metaphorically, saying that " violating the mother referred to lack of filial piety, and violating the child to lack of parental love." The great Watarai Nobuyoshi [1615–1690] interpreted the section literally: " violating one's own mother and violating one's child were sexual acts." Also Yamazaki Ansai [1618–1682], in his *Fū-sui-sō* (Wind and Water) accepted this literal interpretation while rejecting the analogies of Urabe and others. (Considering his general outlook, this was a strange position to take.) Although Kamo Mabuchi, in his *Norito kō* (Study of Shinto Liturgy), did not interpret " the *tsumi* of violating one's mother " etc. in terms of such analogies as those cited above, he saw the terms *shirobito* (albinism, literally: " white persons ") and *kokumi* (skin excrescences) as distortions of *shiragi-bito* (people of the Korean kingdom of Silla) and *kokuri-bito* (people of the Korean kingdom of Koguryo); therefore, he interpreted the *tsumi* listed in the Great Purification Prayer as *tsumi* committed by Korean immigrants. This was an interpretation that had been inherited from Kada Azumamaro.

The later interpretation by Motoori Norinaga, on the other hand, was quite different from Kamo's. Motoori said these " earthly *tsumi* " were *tsumi* and pollutions committed in antiquity, the age of simplicity. He wrote:

> It was a gross error for Mabuchi to substitute the character *rai* for *mi* in his *Study* and to interpret " the *tsumi* of violating one's

mother" as *tsumi* of the people of Silla and Koguryo. In the Jōkan (859–877) code the term *kokumi* is written with three different characters, but the reading is still *kokumi*. We could hardly say that the third character in this rendition also was a mistake for *rai*. Furthermore, in the Ise text of the Engi (901–923) code the "earthly *tsumi*" are listed in a different order: cutting living flesh, cutting dead flesh, violating one's mother, violating one's child, transgression with animals, albinism, skin excrescences, drowning, and burning. How can such an interpretation as that of Mabuchi be squared with the fact that "violating one's mother" comes ahead of *shirobito* and *kokumi*? It is clear that "violating one's mother" etc. has no grammatical relationship to *shirobito* and *kokumi*. Mabuchi's statement that sexual relations between mother and child were unheard of at the Imperial Court is beside the point. We can not be certain that such things did not happen among the common people simply because there are no references to them in the *Nihongi* and other ancient accounts. These chronicles, in reporting official matters, purposely did not record insignificant affairs of the people. In later times we can find references to persons violating their own daughters, and such things are not unheard of even today. That there were such in ancient times can be ascertained from this listing of *tsumi* in the Great Purification Prayer. Furthermore, at the beginning of his book, Mabuchi cites the affair of Prince Karu; but the reference is badly garbled. It was garbled because if he had admitted that such *tsumi* had been committed even by such a noble prince, it would have to be assumed that this sort of crime was frequent among the common people. Furthermore, in the *Kojiki* reference to a Great Purification held during the reign of Emperor Chūai, we find the phrase: "sexual intercourse between a parent and a child." It is absurd to say that this referred to acts by immigrants from Silla and Koguryo, for Korean immigration had not yet occurred.

The very clear-cut way in which Motoori exposed the blind spots in Mabuchi's explanation enables us to see the purity and consistency of his scholarly attitude. Such faulty interpretations as those of Kamo Mabuchi and Kada Azumamaro resulted from their scholarship being distorted by Way-consciousness, and also from a confusion of norm-study and exposition-study. We do not have Keichū's interpretation of the Great Purification liturgy, and so we do not know what he would have thought about these "earthly *tsumi*." But if he had expressed his views, it is logical that they would have been in agreement with those of Motoori and not at all like those of Kada Azumamaro and Kamo Mabuchi, for the Keichū spirit was preserved in Motoori's scholarly approach. I think we have evidence to support such a conjecture in a comparison which I once made between Keichū's interpretation of the 49th section of the *Tale of Ise* and those of Kada Azumamaro and earlier commentators.

Finally, with Hirata Atsutane [1776–1843] — the last of " the four great men " — National Learning was developed in a theological direction. Various areas outside and above the interests of Motoori were opened up. His scholarship was probably superior to that of Motoori in ethics, but in other areas he humbly assumed the role of a devoted disciple of Motoori. Ban Nobutomo [1775–1846], another great disciple of Motoori, developed National Learning by giving special attention to its exposition-study side. But I am inclined to see specialization in National Learning after Motoori. And specialization, in a sense, represented the disintegration of the perfected National Learning developed by Motoori. National Learning had its fullest expression in the Motoori Learning that preceded such specialization.

4

With regard to the special character of National Learning (that is, its special meaning when contrasted with other types of scholarship) the constituent elements as outlined above can only be seen by looking at the broad spectrum of the historical development of learning and culture in the Tokugawa Era. At this point, we should consider:

(1) Confucianism as a great force that controlled the learning and culture of the Tokugawa Era; and (2) the meaning of National Learning as a force which was antagonistic to Confucianism. Confucianism, along with Buddhism, had long controlled the learning and culture of our country. More properly, this was a phenomenon which had existed ever since the beginning of the history of Japanese culture, in the full sense of that word " culture." But when we come to the Tokugawa Era, Confucianism almost completely dominated learning and culture since it now rejected the Buddhism with which it had been hitherto closely associated. Various Confucian schools began to compete with each other and there was a succession of great masters. Furthermore, under the protection and patronage of the rulers it came to occupy the position of an official ideology and to be an instrument for popular indoctrination. One result of this prosperity, as mentioned above, was that an Ancient Learning movement arose within Confucianism. And, as has already been mentioned, the outbreak and development of National Learning was set off by this Ancient Learning movement.

From beginning to end, National Learning manifested an anti-Confucian bias. Furthermore, this attitude was consistently translated into action. And it never weakened one iota. The opposition of National Learning to Confucianism can be said to have existed in three areas of emphasis. First, in the advocacy of a Japanism that revered things Japanese and deprecated things foreign — a reaction against a Sinophilism that revered things foreign and deprecated things Japanese, which had emerged from an excessive reverence of Confucianism by certain schools of Confucian scholars. Secondly, in propounding naturalism and simplicity — a reaction against the formalism, scholasticism, and hypocrisy that were by-products of the moralism of Confucianism. As a result of such an emphasis, a release of human feelings was affirmed. Thirdly, in a scholarly aspiration to shed light on the original meaning of the ancient Japanese classics that were written before the introduction of Confucianism (and Buddhism). This was to be achieved by rejecting all the Confucian (and Buddhist) distortions found in the interpretations of the ancient Japanese classics.

When we observe the character of National Learning, with special attention to the first of the three areas of emphasis, the view emerges that National Learning is a study of ethical norms. It is clear that National Learning had as its important mission the advocacy of, and belief in, the morality of Japanism and stated these as its objective. Therefore, it is not at all wrong to regard this emphasis upon Japanism as one of the special characteristics of National Learning. We must not overlook the fact, however, that the National-Learning attacks on Confucianism were not appropriate merely to this emphasis upon Japanism, and that the attacks existed, and were significant, in the other two areas of National-Learning emphasis. Moreover, it must be said that, with the exception of some educational (or special) features of the Confucianism that developed during the Tokugawa Era, Confucianism was not necessarily subjected to such opposition from National Learning. Whether the teachings of Confucianism carried theories that ran counter to Japanese morals — as National Learning scholars often thought — is something that requires additional study. It is certainly a fact that there was an ardent Chinese culturalism in the Ancient-rhetoric School of Ogyū Sorai, and that as a by-product of this there was a certain amount of "reverence for things foreign and deprecation of things Japanese." But National Learning, as philology, was greatly indebted to this Ogyū study of ancient Chinese literary styles. (This is clearly shown in such developments as Kamo Mabuchi's "*Man'yōshū*-ism.") Furthermore, it was common for the scholars of the various Confucian schools — particularly those of the Hayashi Razan's [1583–1657] Chu Hsi school, which was in the main current of Tokugawa Confucianism — to expound upon morality in Japan and to formulate Japanese moralistic doctrines. Such Confucian scholars as Yamaga Sokō [1622–1685] of the Ancient Learning School made assertions that were extreme statements of Japanism. Then when we move from Confucianism to the Confucian-Shinto school that was bound up with Confucianism, we of course find ardent exponents of Japanism. Hayashi Razan and Yamaga Sokō were not unrelated to this sort of Shintoism. The Suiga Shinto of Yamazaki Ansai [1618–1682] was the most notable example of Confucian-Shinto and, with respect to Japanism and Emperorism (*sonnō shugi*), it certainly cannot be denied that Suiga Shinto was an important forerunner of National Learning. Assertions about "reverence for the Emperor" and the Kami Country — these terms proclaimed a Japanese morality that would clarify the concept of the Nation Body — were common to Tokugawa education as a whole. The uniqueness of National Learning in this area of emphasis upon Japanism can be best appreciated by seeing it in relationship to the other two above-mentioned areas of emphasis. I say this because although National Learning was not particularly unique in its stress upon Japanese morality, and was not even a forerunner in this stress, it did assume an attitude of absolute opposition to Confucianism as a whole, to Confucian-Shinto, and even to such a school as Suiga Shinto.

In the second area of emphasis upon naturalness and simplicity, National-Learning affirmations of emotionalism, or naturalism — realized through philological studies, especially of the prose and poetry of the Heian Era — were more fundamentally at variance with the conventional explanations of Confucian morality than were National Learning statements about Japanism. It seems to me that certain comments made by Motoori, in emphasizing naturalness and simplicity, should be considered quite bold and refreshing for that day. This is true of his attacks on, and opposition to, the formalism, scholasticism, and unnaturalness of Confucian morality. At this point in the discussion, the character of National Learning in the cultural history of the Tokugawa Era should stand out more clearly, but we should not overlook the fact that there was in this emphasis upon naturalness a profession of an amoral learning.

In the third area of scholarly aspiration (shedding light upon the original meaning of the ancient classics) — where there is a rejection of the Confucian (and Buddhist) distortions in the study of the ancient Japanese classics, and a pure spirit of scholarship — I think we have the most unique feature of National Learning in Japanese cultural history. We have a characteristic here that was not yet seen in the expositions of Shintoists or Confucian Japanists. With the search-for-truth attitude that appeared first in the studies of Keichū and that had the most pronounced development — surpassing that of Kada Azumamaro and Kamo Mabuchi — in the studies of Motoori, we have the appearance of a philosophical spirit that is something almost new in the history of learning in Japan. In the foregoing description of Motoori's scholarship, I have indicated how his intense love of learning led him, in his persistent search for truth, to spurn all utilitarian objectives. By looking into the achievements and writings of Motoori, we can understand how clear was his consciousness of, and reflection about, scholarship. He wrote, for example, that one should honor learning more than the teacher, and should not be wedded to the explanations of the teacher; he took the position that secrets and oral traditions had no meaning for scholarship; he warned that one should be careful about producing unusual and new explanations; and he stated that one should not follow old theories blindly — that there should be progress in learning. The rejection of Chinese (and Buddhist) thinking, advocated consistently in National Learning, was particularly important in this connection. Such a thorough-going scholarly attitude cannot be found in Confucianism or elsewhere. Even in the new Confucianism of Itō Jinsai and Ogyū Sorai, which was similar to National Learning in that it was a product of the Ancient Learning movement, we do not see the pure scholarly attitude that existed in National Learning. This was because the new Confucianism was essentially ethics — its study of the ancient classics and history sprang from an interest in morals. But National Learning took its starting point in independence from this interest in morals. It is here that the anti-Confucian attitude of National Learning had its greatest impact on Japanese cultural history. At this point in the discussion, I feel that we have encountered the most unique quality of National Learning and come into contact with its truest value.

5

National Learning (or Japanese philology) was like philology in the sense that it was a form of scholarship that preceded what may be termed, in the strict sense of that word, specialization. It encompassed scholarly elements which were to be developed through different forms of specialization in the various fields of both the exposition-study and norm-study sides of National Learning. It is therefore natural that what is called national morality (*kokumin dōtoku ron*), national history (*kokushi*), national literature (*kokubungaku*), Shinto, and various other established studies of today should have emerged from National Learning. It is not strange that National Learning should be thought of as the aggregate of these various studies.

To the extent that one attempts to understand the true character of National Learning, as a historical study, by taking up one of the various schools of National Learning — irrespective of whether he has established his own brand of National Learning from his own point of view — he certainly should not overlook the significance of National Learning in our cultural history. Even if we see National Learning principally in terms of the national morality of Japanism, or the clarification of the Ancient Way concept of the Nation Body, we must not forget that National Learning stood on the foundations of, and was explained in terms of, the natural, simple sentiment and sincerity of the national spirit that was revealed by philological research into the poetry and prose of the Heian Era and into the traditions of the Age of Kami. In other words, it is in these foundations that we have the special character of National Learning. It was not simply free-floating theory. This is why, in taking the position that there was nothing about Way in Japanese antiquity, the scholars of National Learning rejected ethical principles. This is also the reason why they did not indulge in discussion and reasoning, assigning such activity to Confucianism and even holding them in contempt. Discussion of creed and dogma about the Ancient Way and the Kami Way (Shinto) was not their principal concern; and they were not adept at it. Their Ancient Way and Kami Way were established spontaneously by pure scholarly research that was completely free from — or that positively rejected — ethical assumptions about the ancient Japanese classics. The contributions made on the national-morals side of National Learning were, at this point, not in such areas as the anti-Confucian debate. Even if "the great man of Suzunoya" [Norinaga] were living today, he would not necessarily by recognized as a proponent of the Japanese spirit.

But this does not mean, of course, that I slight the ethical side which National Learning had or that I consider the ethical development of National Learning as meaningless. Although it was inevitable that the National Learning, being originally a form of learning that preceded specialization, should have matured through specialization in ethics and other fields, the history of National Learning reveals that contributions in these areas were far less significant than they were in European philology.

In Europe all forms of learning — whether philosophy, humanistic studies, natural sciences, or history — evolved from philology, and the latter's primary meaning, as the philological study of ancient texts, came to be thought of as having merely a historical existence. In comparing National Learning with European philology, we cannot say that the development of various Japanese disciplines from National Learning is pronounced. Regrettable though it may be, this is a fact. After the time of Motoori, National Learning studies of course did branch off into various Japanese fields of study, and down until the present day there have been specialists in these various fields; but in general it is difficult to say that any of them have established their independence. They are not yet completely systematized, and the interrelationship between the various subjects of study is still confused. Such a situation stems from a lack of scholarly reflection. In order for National Learning to be perfected as Japanese learning it is necessary that it be subjected to thoroughgoing criticism. And when this is done, it is of primary importance that the confusion between the exposition-study and norm-study sides of National Learning be eliminated and that the special character of each field be clearly defined. For example, on the norm-study side of National Learning there should be greater rationalization of the so-called "Way study," and the studies should be rescued from the consistent theoretical deficiencies of National Learning. The same things should be done in the literary criticism of "poetry study." Then on the exposition-study side of National Learning, the various fields of philological research — where we have the most brilliant achievements of National Learning — should be developed historically as the study of culture. That is, they should be brought to maturity as the history of Japanese thought and culture — as historical studies of art, morality, religion, and other areas of thought and phenomena. In order to accomplish this, we must give thorough consideration to rectifying the following weaknesses of National Learning: the lack of developmental treatment of thought and phenomenon in National Learning resulting from its superficial treatment of the classics; and insufficient recognition of the influence, and the meaning of this influence, exerted on Japanese culture by both Confucianism and Buddhism after their introduction to Japan — a deficiency resulting from undue stress on the rejection of Confucianism and Buddhism. Probably we should also initiate more comparative research in various fields, especially in Japanese language study. This would bring about the scholarly maturation of National Learning. And here it must be said that there is plenty of room, and a great need, for learning from European scholarship and its history. Nowadays we often hear the cry that Japanese learning should free itself from the categories of European scholarship. Granted that there is spirit and feeling in this cry, we should never forget that as a prerequisite for such independence we have to establish — and gain general recognition for — a different kind of epistemology that stands entirely apart from the epistemology created in Europe, and one that also has universal value. Such a fundamental renovation of philosophy — one that would have to be carried out by philosophers of Japan — is a great task for the future. Still, the academic maturation of National Learning should and must be carried out separately. For the good of learning and culture in our country, it is to be regretted if, in carrying out this renovation and maturation, anything obstructs the process of modern scholarly development in those various areas of National Learning where achievements have been made, with much effort, since the Meiji Restoration.

November 18, 1939.

Chapter IV

Kamo Mabuchi and Motoori Norinaga as Thinkers[1]

1. *Kamo Mabuchi*

Kamo Mabuchi was one of several antiquarian thinkers to emerge during the Tokugawa Era. But he was unique in that as a representative of Japanism (*Nihon shugi*) in National Learning — in academic contradistinction to Confucianism or Confucian Learning — he was a poet-thinker of a type rarely seen in the cultural history of our country. And also as a scholar of the classics, he was — like the other antiquarians — thoroughly accomplished.

Antiquarianism is a spiritual disposition to find ideals or norms, for various aspects of culture, in the ancient past. Man, dissatisfied with contemporary conditions and perpetually aspiring to ideals, hangs his hopes on the future; but at the same time he often thinks about the ancient past, his spiritual birthplace. Whether men are disposed to dwell mostly on the past or mostly on the future depends on differences in individual and national character. Nevertheless, antiquarianism, because of this disposition, is also idealism — a common possession of man that has its roots in his essential nature. Consequently, ancient cultures have been idealized not only in cases where a superior culture actually emerged in antiquity, but also when this was not necessarily so. Manifestations of such idealization have appeared in the intellectual history of almost all cultured peoples.

With respect to the direct causes of these manifestations, we note manifold differences. In some cases people, repelled by the complexities of the culture of later ages, may yearn for the original forms

---

1) [First published in Nos. 1 and 2 of *Sekai shichō* (World Thought) in February and April of 1928 and included in *Zōtei Nihon shisō shi kenkyū*, 164–230.]

of human nature which are seen in the natural simplicity of the ancient past. In other cases, loathing the prosaic quality of later ages, they come to extol the harmonious beauty of the ancient past. Or the manifestations of idealization may emerge from a sound evaluation of some of the fruits of ancient culture. It is from such various causes that peculiar features of antiquarianism emerge in the intellectual history of both the Orient and the Occident. In Europe we have the notable examples of: humanism in various countries at the time of the Renaissance (when there was a yearning for Greco-Roman culture); new humanism in Germany from the last half of the eighteenth century on into the nineteenth; and the return to original Christianity during the Reformation. In comparison to Europe (where there tends to be an emphasis upon development and progress), in India and China non-antiquarian ideas have been the exception rather than the rule. Thought in those countries has been characterized, rather, by a devotion to the past. There the doctrine of indebtedness to ancestors and return to beginnings (*hōhon hanshi*) was preached; and such terms as " age of attenuation " (*gyōki*) and Final Age (*mappō*) were commonplace.

If we consider antiquarianism in Japan — putting aside the fact that its germination can be traced back to the concept of the Age of Kami in antiquity — we can say that it was introduced early, along with Chinese and Indian thought. But we see conspicuous examples of antiquarianism as an indigenous intellectual product first in the Final-Age idea of the Middle Ages and, later on, in the Ancient-Learning movement of the Tokugawa Era. During the Tokugawa Era antiquarianism was represented by a particular academic school and was an extremely prominent intellectual current, penetrating the whole of intellectual history. It even had an effect on political movements.

However, if we were to examine in appropriate breadth and detail all that is comprehended in the ideas of antiquarianism in the Tokugawa Era, we would have to extend the investigation to all aspects of culture. But looking at the matter from the viewpoint of the history of thought, the most significant developments will be found in Confucian Learning and National Learning. Although both occupied an important position in learning during the Tokugawa Era, Confucian Learning as antiquarianism comes first both in chronology and in importance. National Learning might be said to have been stimulated by Confucian Learning. Still, National Learning, inheriting the Confucian tradition, completed the antiquarian development, manifesting within itself the culmination of Tokugawa thought. And the thought of Mabuchi virtually supplied the foundations for the antiquarianism of National Learning.

Within Confucianism — which has had a long history since its introduction to Japan — there was born, at the beginning of the Tokugawa Era and from Confucianism's own classical nature, a separate, new antiquarian movement. Etiologically this development should be thought of within the context of all cultural movements. Presumably the Age of Wars (*sengoku jidai*) — a period of feudal decentralization which followed the Ōnin (1467–1469) war at the end of the Middle Ages — ushered in social reform, the breakup of classes, and the liberation of the individual. Then with recovery under Oda Nobunaga [1534–1582] and Toyotomi Hideyoshi [1536–1598], and further unification under the Tokugawa, the people came to enjoy peace for the first time after the battle of Osaka in 1615. And culture took on its Tokugawa-Era form as the Tokugawa clan became immersed in its cultural and educational policies.

Two principal characteristics of Tokugawa culture distinguish it from Medieval culture. First, Tokugawa culture was liberated from the special possessors of culture, the priests and nobles; and at the same time it was freed of their traditionalism. Secondly, Tokugawa culture was secular — it had extricated itself from mystical and Buddhist otherworldly tendencies. The anti-Buddhist trend of the Tokugawa Era may be taken as the most notable example of the fusion of these two characteristics. But they were also manifested early in Confucianism, which the Bakufu regarded as the fundamental principle of the policy of "rule through culture and learning" (*bunkyō seiji*). The espousal of Chu Hsi Learning (the Confucianism of the Tokugawa Era) by Fujiwara Seika [1561–1619] and Hayashi Razan [1583–1657], who were apostate Buddhist priests and commoners — and particularly their expressions of anti-Buddhism — were, in this sense, really a reaction against Medieval culture as well as a release from it. And with the passage of time this trend became more pronounced and spread to the whole of culture. Within Confucianism itself this was manifested in the school of Yamazaki Ansai [1618–1682] — a new branch of the Chu Hsi School — and in the Yang-ming School (*yōmei gaku*).[1] By about the time of the fifth Tokugawa Shogun, Tsunayoshi [1646–1709] — toward the end of the seventeenth century and after two-thirds of a century had elapsed since the battle of Osaka in 1615 — Tokugawa culture had therefore emerged at its first stage of growth.

As freedom and liberation arose in all areas of culture, there appeared first of all the Ancient-Meaning School, the earliest representative of antiquarianism within Japanese Confucianism. The originator and representative scholar of the Ancient-Meaning School was Itō Jinsai [1627–1705].[2] A member of a Kyoto merchant family, Jinsai developed a special interest in Confucianism. At first he embraced Chu Hsi Learning, but in his mature years he espoused the Ancient-Meaning School on his own, finally achieving fame. The reason it was called the Ancient-Meaning School was that it constituted a reaction to both the Chu Hsi and Yang-ming Schools.

In the final analysis, Chu Hsi Learning was a philosophic development of the teachings of Confucius based upon the stimulus and

---

1) [The Confucianism of Wang Yang-ming (1472–1529) asserted that moral truths were discoverable by introspection, rather than by exhaustive study of the classics and histories, as Chu Hsi (1130–1200) had maintained. This school was introduced into Japan by Nakae Tōju (1608–1648) and Kumazawa Banzan (1619–1691). See various studies by Galen Fisher.]

2) [Cf. Joseph J. Spae, *Itō Jinsai*. .... (Peiping; 1948).]

influence of Buddhist and Taoist philosophies. From the standpoint of that School, its learning achieved an understanding of Confucius by transcending Confucius. That is, by achieving philosophical depth, it was able to bring out the true meaning of Confucius. But this certainly was not original Confucianism. The Chu Hsi School of Japan generally did not go beyond the expositions of Chu Hsi; and their learning was not necessarily based upon a desire to understand original Confucianism as it really was. In spite of having a Tokugawa-Era significance, with its anti-Buddhist attitude and its refusal to follow blindly the traditional Confucianism of the Imperial Court, it is not at all unfair to say that Chu Hsi Learning in Japan had not yet become academically free, since it was centered exclusively on the inherited teachings of the founders of Sung Philosophy and did not venture toward independent inquiry.

But Jinsai, although steeped in Chu Hsi teachings, came to doubt whether this was original Confucianism. Veering away from the Chu Hsi interpretations, he attempted to bring out the true character of original Confucianism through first-hand study of the classics, especially the *Lun-yü* (*Analects*), containing the sayings of Confucius, and the *Meng-tzu* (*Book of Mencius*). He wrote that Chu Hsi School preached a distinction between Primary Nature (*honzen no sei*) and Physical Nature (*kishitsu no sei*) on the basis of a cosmological theory about Principle (*ri*), Ether (*ki*), and the Supreme Ultimate (*taikyoku*); that its methods of self-cultivation were based on the maintenance of respect (*kei*) and an exhaustive study of Principle; and that it expounded views of morality in terms of a return to Primary Nature, according to which the noumenal Principle and the Primary Nature were identical and morality consisted in a return to Primary Nature through a transformation of Physical Nature. Jinsai asserted that in such teachings the Chu Hsi School held morality to be a realization of Principle that was to be achieved through self-reflection that emphasized speculative discipline.[1] He took the position that the Chu Hsi School did not accept the work of Confucius and Mencius objectively, but wasted time on subtilization and forced analogies based on Buddhism and Taoism, distorting the words of the sages by personal bias. The original sense of Confucian doctrine could never be learned, he claimed, from the Chu Hsi commentaries. It was therefore necessary to reject completely personal opinions colored by the Chu Hsi commentaries and to go directly to the *Analects* and the *Book of Mencius*, the most important Confucian classics, and to attempt to understand Confucianism in its original sense by accurate interpretations of words and their meanings. According to the basic principles of Confucianism ascertained and clarified in this way, said Jinsai, the original ideas of Confucius and Mencius consisted of morality put into practice — of Benevolence (*jin*) in the sense of an active Love (*ai*) of others. Love was ultimately the actualization of the Way of Heaven (*tendō*) or "natural Way"; and the Way of Heaven was the unceasing, external activity of the monistic Ether, the basic principle of the cosmos. Man embodied this cosmic activity as a microcosm. In this way, morality was not achieved by an exhaustive examination of Principle, as maintained by the Chu Hsi School, but by practice itself. The aim of scholarship and self-cultivation, Jinsai said, was to become, first of all, a practitioner of Love. The *Analects* spelled out this practical morality by presenting it in different concrete cases; and the *Book of Mencius* elaborated on it. Jinsai maintained that systematized investigations, such as those which had been attempted in the Chu Hsi School, were academic trifles and obviously unimportant, but also that any view which could accept speculative interpretations, like those of the Chu Hsi School, was certainly not in accord with the writings of the sages.

---

1) [For an exposition of Chu Hsi Confucianism see Joseph Percy Bruce, *Chu Hsi and His Masters* (London, 1923); Fan Yu-lan, *History of Chinese Philosophy*, Vol. II (Princeton, 1953); and especially A. C. Graham, *Two Chinese Philosophers* (London, 1958).]

In this way, Jinsai's principal emphasis was upon the original significance of Confucianism and, at the same time, on the true meaning of morality. With this emphasis, an antiquarianism rooted in the writings of Confucius and Mencius was established. Viewed historically, Jinsai not only fell heir to the new trends of Tokugawa culture and to Chu Hsi Learning, but brought further development to both in the sense that his was a new school proclaimed in a spirit of free inquiry, in rivalry with the dominant Chu Hsi School, and also in the sense that he persisted in emphasizing social ethics, in opposition to the other-worldly tendencies of Buddhism. When we look at his School as antiquarian thought, two distinguishing features — manifestations of this Tokugawa culture — are worthy of attention. First, there was a truth-seeking urge to elucidate the real meaning of ancient ideas. Secondly, there was a moralistic, practical, non-Principle urge — in contradistinction to the philosophical, speculative and Principle-oriented emphasis of the Chu Hsi School.

Jinsai's Learning was inherited by his son, Itō Tōgai [1670–1736]. The scholarship of these two, known as the Horikawa School, became a great power in the Kyoto-centered scholarly world. Among the adherents there were many "possessors of the conversion experience" who had left the old Chu Hsi and Yang-ming schools to enter the faith of the Ancient-Meaning School.

With Ogyū Sorai [1666–1728],[1] a generation after Jinsai, antiquarian thought within Confucianism was further developed — almost to the ultimate. In contrast to Jinsai, who spent his life as a non-official teacher in Kyoto, Sorai came to serve the Edo military government and was favored even by Tsunayoshi [1646–1709] and Yoshimune [1684–1751]. He too studied the teachings of the Chu Hsi School in the beginning, but in his mature years he was stimulated by Jinsai and entered Ancient Learning. Later he came under the influence of the Ming scholars, Li P'an-lung and Wang Shih-chen, and

---

1) [Cf. J. R. McEwan, *The Political Writings of Ogyū Sorai* (Cambridge University Press; 1962.]

studied ancient Chinese rhetoric. Finally he founded his own antiquarian school, Ancient Learning, that included the study of ancient Chinese rhetoric.

Sorai's teachings were similar to those of Jinsai in that he maintained that the Principle-oriented philosophy of the Chu Hsi School was not — because of the later influence of Buddhism and Taoism — the main point of Confucianism. But he felt that Jinsai's " natural Way " thought still had traces of such Buddhist and Taoist influences. While rejecting the arguments of Mencius, he returned afresh to Confucius and maintained that the Way of the Former Kings, taught by Confucius himself, was the true Confucianism. According to the Way of the Former Kings, the sage kings — Yao and Shun — and the sage kings of the three dynasties — Hsia, Yin, and Chou — received the mandate of Heaven (*temmei*) and became kings of the land because of their virtues of enlightenment and wisdom. With the object of tranquilizing the land, they devised the Way by using their hearts and strength to the utmost and by exercising ultimate skill and wisdom. This Way of the Former Kings, according to Sorai, was definitely not the natural Way of Heaven and earth, nor was it to be equated with Benevolence and Right-doing (*gi*). In other words, the Way of the Former Kings, having developed from a way of utility and welfare, was none other than ancient culture endowed with the splendor of Rites (*rei*), Music (*gaku*), Punishment (*kei*) and Law (*sei*). Way and Virtue (*toku*) were both creations of the early sages and did not exist outside Rites, Music, Punishment, and Law. The purpose of Confucianism, as Sorai saw it, was to clarify this Way of the Former Kings and to have the land governed in accord with this model. And Sorai claimed that the Way of the Former Kings was transmitted to the present through the Six Classics: the *Shih-ching* (Book of Poetry), the *Shu-ching* (Book of History), the *Li-chi* (Record of Rites), the *Yüeh-chi* (Record of Music), the *I-ching* (Book of Changes), and the *Ch'un-ch'iu* (Spring and Autumn Annals).[1] He considered the Six Classics to be instruments for the administration of the nations of the world, encompassing all aspects of ancient culture. The essence of the Way of the Former Kings, according to Sorai, is found in words (辞 *ji*) and deeds (事 *ji*). By these the Way of the Former Kings can be represented: poems and history are the "words," and Rites and Music the "deeds." Of course, the hearts and minds of the ancient sages cannot be known apart from the sages themselves. All we can do is to clarify their words and deeds. And since their words and deeds can be gleaned only from the Six Classics, it is first necessary to clarify the ancient words and sentences found in these Classics. For this purpose, we must avoid personal opinions and arbitrary judgments, reject commentaries written in later ages — like those of Chu Hsi — clarify the words and meanings in the original texts, and finally make our interpretations in terms of the hearts and minds of the ancient people. In order truly to understand the feelings and thoughts of the Classics through the meanings of words, we must compose classical rhetoric ourselves. Such philological and literary preparation is particularly important for scholars in our country, since the Six Classics are foreign classics. Furthermore, it is necessary to have drills in the Chinese language. In studying Chinese rhetoric one should by all means take lessons in the ancient rhetoric of Li and Wang, and aim for the elegance

---

1) [The *Shih-ching* is a collection of folk songs, religious odes, and dynastic hymns, the most recent of which probably predate the birth of Confucius in 551 B.C. The *Shu-ching* consists of speeches and exhortations attributed to kings and ministers from the legendary Yao down through the first three hundred years of the Chou dynasty. The *Li-chi,* which in its present form dates from the Former Han (202 B.C.-A.D. 8), gives an ideal description of the rituals and institutions of the Chou dynasty, which ended in 249 B.C. The *Yüeh-chi* survives in fragments, which are included in the *Li-chi.* The *I-ching* contains formulas and diagrams accumulated during the Chou dynasty as a handbook for diviners. The *Ch'un-ch'iu* is a chronicle of events in the feudal states from 721 to 481 B.C., arranged after the chronology of Confucius' native state of Lu. For analyses and translation references see Burton Watson, *Early Chinese Literature* (Columbia University Press, 1962).]

and correctness of the ancient literature of the period during and before the Former Han [202 B.C.–A.D. 8], which Li and Wang took as their model. The inferiority, and Japanese flavor, of the poems and prose written in the past by scholars of our country have been due, Sorai said, to their following models of later ages. Thus he strongly advocated " literary restorationism."

Sorai's School, known as the Ken'en School, came into vogue in Edo during the second and third decades of the eighteenth century, and during the '30s and '40s it flourished to such a degree in Kyoto that it appeared to dominate the scholarly world, replacing Jinsai's Ancient-Meaning School. Many superior scholars appeared among the adherents of this Ken'en School, but they were divided generally into two groups: those who studied the classics and those who studied literature.

A representative figure of the " classics-study " group was Dazai Jun (Shundai) [1680–1747].[1] He, too, entered scholarship through Chu Hsi Confucianism. Harboring doubts, he then shifted to Jinsai's school and then to Sorai's. It was after thirty years of work that he found his place in Sorai's school; and it appears that he brought the School to its ultimate stage of development with his extreme utilitarian theory of morality and his anti-Principle attitude of respect for the Six Classics and the ancient sages. He was not weak in Japanese literature either. His discussion of Japanese poetry in his miscellany, *Dokugo* (Solitary Words), deals with Japanese poems from the point of view of Chinese poetry, in which he was well versed. He stated that there were changes even in Japanese poetry styles: the style of the *Man'yōshū* combined elements from the *Book of Poetry* and from old-style poems of the Han and Wei dynasties, and also incorporated — to some extent — stylistic elements from T'ang-dynasty poetry; and the poetry of the *Kokinshū* (Anthology of Ancient and Modern Times) [2] contained poems directly from the T'ang period.

1) [See studies by R. J. Kirby in TASJ.]
2) [The first of the 21 Imperial anthologies, compiled in ca. 905 A.D. by order of Emperor Daigo. It contains 1,111 poems. Translated by T. Wakameda, *Early Japanese Poets, Complete Translation of the Kokinshū* (Tokyo, 1929).]

With regard to such changes and developments in Japanese poetry, he maintained that one should recognize the existence of Chinese poetic influence and, disregarding the explanations of teachers who lived in later times, should use the *Man'yōshū* and *Kokinshū* as models and also study Japanese poetry of the past, poetry which avoided falseness and gave expression to true feelings.

With Hattori Nankaku [1683–1749], a representative of the " literature-study " group of the Ken'en School, the literary-restoration side of Sorai Learning was developed — a special emphasis being placed on Chinese poems and prose. He thought this type of study, rather than study of the classics, was the essence of Sorai Learning. He too was deeply grounded in Japanese poetry. Shundai wrote of him: " After understanding Japanese poetry, he studied Chinese poetry; and perceiving the way of Chinese poetry, he eventually acquired fame as a master."

And so in comparing Sorai Learning with that of Jinsai, it must be said that, as Confucianism and moral teaching, the Sorai School — with Jinsai Learning as preparation — was a culmination of the teachings of Jinsai in their objective or external aspect — that is, in literature rather than in human nature and the Way of Heaven. If we look at Sorai Learning as antiquarianism, we can see three advances: methodologically, there was philological and literary preparation for the investigation of ancient Chinese rhetoric; in content, there was advance from the morality of the *Analects* and *Book of Mencius* toward an emphasis upon various cultural values — political, literary, economic, etc. — which were represented in the Six Classics; and chronologically, there was a moving back from Confucius and Mencius to the Former Kings. Furthermore, we can see in Sorai Learning a further enhancement of the fundamental power of antiquarian thought in its faith in ancient culture and its idealization, or rather beautification, of ancient culture, as well as in its infatuation with ancient culture based on the attitude of beautification. This resulted in a fervent worship of ancient Chinese culture and a neglect of national feeling.

There even emerged the phenomenon of Sorai's calling himself an "Eastern Barbarian", which, like other indications of China-copying, can be compared to the Greek mania of modern Europe.

In contradistinction to this trend in Confucianism there were beginnings, at about the time of Jinsai, in another direction — in the area of Japanese Learning (*wagaku*) — with the work of Keichū [1640–1701] in Osaka. The scholarship of Keichū centered in exegetical research in the ancient Japanese classics (especially in the *Man'yōshū*) and in philology (particularly in establishing the way to use the *kana* syllabary). In both endeavors he avoided the traditional erroneous views of the Middle Ages, threw out completely the forced analogies and arbitrary views of later commentators, and tried to bring out the true meaning of ancient words (especially in the *Man'yōshū* and ancient classics) and to get at the truth of the ancient classics. Keichū's attitude of free inquiry was the same as that in Confucianism. In comparison to Jinsai's, however, it was more thoroughgoing as an attitude of scholarship, for Jinsai was still somewhat hampered by the moralistic character of Confucianism which he emphasized, and he can hardly be said to have carried free inquiry to its furtherest limits. At the same time, there was, intellectually, not yet any positive antiquarian assertion in the writings of Keichū. Even his anti-Buddhism and anti-Confucianism were merely implied in his rejection of erroneous interpretations of ancient classics. Furthermore, as far as his study of the ancient classics was concerned, neither his career nor his training as a scholar-priest of the Shingon Sect, profoundly learned in Buddhist and Confucian scripture, ever had the slightest adverse effect on the scholarly spirit with which he approached the Japanese classics. Rather, with his thoroughgoing commitment to search for truth, he stimulated the development of antiquarian thought.

Keichū's successor as an antiquarian thinker in the sphere of Japanese Learning was Kada Azumamaro [1669–1736]. A son of the Superintendent Priest of the Inari Shrine in Kyoto, he came a generation after Keichū and died in the same year as Tōgai. He was the first advocate of what was called National Learning — national scholarship which attempted to make clear the ancient culture of Japan (in religion, literature, ethics, law and all other areas) through the *Kojiki, Nihongi, Man'yōshū* and other classics. At the roots of his scholarly urge moved an ardent national "restorationism." In considering the influence of predecessors, we begin first with the fact that he was stimulated by the writings of Keichū in studies of ancient words and classics; and then we note that Azumamaro's mature years coincided with the heyday of the Ancient-Meaning School. But the influence of Sorai's School, in particular, is clearly recognizable. Azumamaro first went to Edo in 1699 at the age of thirty-one; and he stayed there for fifteen years. After that he went to Edo two more times and during this period became known to Shogun Yoshimune for his Japanese Learning. At about the time Azumamaro was going to Edo, Sorai Learning had reached its apogee in that city. Azumamaro's ideas on the above-mentioned National Learning were advocated in his "Proposal for the Founding of a National Learning School"[1] which he submitted to the military government in 1728, several years after he had returned home from his last trip to Edo. In the emphasis and thought, and even in the phraseology, of that document the influence of Sorai Learning stands clearly revealed. Furthermore, we can see here another stage in the rise of a Japanist national consciousness, something that had been gradually boiling up (especially within Shinto) over since the beginning of the Tokugawa Era, and that was now stimulated by the Sinophilism of the Sorai School. This being so, Japanese Learning certainly was a reaction against the influence of Sorai Learning.

The above is a general survey of Tokugawa antiquarian thought down to Kamo Mabuchi [1697–1769].

---

1) [Translated into German by Heinrich Domoulin, "Sō-gakkō-kei ..." *Monumenta Nipponica* III, 2 (1940), 230–49.]

Kamo Mabuchi was born in Hamamatsu, midway between Edo (where Sorai and his disciples worked) and Kyoto (where Jinsai, Keichū, and Azumamaro were influential). He was born in 1697, at a time when Sorai and Azumamaro were at the prime of life and Jinsai and Keichū were growing old. Mabuchi's father, Sadanobu, was a Priest of the New Shrine of Okabe in Iba Village and took "Okabe" for his family name. Masada, one of his ancestors (five generations earlier), had distinguished himself in the service of Tokugawa Ieyasu [1542–1616] at the battle of Mikatagahara in 1572.

As a child Mabuchi was adopted by Masamori, the husband of an elder sister. Subsequently he was adopted by, and married to the daughter of, Masanaga, a kinsman; but when he was twenty-eight, his wife died and he left that family. He wanted to become a priest of the Shingon Sect of Buddhism, but not receiving permission from his parents, he was unable to do so. Some time later he was again adopted by, and married to a daughter in, the Umeya household, innkeepers of Hamamatsu, where he remained for some ten years.

We do not know much about Mabuchi's scholarly preparation during his life in Hamamatsu. But two or three things are worthy of attention. First, as a child he was taught (by his mother) the beauties of "serenity" (*yasurakeku*) and "refined elegance" (*miyabika*) in ancient poetry, through exposure to several of the best poems in the *Man'yōshū*. Secondly, he was drawn to Chinese studies and composed numerous Chinese poems—he even studied under Watanabe Mōan [1687– ?] who was a student of Dazai Shundai and who later, in 1743, wrote *Rōshi gudoku* (Humble Reading of Lao-tzu). Thirdly, he was able to establish contact with Kada Azumamaro. Having such disciples in Hamamatsu as his niece's husband, Sugiura Kuniakira [1678–1740] (who was a priest at the Suwa Shrine) and Mori Terumasa [1685–1752] (who was a priest at the Gosha Shrine), Azumamaro stopped at Hamamatsu several times on his way to and from Edo. At the time of his return from his first trip to Edo, and also at the time of his second trip, Mabuchi was seventeen or eighteen years old; and at the time of Azumamaro's third trip, Mabuchi was twenty-seven. Even if Mabuchi may not have received formal instruction from Azumamaro, there is no doubt but that the two became intimate and that the contact stimulated Mabuchi's young mind. Moreover, Mabuchi established closer contacts with his two seniors, Kuniakira and Terumasa, and learned much from them. Then in 1733, at the age of thirty-seven, he made up his mind, at the urging of these seniors, to go to Kyoto for study under Azumamaro.

Mabuchi studied with Azumamaro until the latter's death. (During this period of study under Azumamaro, he frequently returned home to Hamamatsu.) The period lasted only four years, but it was at a time of Azumamaro's maturity as a scholar and thinker, and Mabuchi was able to imbibe fully from his store of knowledge. From this time on Mabuchi became more and more deeply involved in the main currents of the Ancient-Learning movement of the Tokugawa Era.

In 1737, the year after Azumamaro's death, Mabuchi — at the age of forty-one — returned home; and in the year after that he went back to Edo. It was then that he discarded the name of Umeya and took back the name of Okabe. He then opened up a private school in Edo where he taught Japanese poetry and prose. After about ten years, he became known to Tayasu Munetake [1715–1771], a patron of art and literature who was a son of the Shogun Yoshimune and the position formerly held by Kada Arimaro [1706–1751], the son of Azumamaro. Mabuchi served here until 1760, when he was sixty-four years old. He lived on for ten more years after retirement and died in 1769 at the age of seventy-three. Mabuchi lived from 1697 to 1769, roughly at the time of the German antiquarian, Johann Joachim Winckelmann (1717–1768).

In tracing the development of Mabuchi's scholarship and thought after he went to Edo, we note three separate periods of about a decade each: before, during, and after his service in the Tayasu household. In looking for characteristics of these periods in his writings, we find him saying that when he was " over fifty " — as a result of tremendously hard work after being first inspired by Azumamaro to take up Ancient Learning — he felt that " he had achieved some familiarity with numerous matters of antiquity and with the meanings of the ancient texts."[1] Again he wrote that " when he was sixty " he was awakened to the value of the *Man'yōshū* and perceived that one could learn the thinking of the ancients by studying ancient poetry, finally completing his work on the *Man'yōshū*.[2] Then " after passing through manifold labors," he said that " now that he was seventy," he had penetrated the heart of the Way and reached a stage where " I feel as if I have mastered many things."[3] The first ten-year period came when the Sorai School had already passed its zenith, but had not yet lost its momentum. The second coincided with the last stages of Sorai Learning when Hattori Nankaku, who was a close friend of Mabuchi's, was carrying on work in Chinese literature. The last period — from the standpoint of antiquarianism — was when Mabuchi appeared to take advantage of the decline of Sorai Learning and to replace it with his own Learning. After Mabuchi took up his residence in "*Agatai*" (House in the Fields) in the Hama Ward of Edo in 1764 at the age of 68, his so-called " Agatai School " became a new force in the scholarly world of Edo. The " Old Man of Agatai" was symbolic of the movement of culture eastward from Kyoto to Edo. It was then that he inherited the antiquarianism of the Tokugawa Era.

In viewing Mabuchi as a poet-thinker, we certainly should not neglect his achievements in scholarship. His studies of the Japanese classics ranged from the literature of the Nara Era (including the *Man'yōshū*, the Shinto liturgies, and the early Imperial Edicts)[4] to

---

1) *Bun'i kō* (Study of Textual Meaning) [*Zōtei Kamo Mabuchi zenshū* (Tokyo, 1927–32), X, 331.]
2) *Man'yō kō jo, hitotsu* (Preface to 'Study of the *Man'yōshū*,' Part One) [*Kamo Mabuchi zenshū* XII, 49.]
3) *Manabi no agetsurai* (Discussion of Learning) [*Kamo Mabuchi zenshū* XII, 308.]
4) [See G. B. Sansom, "The Imperial Edicts in the Shoku Nihongi (700–790 A.D.)," TASJ 2nd Ser., I (1924), 5–39.]

the literature of the Heian Era — including the *Genji monogatari* (Tale of Genji), the *Ise monogatari* (Tale of Ise),[1] the *Kokinshū* (Anthology of Ancient and Modern Times), and the *Hyakunin isshu* (One Hundred Poems by One Hundred Poets).[2] In expositions and commentaries, he not only followed the example of his antiquarian predecessors in concentrating on a search for the true meaning of the ancient classics (and in adopting a truth-seeking attitude), but in his philological research he carried on the work of Keichū in particular and added refinements to it. All his studies provided a strong foundation for, and the underlying power of, his thought.

In order to assess the thoroughness and intensity of his scholarly approach, there is certainly no need for us to scrutinize here his separate achievements in such works as the *Kanji kō jo* (Preface to Study of Poetic Epithets), the *Man'yō kō* (Study of the *Man'yōshū*), or the *Norito kō jo* (Preface to Study of Shinto Liturgy). Let us consider Mabuchi's reply to a dissenting opinion on the *Man'yōshū* (sent to him by his disciple, Motoori Norinaga) in which he rejected his disciple's view with the following words: "One can not understand a work of literature well unless he has studied it 20 years."[3] And let us add the following paragraph which he wrote about the way one should study the *Man'yōshū*:

> In reading the *Man'yōshū*, we should read one poem five times, using the modern edition marked to indicate the Japanese readings (*tempon*), but without trying to get the meaning. As we do this, we can natually understand the readings and word usages by comparing them back and forth. After that we should read the poem again and then write the variant characters into the movable-type edition and

---

1) [See Frits Vos, *A Study of the Ise-monogatari, with the text according to the Den-teika-hippon and an annotated translation* (The Hague, Mouton and Co.; 1957), 2 vols.]
2) [See Kenneth Yasuda, *Poem Card (The Hyakunin-isshu in English)* (Tokyo, Kamakura Bunko; 1948).]
3) [Mabuchi to Norinaga, No. 64 in *Agatai shokan zokuhen* (Agatai Letters, Continued) [*Kamo Mabuchi zenshū* XII, 516.]

read it again without the marks.¹⁾ At first it will probably be difficult to understand, and previous readings will no doubt come to mind unconsciously. If there are difficult passages, we can refer again to the marked edition. At this point we will find many passages the readings of which we really feel are correct in the marked edition. After going over them several times in this way, we should make a cursory examination of the other ancient works from the *Kojiki* on down to the *Wamyō ruijū shō* [a Japanese dictionary compiled around 935]. If we read the *Kojiki*, the *Nihongi*, the Shinto liturgies in the *Engishiki*, and the texts of the Imperial Edicts of the various reigns, and then take up the unmarked edition of the *Man'yōshū* again, we should be able to understand most of it. At this stage we should be able to tell that certain current readings are questionable, that another is correct, and still another is definitely wrong; and we will no doubt develop suspicions concerning possible errors, interpolations, and deletions. But even when we have our doubts, we make mistakes when we try to reach a conclusion too quickly. On the other hand, when we keep all our doubts in mind, it often happens that we get answers each time we read other literature, even when we listen to modern dialects and slang of the various provinces. Only after this, as we turn the possibilities over in our mind, do we arrive at definite opinions unexpectedly. Then the marked edition will become a complete nuisance. The person who has achieved such understanding of the *Man'yōshū* poems will now be distracted by the readings

---

1) [The difficulty of the *Man'yōshū* is due not so much to the archaic language as to the fact that it is written in Chinese characters. In some cases characters are used phonetically to represent Japanese words syllable by syllable, while in other cases they are used semantically. When they are used semantically, the commentator must find an appropriate Japanese word that was in use at that period and that has a length that fits the meter. It is this situation that gives rise to variant readings. Mabuchi is describing a method of study in which the student begins with a marked or annotated edition and progresses toward an ability to use an unannotated edition—in this case a movable-type edition based on the research of Sengaku in the Muromachi Era, but without Sengaku's notes.]

written beside the original text, and this will constitute a hindrance to reading, since it may cause him to overlook words which should be noticed.[1]

But we also note that Mabuchi — with an excess of intuitive insight — rushed boldly into very arbitrary conjectures. For example, he tried to guess the period when Shinto liturgies were composed through an appreciation of their style. Also, he evolved the idea of "an original *Man'yōshū*" by surmising — with his own subjective evaluation of poetry as his main standard — that there was an original compilation and a supplementary one. Also, when concerning himself with the archaic Japanese readings of Chinese characters, he often insisted, when he came across difficult words, that the characters were wrong; and he tried rashly to correct them. Furthermore, in attempting to explain archaic meanings of poetic epithets (*makura kotoba*), he would give free reign to his inventiveness. Thus his character as a poet-thinker stands revealed in his scholarly approach.

The object of Mabuchi's entire activity — his research, thought, and writing — was really the *Man'yōshū*. As to why he selected the *Man'yōshū* from among the ancient classics for study, he wrote: "Events of the remote ages, when divine Emperors assumed the rule of the Heavenly Sun Succession, are recorded in the books of successive reigns of antiquity. And yet when one examines these vague generalities, the ancient legends are as remote as the sound of the wind, and the spirit with which these Emperors ruled is shrouded in a gloom of uncertainty. Therefore, when men speak of these writings in later ages, they doubtless discuss them from their individual and differing viewpoints. And so it is only the poetry of the ancient age which carries the feeling and expression of the men of antiquity."[2] From such as this we see why he considered the *Man'yōshū* the most suitable subject for research.

---

1) *Man'yō kai tsūshaku narabi ni shakurei jo* (Preface to General Interpretation of the *Man'yōshū*, with Examples) [*Kamo Mabuchi zenshū* IV, 495–6].
2) *Man'yō kō jo, hitotsu* [*Kamo Mabuchi zenshū* XII, 48].

As to what he thought of the *Man'yōshū* as a repository of ancient poems, and as a masterpiece of ancient Japanese culture, we read:

> Here stands a huge tree. Its topmost branches spread over the sky; its middle branches spread over the distant east; its lower branches spread over our rustic fields. Even the tall trees on Tsuki River and at Mike are tiny branches by comparison. From the morning sun to the evening sun, sky-shining, there was no place where it did not cast its shadow — in Tsukushi, Mutsu, Tosa or Koshi. Its seed was produced from the two Kami who descended from Heaven, and passed to the Imperial Palace at Kashiwara. It began to grow at the Palace of Naniwa and spreading luxuriantly over the White Wisteria Plain [Fujiwara, location of the Imperial Court from 694 to 710], it flourished even at the Imperial Palace of Nara of much-leveled earth. The multitude of its branches (poems) from the topmost to the nethermost — some long, some short, some of the Palace style, and some of the rustic style — numbered four thousand one hundred. Much more the multitude of its leaves (words) which were myriads without end; and so it was called an *Anthology of a Myriad Word-Leaves* (*Man'yōshū*).[1]

Such was the grandeur with which Mabuchi depicted so graphically the image of this great *Anthology* as it was reflected in his heart. Thus, after years of studious devotion and creative effort during which " I pass the years and months in converse with these *Myriad Leaves* of words, and desirous that the words and spirit of my own poetry be perfect in their likeness to the *Myriad Leaves,* among them I stroll in spare moments away from the workaday world, now looking, now reciting,"[2] Mabuchi was at last able to grasp the essence of the *Man'yōshū* style. As for what this " essence of the *Man'yōshū* style " meant, he explained it again and again in his numerous works,

---

1) *Man'yo kai jo* [*Kamo Mabuchi zenshū* IV, 48].
2) *Man'yō kō jo, hitotsu* [*Kamo Mabuchi zenshū* XII, 48].

but perhaps it is best summarized in the opening paragraph of his *Niimanabi* (Primary Learning):

> Poems in ancient times emphasized tone, for they were meant to be sung. The tones as a whole emerged in whatever way individuals took hold of them — whether soft, bright, clear, or dusky — but through them all runs a lofty (*takaki*) and direct (*naoki*) spirit. In their loftiness we find elegance (*miyabi*); in their directness, a manly (*o-oshiki*) spirit."[1]

These words explain the Sincere Heart (*magokoro*), which Mabuchi set forth as the spirit of the *Man'yōshū* poems. Probably the phrase " in whatever way individuals took hold of them" referred to a naturalness, in contradistinction to the contrived artificiality of later poetry. If we take this as a formal definition of the "sincere heart," we can regard the words "lofty" and "direct" as definitions of content.

"Lofty" referred to what was divorced from the tediously vulgar — to the large as opposed to the small, the broad as opposed to the narrow, the simple as opposed to the complex, and the laconic as opposed to the verbose. Its beauty was recognized as "elegance." Here we see demonstrated the greatness of that which had simple purity.

"Direct" referred to a frankness of feeling which was devoid of ostentation — the straight as opposed to the stooped, the regular as opposed to the bent, the erect as opposed to the twisted, and the easy as opposed to the labored. On that foundation he recognized a manliness that did not permit effeminacy. Here we see an understanding of the literary value of simplicity, in contrast to sentimentality.

This was what he appreciated in the good poems of the *Man'yōshū*; and the good poems were, for him, principally those composed in the reigns of Empress Jitō and Emperor Mommu [690–707]. In the pre-

---

1) *Niimanabi* [*Kamo Mabuchi zenshū* X, 311].

face to his *Man'yō shinsai hyakushu kai* (Understanding of One Hundred Poems Newly Extracted from the *Man'yōshū*),[1] he discussed three changes in poetic styles since antiquity. He dismissed the poems of the Tokugawa Era, which had lost the " true feeling,' ran to excesses of artificiality and elaboration, and had become just like landscapes in miniature gardens. While there was still a certain naturalness in the poems of the Heian Era, he did not approve of their maidenly " extremes of elegance like the smoothness of a polished mirror and the sheen of a painted eye-brow." Rather, he extolled " the sincere and rare quality " of the *Man'yōshū* poems " as if we today were viewing those times again; for they are like the seas and mountains created by Heaven and earth, and were sung to the shifting scenes of clouds and wind, blossoms and tinted foliage as they changed with the movements of the sun and moon."[2] He had an especially high regard for the poetic styles of the Court at Fujiwara [694–710], styles that were represented in the heroic sweep of Hitomaro and the lofty, limpid qualities of Akahito.

Another aspect of these writings on the *Man'yōshū* is that Mabuchi was the first *Man'yōshū* poet after Minamoto no Sanetomo [1192–1219]; his poetic gifts enabled him to do what neither Keichū (the *Man'yōshū* scholar) nor Azumamaro (the champion of a *Man'yōshū* restoration in National Learning) had been able to accomplish. There are many short and long poems in his collected poems (*Kamo-ō kashū*) and fragmentary manuscripts, but there is no need to describe or illustrate his scholarly mastery of the diction and form of the *Man'yōshū* poems. On the other hand, the poetic style of Mabuchi was not identical with that of the *Man'yōshū* poems. In his poems we can see, clearly and throughout, traces of the style and tastes of the Tokugawa Era. But I think this was natural. He showed that he had achieved true mastery of the *Man'yōshū* poems without becoming

---

1) [The author says "preface to the *Man'yō kō*, but the comments are from the *Man'yō shinsai hyakushu kai*.]
2) *Man'yō shinsai hyakushū kai* [*Kamo Mabuchi zenshū* XII, 47].

a *Man'yōshū* imitator. Thus his understanding of the *Man'yōshū* poems enabled him to become a good poet; and at the same time, his ability as a poet enabled him to achieve a deep understanding of the *Man'yōshū* poems.

Such expression and exercise of the *Man'yōshū* style were for Mabuchi nothing less than mastery of the highest values in the *Man'yōshū* spirit. This mastery awakened him vigorously to the values of the ancient Japanese civilization that had produced the *Man'yōshū*. The various thoughts and ideas which were contained in the antiquarian intellectual currents of the Tokugawa Era — the National Learning of his teacher Azumamaro and the study of ancient rhetoric in the Sorai School — were reborn with a new vitality in the heart of Mabuchi. We see in this *Man'yōshū* scholar an antiquarian thinker as well.

Mabuchi said: "How obvious it is that the beauty of literature is the very balm of government!" And the fact that *Man'yōshū* poetry revealed such beauty was because " the august government of all under Heaven flourished in its perfection at Fujiwara," and Japan in high antiquity had a culture that was excellent."[1]

The reason why the culture was excellent lay in the fact that " the Emperor displayed majesty and manliness in accordance with the Way of the Heavenly Kami, and the ministers governed in his service, professing valor and directness over all " — that is, both the Emperor and his ministers acted with hearts that were direct and manly.[2] This was the picture of our ancient civilization before it was damaged by the influence of Confucianism and Buddhism; but later, he claimed, these two teachings were propagated and the people came to take pleasure in intellectual trivialities and to turn to elaboration. More and more the prestige of the Imperial Court deteriorated and the

---

1) *Engishiki norito kai jo* (Preface to an Understanding of the Shinto Liturgies in the *Engishiki*) [*Kamo Mabuchi zenshū* XII, 56].
2) *Man'yō kō jo, futatsu* (Preface to a Study of the *Man'yōshū*, Part Two), [*Kamo Mabuchi zenshū* XII, 49].

spirit of the people degenerated. And Mabuchi explained that this was why poetry, in later ages — especially after the capital was moved to Heian — became effeminate and increasingly decadent. Possibly it was in this sense that his "*Man'yōshū*ism" meant "ancient culturism." And yet "*Man'yōshū*ism," in which the *Man'yōshū* poems were understood and composed, was not simply, for Mabuchi, an instrument for the advancement of antiquarianism. It was antiquarianism itself. Someone once said to Mabuchi: "I have no interest in such small matters as poetry, but rather in the way of China [Confucianism] which seeks to govern society with good order." In response to which Mabuchi explained that it was poetry which constituted the true Way, while the teachings of China were the small Way.[1] He meant that poetry came spontaneously from human feeling and did not conform to logic. Although it appeared to be useless, it did not make sharp distinctions and it gentled the heart. It was for this reason that poetry fell naturally into harmony with the spirit of good government and was in keeping with the Ancient Way. For, as Mabuchi wrote:

> When things are fully exposed to logic, they die, as it were. It is only when they are in a natural interplay with Heaven and earth that they live and move. I do not mean that it is bad to have a general knowledge of numerous matters, but it is a weakness of man's mind to go one-sidedly in that direction. The best thing to do is to learn things, then leave them. Indeed, poetry ranges over all things. Even if a poet gives expression to improper and wrong entreaties, one's mind is not disordered, but gentled.[2]

And so the like of Confucianism was definitely not a Way to keep order in the world, but rather a dead Way that ought to be learned, then discarded. Thus Mabuchi's study of the *Man'yōshū* and poetic composition were fused in antiquarianism, and from this emerged his

---

1) *Koku-i kō* (On the Spirit of the Nation) [*Kamo Mabuchi zenshū* X, 359].
2) [*Kamo Mabuchi zenshū* X, 361.]

concept of the Ancient Way. Looking at this Ancient Way from the point of view of the *Man'yōshū* poems, he wrote:

> Indeed, for men born of the womb of Heaven and earth who have been unchanged for fifteen generations, what is there to tell of the ancient past but words and feelings! When we succeed in expressing ancient words and feelings, we will be transported to antiquity, even though we live in a later age.[1]

And from the point of view of the Ancient Way, he wrote:

> In revering the august Emperor, one thinks of bringing peace to the world. By so thinking, he cannot help but revere the Imperial reigns of the ancient past. By revering the ancient past, he will read the books of the past. When he reads the books of the past, he will want to know the words and feelings of the past. In wanting to know the words and feelings of the past, he will try to become familiar with the poems of the past. And in trying to become familiar with the poems of the past, he will turn first to the *Man'yōshū*.[2]

Essentially we have here a restorationism of the past and an idealism in which restoration is realized by being able to put the past into the words and feelings of poems. When Mabuchi completed the manuscript for his *Man'yō kō,* he made the comment that in his youth he "thought of the *Man'yōshū* as being merely a collection of old poems, and did not realize that by means of old poems one could understand the spirit of antiquity." He had devoted his energies primarily to the study of poetry and literature in the Heian Era, but now he knew that these had the effeminate graces of a later age: " They lack virile, manly qualities and do not accord with the majestic reigns of the glorious past." After he appreciated this fact, he "knew that

---

1) *Man'yō kō jo, hitotsu,* [*Kamo Mabuchi zenshū* XII, 48–9].
2) *Man'yō kō* (Study of the *Man'yōshū*), preface to scroll 6 [*Kamo Mabuchi zenshū* XII, 54].

all that counted was the *Man'yōshū,* and after passing through multifold changes from summer to winter wear," he completed the work at the age of sixty. He often likened the gains he had made in the *Man'yōshū* to standing on a lofty summit surveying the land. His comment that "if one works from the top down what can he not achieve?" suggests the mental state he had attained.[1]

Mabuchi the poet often depicted, in poetry and in prose, beautiful representations of Japan's ancient spirit. A passage from the *Man'yō kō jo,* illustrates this:

> The Emperors of high antiquity venerated the Imperial Kami within and wielded awesome majestic power without; and thus did they pacify countries that would not submit and soften men of fierce might. By conforming with Heaven and earth, they created a Way of splendor and kept order; and every shortcoming they corrected as soon as it reached the eye or ear. Therefore even the multitudes, teeming as the verdant grass, venerated the Imperial Kami and had no foul recesses in their hearts, stood in awe of the Emperors, and had no vice in their persons. Much more the ministers who served with manly true-heartedness, declaring "True, we may die by the side of our Lord, water-soaked corpses if on the sea and grass-covered corpses if in the mountains, but we will not go down without a fight." And so did they govern the land ruled by our Emperors, long as Heaven is eternal and placidly as the earth is level.[2]

Also he praised the Province of Yamato, cradle of the ancient culture:

> Our supreme Lords, noble progeny who have ruled the Sun Succession of Heaven since the divine Age of Kami, saw to their outer affairs with manliness and valor, and attended to their inner affairs with directness and calm; so that their many countries grew ever broader and their countless ministers flourished ever more splendidly. The

---

1) *Man'yō kō jo,* Vol. 1, [*Kamo Mabuchi zenshū* XII, 49].
2) [*Ibid.,* 49.]

white clouds rise serenely far and wide over the province of Yamato seen from the sky. Look at its mountains: how tall they are! Look at its hamlets: how peaceful they are! A land delightful with spring flowers! Here with good reason did our Emperors extend their power; and with good reason did their many provinces prosper. Oh, to see again the perfect age, that age of august majesty long ago! Rich and full are our hearts, even the hearts of us, the people, treasures of our sovereign, living here in the land of Hidakami [the northeast], after viewing the plains of Yamato in spring.

As has already been stated, Mabuchi's idea of " the perfect age, an age of august majesty long ago," which he saw in the *Man'yōshū*, referred to the " age of the flourishing of Fujiwara, the Wisteria Plain " [694–710]. This is further verified in *Engishiki norito kai jo*, which he wrote at the age of fifty:

> After the period when the Court was at Ōtsu in Ōmi, there came the majestic age of the abode at Fujiwara in Yamato. Imperial rule filled out in all its plentitude and reposed in all its tranquility as far as the clouds lie beyond and as close as the circuit of a toad's crawl; so that this was the time when the beauty and elegance of literary expression existed complete.[1]

I think that we can see here, in the rich beauty of his idea of the past, the essence of the antiquarianism of Mabuchi, the poet-thinker. But Mabuchi's idea of the ancient past could not fail to show development in other directions as well. For example, he could not fail to proceed from an enhanced aestheticism to an enhanced morality. Likewise, he exhibited, more and more, the personality of a philosopher. It is however not possible to differentiate between such developments with absolute precision; rather it is more appropriate to understand them as a movement of the center of gravity in his total personality. In a general way, we can pursue these in the thought of the last period of

---

1) [*Kamo Mabuchi zenshū* XII, 55.]

his intellectual life — in his declining years, or during the last of the two periods mentioned above, when he was in his seventies. These developments appear in three areas.

First, there was a tendency to return to a more ancient past. Although he reiterated the glories of the Imperial Court of Fujiwara (glories which he saw through the *Man'yōshū* poems), yet because of a view of cultural history in which he explained the degeneration of the ancient spirit as due to the influence of Confucianism and Buddhism, he went farther back and placed the golden age in the period before Empress Jingū's invasion of Korea and was willing to regard the reigns of Emperor Kōtoku [645-654] and Empress Saimei [655-661] as, on the whole, part of that age. But the period from Emperor Tenji [668-671] on, he saw as one of change.[1] In his *Agatai shūgen roku* (Collected Utterances at Agatai) and also in his *Koku-i kō* (On the Spirit of the Nation) he compared Japan, the country where the sun rises, with China, the country of the sun at its apogee, and India, the country of the setting sun. He described the national character of Japan as corresponding to spring — in contrast to the summer and autumn of China and India; to morning — in contrast to the noon and night of China and India; and to youth — in contrast to the maturity and old age of China and India. The people in those countries were disposed to set great store on reasoning and to play the wise man. They ran to excesses of fallacy and concentrated on elaborateness. In contrast, the minds of the Japanese were smoothly flowing with no sharp edges, and direct by nature. Therefore the Japanese had no pompous doctrines like those of Benevolence, Right-doing, Propriety, Wisdom, and Good Faith [the five constant virtues of Confucianism]. There was not even any writing. Nor was marriage between brothers and sisters of the half blood necessarily avoided. There was no splendor of palace halls and garments, and all was natural and simple — wooden roofs, earthen walls, and clothes of bark cloth and hemp. Moreover, the way of behavior existed naturally, just as ways and paths formed naturally in the virgin hills and moors. Therefore, since the Emperors

---

1) Postscript to *Man'yō shinsai hyakushu kai* [*Kamo Mabuchi zenshū* IV, 483-5].

from the Imperial ancestral Kami on down ruled above in accord with the spirit of Heaven and earth, the ministers served with faithful hearts below. Of course this did not mean that no evil persons appeared to bring disturbances to the world; but since this was an age of direct minds and hearts, nothing was concealed; and evil was crushed at once so that there were no serious disorders. Even though no century went by without some slight tremor, a whole millennium was kept in order with considerable tranquility. Apart from minor difficulties, the Emperors succeeded in a single line and were not thrown into confusion. And their rule manifested a virile spirit because they stressed simplicity and martial spirit, without a hint of cultural meretriciousness. Being devoted to valor, it had nothing in it that was effeminate or devious. This picture he contrasted with conditions in China, where despite the preaching of a pompous and meticulous Confucianism, the throne passed from one usurper to another, and in the end the country was seized by neighboring barbarians; and when despite the fact that they had in high antiquity the so-called peace of Yao and Shun and the Three Dynasties, this did not endure. Thus, in propounding the idea that Japan was a country which conformed to the true Way of Heaven and earth, Mabuchi set as his ideal the conditions of simplicity and martial spirit which had prevailed in Japan's ancient past.

Perhaps it was in this way that the lofty summit of the *Man'yōshū*, where he stood and looked down upon the world, became the stairway by which he would ascend to the heights of the Age of Kami. His study of the *Man'yōshū* poems was preparation for his study of the Age of Kami; and his knowledge of ancient poems permitted him to push farther back and appreciate the Age of Kami. And so, even as he lamented that he had come to the final years of his life, he poked fun at the far-fetched interpretations put on the Shinto classics [*Kojiki, Nihongi,* etc.] in Sung Confucian theories of later generations. He turned his mind to the world of the Shinto classics of which he had once said: " The ancient stories passed on are as remote as the sound of the wind, and the spirit with which those Emperors ruled is shrouded in a gloom of uncertainty." There was the same tendency to throw himself into the study of Shinto liturgies in the closing years of his life. About them he said: "These are the model of ancient style. They have never been touched by the dead hand of later Confucianists. They make you feel as if you had purified yourself on the Plain of Ahagi." Of the "divine congratulatory words of Kuni-no-Miyatsuko of Izumo" and the "Great Purification" in particular, he wrote, "These should be studied first of all to understand the Way of Kami."[1] Concerning the date of their composition, Mabuchi claimed in his *Engishiki norito kai* that they had been written during the reigns of Emperor Temmu and Empress Jitō [673–696]; but in his *Norito kō* he placed the writing of the "divine congratulatory words" during the reign of Emperor Jomei [629–641] and the "Great Purification" sometime during the reigns of Emperors Tenji [668–671] and Temmu [673–689]. This shift reflects his tendency to go farther back in time for his idea of the ancient past. Also, the same trend is seen in his poetic interests. As he approached the end of his life, he was less content with the *Man'yōshū* poems, and came to idealize an even older style "which was lofty, without artificality and beyond the conception of other men."[2]

The second development, during the last period of Mabuchi's intellectual life, was the establishment of a philosophical base for his antiquarianism. His return to a point further back in time for his

---

1) [Mabuchi to Saitō Nobuyuki in *Agatai shoken, Kamo Mabuchi zenshū* XII, 446. The "divine congratulatory words of the Kuni-no-Miyatsuko of Izumo" were recited in the Imperial Court whenever a new Kuni-no-Miyatsuko (Provincial governor who after the Great Reform of 645 devoted himself largely to religious matters) was appointed for the Province of Izumo. This liturgy is translated by Donald L. Philippi, *Norito, A New Translation of the Ancient Japanese Ritual Prayers*, 72–5. The "Great Purification" liturgy was recited on the occasion of a general exorcism held twice a year, on the last day of the sixth and twelfth months. The purpose was to remove *tsumi*. This too has been translated in ibid., 45–9.]
2) Preface to *Kamo-ō kashū* (Collected Writings of the Old Gentleman, Kamo), [*Kamo Mabuchi zenshū* XII, 1].

idea of the ancient past was naturally accompanied by a deepening of philosophical reflection about this idealization. His philosophy, which had within it elements of Lao-tzu and Chuang-tzu, should be considered a natural drift, and not at all an imitation. He often expressed approval of Lao-tzu, as in the following passage: "It is the utterances of the man called Lao-tzu, spoken in accord with Heaven and earth, which conform with the Way of all under Heaven."[1] His exposition of "spontaneity and non-activity" (*shizen mui*) and "nothingness and quietism" (*kyomu tentan*) meant of course that he rejected the Confucian ideals of the Worthy (*ken*), the Sage (*sei*), Learning (*gaku*), and Wisdom (*chi*); and that he disclaimed Benevolence and Right-doing. On the other hand, he extolled muteness and taciturnity and valued thrift — all of which are reminiscent of the language of the *Tao-tê-ching* (Lao-tzu). We see this especially in his basic concept of Heaven and earth, and of father and mother. He referred especially to the following phrases in the Empress Saimei [655–662] section of the *Nihongi* where Hakatoko answers questions raised by the Emperor of China about the condition of Japan: "She [the Empress] gets her good health naturally, by bringing her inner powers into conformity with Heaven and earth..... Since the government is in accord with Heaven and earth, there is no trouble among the people." "This," he said, "really describes the Great Way of our country." That is, the Kami Way (Shintō), as he understood it, was precisely this Great Way; it took its models from the natural forces of Heaven and earth which undergo gradual transformation through the interaction of the four seasons.[2] And as to the Kami, he took the position that faith in the power of the Kami to fulfill requests, like the Buddha faith, was a useless thing; it was a foolish superstition which showed a childish unawareness of the permanent, fundamental Way of Heaven and earth. And, of course, he held that " such ideas as hell (*jigoku*) and the after-

1) *Koku-i kō* [*Kamo Mabuchi zenshū* XII, 365].
2) *Manabi no agetsurai*, [*Kamo Mabuchi zenshū* XII, 309].

world are all the words of robbers ". The Kami were merely to be revered and worshipped.[1]

It is evident that Mabuchi's Way of Kami, or Shinto, was nothing other than an atheistic natural philosophy. Moreover, opposing the idea that man is the lord of creation, he said: " In the eyes of the father and mother which are Heaven and earth, man, beasts, birds, and vermin are all the same thing." Again he said " When considered in comparison with the duration of Heaven and earth, five hundred or one thousand years are less than the blink of an eyelid." He preached the goodness of that which is " round " in conformity with the metaphoric figure of Heaven and earth, and considered everything that is angular, precipitate, crabbed, or extreme as characteristic of those Confucian teachings that were bogged down in Principle — thus did he attack the unnaturalness of Confucianism.[2] All such ideas were conceived from his view of Heaven and earth. Nor did he consider the Ancient Way as simply a way that prevailed in the past. He thought of it as a Way that emerged out of the past to be followed in the present. In this respect he agrees with Lao-tzu's view of the ancient Way, and appears to have adopted it.

The third change that occurred during the last stage of Mabuchi's intellectual life was the rise of a political emphasis in his antiquarian thought. He fervently advocated a return to antiquity:

> When even China, the country that changes its masters, is said to admire a return of everything to antiquity, shall this great country, whose rulers have descended in the same Sun Succession of Heaven, fail to return to the usages of the grand age, lofty as the clouds in the sky, which was established by the Imperial ancestors in all their glory; and shall it hold to nothing but the present which has come down like the descent of a mountain stream to the plain?[3]

---

1) Mabuchi to Umeya Ichizaemon Mashige, no. 50 in *Agatai shokan, zokuhen*, [*Kamo Mabuchi zenshū* XII, 506].
2) [*Koku-i kō, Kamo Mabuchi zenshū* X, 365–67, 368–69.]
3) *Ka-i kō* (On the Spirit of Poetry), [*Kamo Mabuchi zenshū* X, 323].

But since the advocacy here was *Man'yōshū*-ism, that is, gaining an understanding of ancient words and meanings, what is seen in this passage is rather an expression of antiquarian idealism. Moreover, concerning conditions of his own day, Mabuchi gave vent to eulogies of the Tokugawa military government, which had existed since the time of Ieyasu, and even praised this period as an age of return to antiquity. In one sense, this attitude was a product of his lineage and environment; but it was definitely a product of his idealism as a poet-thinker as well. On the other hand, his Ancient Way naturally tended to contain some stress on a restoration of Imperial rule; and this shows that his idealism was moving in a practical direction. The most prominent manifestation of this is found in a section of the *Agatai shūgen roku* (Collected Utterances of Agatai) where he talks about moving the Imperial capital. There he wrote that at times it is necessary to move the capital — even though this may involve considerable trouble — in order to reinvigorate the spirit of the people. He cited a case in history: When the Imperial capital was located in the Province of Yamato, Imperial prestige was great; but after the capital was moved to the city of Heian, there was deterioration. This was due entirely, said Mabuchi, to a weak, effeminate national character. For this reason, he advocated a political program of Imperial restoration, saying that if the Court could achieve the strong spirit of the eastern provinces by moving the Imperial capital to the east, the country would be put in order as a matter of course and the Imperial prestige would be enhanced.[1] In the conclusion to his *Koku-i kō* he wrote: " All I do is talk on and on, hoping that one day a good ruler will appear. If there should emerge a man on high who loves antiquity and who hopes to put the world right, the world will be entirely put right within less than ten or twenty years. It is too soon to think it cannot be put right easily. Through the thought and feeling of one man on high, the world can certainly be changed."[2] Here he hints that as a teacher of a good ruler he would like to actualize the past.

---

1) [*Agatai shūgen roku, Kamo Mabuchi zenshū* XII, 412.]
2) *Koku-i kō,* [*Kamo Mabuchi zenshū* X, 375].

It is clear that through such developments in Mabuchi's conception of the ancient past, his philosophical style as a teacher of the Ancient Way became ever more pronounced. It has already been pointed out that this was not something to be seen only in his declining years. After considering the course of his life as a poet-thinker, I feel that it was an appropriate intellectual development.

Now, I can bring the discussion in this section to a close with a few words concerning Mabuchi's position in the antiquarian intellectual movement of the Tokugawa Era, described at the beginning of this essay. It is obvious that Mabuchi, as an antiquarian, owed much — academically, intellectually, and spiritually — to his predecessors in Confucianism and National Learning. But at the same time, he differed from them, for he had achieved a unique individuality in which the influence of his predecessors was fused. In comparing him to Keichū, we find that Keichū was more of, if not purely, a scholar; whereas, Mabuchi was more of a thinker and poet. When we compare him with Azumamaro, his immediate teacher and the man who is thought to have exerted the greatest personal influence on him — and leaving aside the difference in achievement in the sense that one was the originator and the other the perfecter — we can still see in their aptitudes that as a poet, scholar, and thinker Mabuchi was, in all areas, more gifted.

From various points of view it is probably Sorai who makes the best contrast. Not only in doctrines and tendencies, but also in ability, the two were very much alike. But in contrast to Sorai, who went from ethics to literary style and developed the externals of Confucianism to their highest point, Mabuchi went from poetry to morality and gave to National Learning an ethical content. Both idealized the past, but Sorai expounded the Way of the Former Kings and moved toward culturalism; whereas Mabuchi proclaimed anti-culturalism and drew close to Lao-tzu. Although Mabuchi established a "*Man'yō-shū*-ism" under the influence of Sorai's emphasis on ancient Chinese rhetoric, he did not connect his Ancient Way with the Way of the Former Kings. Instead, he took a negative attitude:

Yao and Shun, for example, have been apotheosized by Ogyū Sorai, as have been Amida and Shaka among the Buddhists; and the dynasties of Hsia, Yin and Chou that came after them are cited as canonical authority. Neither Yao and Shun, nor the dynasties of Hsia, Yin and Chou, were as the oral traditions have made them out to be, and they must have had many evils in them. But assuming that this fact would not be edifying, they have obscured the origins and thereby deluded mankind. Thus the tradition was handed down, and in due course such things were spoken and believed in this country as well. But in my opinion the people of the world do not understand these things well. Let us reveal everything that happened in the ancient age without the slightest falsification, and let us make known that such things have never existed anywhere. But in the present age we shall be able to set up teachings properly about what ought to be and what one ought to do.[1]

By this declaration he aspired to elucidate, in a scholarly way, the true situation of the ancient past in our country, and thereby to bring out its values. And because of his power of discernment he was able to grasp, in an admirable way, the permanent values inherent in simplicity; and to recognize, in the special character of our Nation Body — predicated on the unbroken line of Imperial descent — a symbol of those values. The teachings of Lao-tzu were also adapted to this purpose. Thus he demonstrated a truth-seeking attitude which is a special characteristic of modern antiquarianism. National Learning best represented this attitude. In this way he was able to preserve his own originality of thought and, at the same time, to achieve intellectual results. It is this more than anything else which has produced the enduring significance of Mabuchi's thought and the resultant influence on later generations.

Bibliographical Note:

The following works by Mabuchi constitute the major source material for an understanding of him as a thinker:

---

1) *Koku-i kō* [*Kamo Mabuchi zenshū* X, 369].

(1)   *Engishiki norito kai jo* (Preface to 'An Understanding of the Shinto Liturgies in the *Engishiki*') [*Kamo Mabuchi zenshū* V, 273–8], and

Bun'i kō (Study of Textual Criticism) [*Kamo Mabuchi zenshū* X, 329–34];

written in 1746, age 50.

(2)   *Man'yō kai tsūshaku narabi ni shakurei jo* (Preface to 'A General Interpretation of the *Man'yōshū*, with Examples') [*Kamo Mabuchi zenshū* IV, 487–88];

written in 1749, age 53.

(3)   *Kanji kō jo* (Preface to 'A Study of Poetic Epithets') [*Kamo Mabuchi zenshū* V, 1–5];

written in 1757, age 61.

(4)   *Man'yō kō narabi ni bekki jo* (Preface to 'Study of the *Man'yōshū*' and 'Supplement to Study of the *Man'yōshū*') [*Kamo Mabuchi zenshū* I, 1–24];

Tatsu no Kimie, Kamo no Mabuchi toi kotae (Questions and Answers between Tatsu no Kimie and Kamo Mabuchi) [*Kamo Mabuchi zenshū* XII, 215–44];

both written in 1760, age 64.

(5)   *Ka-i kō* (On the Spirit of Poetry) [*Kamo Mabuchi zenshū* X, 321–8];

written in 1764, age 68.

(6)   *Nii manabi* (Primary Learning) [*Kamo Mabuchi zenshū* XI, 311–20];

written in 1765, age 69.

(7)   *Manabi no agetsurai* (Discussion of Learning) [*Kamo Mabuchi zenshū* XII, 306–11];

written in 1766, age 70.

(8)   *Norito kō jo* (Preface to 'Study of Shinto Liturgies') [*Kamo Mabuchi zenshū* V, 401–4];

written in 1768, age 72.

(9) *Go-i kō* (On the Meaning of Words) [*Kamo Mabuchi zenshū* X, 339–58];

written in 1769, age 73.

(10) *Koku-i kō* (On the Spirit of the Nation) [*Kamo Mabuchi zenshū* X, 359–76];

Agatai shūgen roku (Collected Utterances of Agatai) [*Kamo Mabuchi zenshū* XII, 407–14]; and

Sho-i kō (On the Meaning of Japanese Classics) [*Kamo Mabuchi zenshū* X, 335–38];

all written in the last years of his life.

Note: With the exception of the *Agatai shūgen roku*, all of the above are included in the *Kamo Mabuchi zenshū* (Collected Works of Kamo Mabuchi).[1] The *Agatai shūgen roku*, which can be considered the original draft of the *Koku-i kō*, has come down to us in manuscript form. Perhaps because of the intricacy of Mabuchi's style, there are numerous errors not only in the *Kamo Mabuchi zenshū*, but in other publications as well. The *Koku-i kō* is the worst example of this, and so it should be read with caution. I think that the errors in the older publications will be corrected in the *Zōtei Kamo Mabuchi zenshū* (Enlarged Edition of the Collected Works of Kamo Mabuchi). [This was published in 1927–32.] There are also several editions of his collected poems, but the most complete is *Kamo-ō kashū* (Collected Poems of the Old Gentleman, Kamo) — the preface by Tachibana Chikage is dated 1801. The *Kamo-ō kashū* is included in the *Kamo Mabuchi zenshū*.

2. *Motoori Norinaga*

Motoori Norinaga, as an antiquarian thinker of the Tokugawa Era, was Kamo Mabuchi's foremost disciple and his immediate successor. As a matter of course, the antiquarian thought of Norinaga

---

1) [The *Agatai shūgen roku* is included in the *Zōtei Kamo Mabuchi zenshū*.]

was not merely an extension of Mabuchi's, but a further development, and we should note that "development" in this case meant a distinct enhancement of uniquely individual qualities. The fact that the development of thought does not necessarily take place solely in accord with the dictates of logic and has a variety of factors working within it is often seen in the history of thought and philosophy, and constitutes, moreover, a fascinating aspect of historical research. We can recognize a striking example of this in Norinaga's thought.

Norinaga was born in 1730 (halfway through the administration of the eighth Tokugawa Shōgun, Yoshimune) in the family of a certain cotton wholesaler of the city of Matsuzaka in the Province of Ise. This was about thirty years after the death of Keichū and Jinsai, two years after the death of Sorai, and in the declining years of Azumamaro — but in the mature years of Mabuchi. As a child he received a literary education at home that was typical in merchant families of the Kyoto-Osaka area. Between the ages of twenty-three and twenty-eight he studied in Kyoto, where he was trained in Confucianism and medicine. In the tenth month of his twenty-eighth year he returned home, where he practiced as a pediatrician and, at the same time, lectured on poetry and literature. Finally he became famous for his National Learning and was eventually called into the service of the feudal lord of the Province of Kii.

Except for the above-mentioned years of study in Kyoto and for occasional trips — particularly in his declining years when he often went to Nagoya, Wakayama, and Kyoto — Norinaga spent most of his long life of seventy years in his native town of Matsuzaka. On the whole, his academic authority during his lifetime centered in the Kansai area — in contrast to Mabuchi's influence in the Kantō. He died in 1801, in the fifteenth year of the fifty-year administration of the eleventh Tokugawa Shogun, Ienari [1773–1841], and nine years after the resignation of Ienari's counsellor, Matsudaira Sadanobu [1758–1829]. This was sixty-six years before the Meiji Restoration. Norinaga's lifetime coincided with the lives of Johann Gottfried von

Herder (1744-1803) of Germany and Edward Gibbon (1737-1794) of England.

As is usually acknowledged, the principal factor in Norinaga's development as an antiquarian thinker was his association with Mabuchi. Because of Mabuchi, Norinaga was thrown completely into the stream — in fact into the main stream — of antiquarian thought in the Tokugawa Era, and he became the leader of the entire movement. The beginning of Norinaga's association with Mabuchi came when the former was twenty-eight years old, at about the time of Norinaga's return from Kyoto; for it was then that he happened to read Mabuchi's famous book, the *Kanji kō* (Preface to Study of Poetic Epithets) and was impressed by the depth and precision of Mabuchi's scholarship.

Then, six years later, when Norinaga was thirty-four years old, Mabuchi (who had left the service of Tayasu Munetake the preceding year) happened to be travelling in the Kinki area, and stopped overnight at an inn, Shinjō-ya, in Matsuzaka on his way home from a tour of old cultural remains that he had longed to see. With eager anticipation, Norinaga visited Mabuchi that night and received personal instruction from him. For Norinaga, and also for the history of antiquarian thought in Japan, this was an event of very deep significance. Mabuchi was then sixty-seven years old, and his *magnum opus*, the *Man'yō kō*, had been completed several years before. Now that he had reached the "summit of the *Man'yōshū*," Mabuchi was already gazing up at the lofty peaks of the Age of Kami, farther away beyond the clouds, where he let his thoughts run free. Mabuchi was overjoyed to hear that Norinaga wanted to investigate the *Kojiki*, and not only rewarded him liberally with encouragement and advice, but even entrusted the work to him. About these matters we are well informed as a result of the impassioned words written by Norinaga himself, when recalling this period, in the chapter "Words of Counsel from the Master of Agatai" (included in the second volume of *Tama katsuma*). Norinaga was to meet Mabuchi only this one time, but he immediately, and formally, entered his name on the roll of Mabuchi's students.

For six years thereafter (until the death of Mabuchi in 1769 when he was seventy-three years old and Norinaga was forty) there was between them a regular exchange of letters in which problems were examined, advice sought, and views argued. We know how earnest these men were about their scholarly study during this period from the letters which they wrote to each other, especially from the books *Man'yōshū monmoku* (Questions about the *Man'yōshū*) and *Senmyō monmoku* (Questions about the Ancient Imperial Edicts) in which their questions and answers were compiled. The extreme poignancy of Norinaga's grief at the time of Mabuchi's death, and the depth of his feelings of reverence for Mabuchi, which he expressed often after that, make us realize how strong Mabuchi's influence on Norinaga was.

In his study of ancient books and words, centered on research in the *Man'yōshū* — that is, in the field of textual study — Norinaga owed much to the mature scholarship of Mabuchi. Norinaga himself often spoke of this. Moreover, this fact is evident in his work on the *Kojiki den* (Commentary on the *Kojiki*) and thereafter; but I will not go into the details here. Our problem, in this connection, is: how did Mabuchi influence Norinaga in the area of antiquarian thought? On this point we can say that Norinaga acquired two things from Mabuchi: Mabuchi's idealism, in which the acts, words, and spirit of the ancient past were seen as a unit; and Mabuchi's doctrine of simplicity, in which "spontaneity and non-activity" were seen as the spirit of the Ancient Way, and Confucian theories about reason and morality were rejected as artificial. In the abovementioned "Words of Counsel from the Master of Agatai" by Norinaga, Mabuchi is quoted as saying: " I, too, aspired from the outset to unravel the sacred classics of the Kami. But to do this, one must first free himself from the Chinese spirit before he can seek the true spirit of antiquity."[1]) To understand and bring into play the idea of freeing oneself from the Chinese spirit, and to understand and bring into play the concept of the true spirit of antiquity — this was the object of Mabuchi's constant endeavor, and clearly it became the motive force that runs through the whole of Norinaga's antiquarian thought. But in order to carry forward the logical development of Mabuchi's thought, Norinaga could not stop here.

In the closing years of Mabuchi's life, after he had gone as far as he could with his study of the so-called "age of man" by exhausting the possibilities of the *Man'yōshū*, and when he was endeavoring to go farther back into the Age of Kami as reflected in the *Kojiki* and the *Nihongi*, his thought took on philosophical depth as he plumbed deeper into the past for his idea of antiquity and even went so far as to adopt some of the thinking of Lao-tzu. Although Norinaga was in touch with Mabuchi in this last period of his intellectual development, he was concerned chiefly with the Age of Kami as reflected in the *Kojiki* and refused to carry on the logic of this sort of philosophical development. Actually he harbored feelings of discontent about the direction taken by Mabuchi. Norinaga wrote this passage about Mabuchi under the heading: "How I received the Teachings of the Master of Agatai."

> To begin with, it seems pointless to refer again to the credit that is due this Great Teacher for having opened up the Way of Ancient Learning. On the other hand, as he said in his words of counsel, so exclusively did he devote his energies to the *Man'yōshū* all his life that, with respect to the *Kojiki* and the *Nihongi*, his studies were not yet broad enough or deep enough, and refinement was lacking in many places. Therefore, since he did not analyze the Way in detail, the over-all significance did not emerge very clearly either, and all he did was comment disconnectedly on

---

1) *Tama katsuma* (Jeweled Wicker Basket) *kan* 2, [*Zōho Motoori Norinaga zenshū* (Enlarged Edition of the Collected Works of Motoori Norinaga) (Tokyo, 1937–38), VIII, 59].

problems as they came up. Moreover, he still had not succeeded in making a clean break from the Chinese spirit, so that there are still evidences, though infrequent, of his having fallen naturally under that influence.[1]

His intent was not merely to criticize the immaturity of Mabuchi's philological research in the *Kojiki* and *Nihongi*. We know from the words in the last part of the quotation that he also found it difficult to agree completely with Mabuchi's conception of the Ancient Way, or rather with his conception of the Kami Way. When Norinaga wrote that Mabuchi had not succeeded in making a clean break from the Chinese spirit, so that he fell naturally under that influence, he was referring to the Lao-tzu tendencies in Mabuchi's thought.

Therefore Norinaga did not express approval of Lao-tzu as Mabuchi did. In his book *Kuzubana* (Arrowroot Blossoms), Norinaga compared Lao-tzu with the Ancient Way and emphasized that similarities between the two were merely fortuitous, that essentially they were quite different:

> Lao-tzu and Chuang-tzu have as a matter of course many resemblances to the Kami Way. This is because they shunned artificial cleverness and esteemed naturalness. What is natural should be thought of in roughly the same terms in both countries. But their naturalness is not true naturalness, because their Way began as a deliberate attempt, out of a hatred of artificial cleverness, to set up a principle of naturalness..... The Way of Kami, on the other hand, is not an attempt to elevate naturalness out of hatred for artificial cleverness. It is the original, unaltered Way of Kami.[2]

Mabuchi's sympathy with Lao-tzu, which was in a certain sense the natural outcome of his thought, was — from Norinaga's point of view —

---
1) [*Tama katsuma, kan* 2, *Motoori zenshū* VIII, 60.]
2) *Kuzubana*, [*Motoori zenshū* V, 497].

a relapse into the Chinese spirit and something really deserving of criticism.

The principal reason why Norinaga did not veer toward Mabuchi's philosophical approach was that before he came into contact with Mabuchi he had been exposed to the teachings of Keichū and, as a result, had formulated his studies of the Heian Era and had developed a doctrine of "Heianism" based upon these studies. Keichū, as the originator of National Learning in the antiquarian movement of the Tokugawa Era, condemned the traditionalist fallacies of the earlier scholars. He had established a basic academic approach which sought to get at the true meaning of ancient words and texts by direct study of the texts themselves. Moreover, within this approach there prevailed an inductive and objective trend to ascertain reality from the facts of ancient words and texts; and this had a unique significance for antiquarian study.

Norinaga's contact with the scholarship of this cool-headed scientist began early in his stay at Kyoto. He went to Kyoto in 1752, at the age of twenty-three, and entered the school of Hori Keizan [1688–1757]. While studying Confucianism, Norinaga was introduced by Keizan to the works of Keichū. During the five years of his study in Kyoto he perused and copied such works by Keichū as: *Hyakunin isshu kaikan shō* (Notes on a Re-examination of *Hyakunin isshu*), *Seigo okudan* (Hypotheses about the *Ise monogatari*), and *Kokin yozai shō* (Miscellaneous Notes on the *kokinshū*). And so, through his basic academic style and inductive approach, Keichū brought an early enlightenment to Norinaga's scholarly awareness. In referring to his experiences at that time, Norinaga wrote:

> Master Keichū of Naniwa was the first to achieve a clear vision, and he deplored the darkness that had fallen upon this Way. Basing his work on the ancient texts, he exposed the fallacies of recent times, and was the first to discover the original aspect of things. Until the recent emergence of this man, everyone high and low went about aimlessly as if in a drunken stupor, or dreaming. Some people have at last had their eyes opened by the shock

he has given them. But there are many persons whose eyes have not been opened. Fortunately I read his books and my eyes were opened at once. Therefore, appreciation of this Way has revealed itself to my mind as a matter of course; and I am aware of wrongs such as those perpetrated in recent times. This is altogether a gift from Master Keichū.[1]

The words " this Way " in the above passage refer to Norinaga's study of the poetry and prose of the Heian Era, with which he had been familiar ever since his youth — in short, to the study of Japanese poetry. Norinaga's work in this field, which he had entered because of the influence of Keichū, had already taken form prior to his contact with Mabuchi.

By the time Norinaga met Mabuchi in 1763 (when he was thirty-four years old) his studies had already borne fruit in two distinguished books: one on Japanese poetry, *Isonokami sazamegoto* (Whispered Words of the Past) ; and one on the *Genji monogatari*, *Shibun yōryō* (Essentials of Murasaki's Prose). These books were a product of his philological study of the Heian Era. In these he developed his theory about the primacy of feeling which, he said, was the spirit of the culture of the Heian Era and the essence of its literature. He expressed this concept in the stock phrase *mono no aware* (sensibility to things). With Norinaga this phrase became an objective explanation of Heian literature and culture, and at the same time the main assertion of his own view of literature and life. For in literary criticism he held that the essence of literature lay not in reason or morality, but in feeling and beauty; and on this basis he saw his literary ideal in the sentimentalism of Heian literature, and advocated *Shin Kokinshū* (New *Kokinshū*)[2] principles in the composition of poetry. With regard to his life-view, he considered feeling to be the essence

---

1) *Ashiwake obune* (Punting through the Reed Brakes) [*Motoori zenshū* X, 193].
2) [The *Shin kokinshū*, completed in 1206, is the eighth Imperial anthology of Japanese Court poetry. The best of its poems are appreciated for their subtlety of feeling and atmosphere.]

of man's nature, and held a doctrine of human feeling (*ninjō shugi*) by which he explained the ideal of culture and morality in terms of the development and harmony of emotion. The Confucian view that literature should encourage good and reprove evil, the Confucian moralistic view of life, and the Buddhist otherworldly view of the world, were all rejected by Norinaga. His rejection, from a philological standpoint, of Buddhist and Confucian slanted interpretations of earlier commentators became, at this point, a rejection of all Buddhist and Confucian tendencies and attitudes about human life and the world. And so, both academically and intellectually, this Heian study and "Heianism" became — early in life — an attitude and disposition that directed Norinaga by its positivism as well as its sentimental emotionalism.

Also, it is noted that he had begun to study the Shinto classics while he was a student in Kyoto. After all, he had come from a place near the Ise Shrine, and had had relatives who belonged to priestly families of Shinto; and so he had been interested in the Kami Way (Shinto) since childhood. This created an early desire to study the Shinto classics. But it was actually this scholarly consciousness, received from Keichū, that affected him most remarkably. In recalling this period, he wrote:

> As to my study of the Way, right from the beginning I read everything I could find, old and new, that was in the nature of a book about the Kami — though it was not until the age of twenty that I had any real purpose. I made no special effort to study these books. Then, when I was in Kyoto, I did indeed develop a desire to study. When I reflected on the meaning of the ancient past of the Imperial Country (*kōkoku*) in the light of the discussions in Keichū's books on poetry, I was quick to learn that the doctrines of the so-called Shintoists were all terribly wrong.[1]

Also, in his writings of the Kyoto period he expounded — in frequent references to a "natural Kami Way" — a concept of an ancient Kami

---

1) *Tama katsuma*, kan 2 [*Motoori zenshū* VII, 58].

Way that was independent of Buddhist and Confucian influences and distortions. Here we see an early form of the *Kojiki* Kami Way which he developed in later years.

Keichū and Mabuchi were both representative figures in the Ancient Learning movement that emerged within National Learning. The principal object of research for both was the *Man'yōshū*. Mabuchi owed much to Keichū for his theories. The two men were alike in both scholarly approach and reverence for the past. And yet there were essential characteristics of thought that placed the two men in opposition to each other: the positivism of Keichū was pitted against the idealism of Mabuchi. Of course, as a devotee of the past, Keichū had some idealism within his positivism; and as a scholar, Mabuchi had some positivism in his idealism. Both as an antiquarian and an idealist, Mabuchi moved beyond Keichū. This is why these two figures are regarded as having a developmental relationship to each other.

The same thing can also be said about the relationship of Mabuchi to Norinaga. Nevertheless, such a formal view does not permit us to ignore the individuality of each man. On the contrary, within this view of their development, we can only begin to see the true picture of the process itself by further clarifying the manifestations of individuality in each. Norinaga, before coming into contact with Mabuchi and being influenced by him, had already had his own thoughts shaped by Keichū. And it was quite natural that these Keichū influences should continue to operate as resistant elements in preventing the complete ascendancy of Mabuchi's influence, even after Norinaga had entered all the way into the world of Shinto classics under Mabuchi's guidance.

The question of how Norinaga, when fully entered upon the Kami Way, retained these two tendencies in his thought, I will defer to the following section which attempts a general outline of his thought. It should be noted here that his advocacy of *Shin Kokinshū* principles in poetry, which upheld the emotionalism resulting from his study of Heian life and was representative of his literary views, still remained unchanged even after the perfection of his Ancient Way theories. Even after he had been introduced to the *Man'yōshū* by Mabuchi, and had imbibed *Man'yōshū* principles from him, this advocacy remained unchanged. As a result, he was severely upbraided by Mabuchi, who even told him he was almost beyond redemption. For Mabuchi, who was thoroughly imbued (through his " *Man'yōshū*-ism ") with the principles of Nara-Era simplicity and had disassociated himself completely from later periods, this attitude of Norinaga was something imperfect and incomplete. But for Norinaga, the beautiful sentiments of the *Shin Kokinshū,* which he had found at the roots of his scholarly research in the poetic and prose literature of the Heian Era, were in harmony with tastes and preferences which had been nourished in him since childhood; and even when he became involved with the Ancient Way, these sentiments existed in a separate, inviolable area of his heart. Norinaga could not discard his *Shin Kokinshū* principles in favor of the Ancient Way. This was not merely a matter of taste and preference, for at the same time, in the scholarly awareness he acquired from his philological research in the literature of the Heian Era, there were elements that sustained this attitude. His literary theories were not necessarily inherited from Keichū; rather they went beyond Keichū. And yet we can detect a strong Keichū influence. In fact, if we look at this aspect in isolation, it is possible to say that Norinaga acquired his *Shin Kokinshū* principles from research in the prose and poetic literature of the Heian Era in exactly the same way that Mabuchi acquired his *Man'yōshū*-ism from research in the *Man'yōshū*. However, in contrast to Mabuchi's full commitment to *Man'yōshū*-ism, Norinaga was not necessarily committed to Heianism. Under Mabuchi's influence he also learned *Man'yōshū*-ism, and while he composed poems in the *Shin Kokinshū* style, he composed in the *Man'yōshū* style as well. In his poetry anthologies there are poems of both the ancient and modern variety. This too provides strong proof that the character of Norinaga's thought differed from that of Mabuchi.

After coming into contact with Mabuchi, Norinaga devoted his energies principally to research in ancient classics written in the Nara Era. And the *Man'yōshū* was of course one of those classics. As far as the *Man'yōshū* was concerned, Norinaga got his guidance from Mabuchi. But the object of his main effort was the *Kojiki*. By 1786 — twenty-three years after he had met Mabuchi and when he was fifty-seven years old — Norinaga had completed his commentary on the first volume of the *Kojiki*, the section on the "Age of Kami." Before that — in 1771, when he was forty-two years old — he produced, in a book entitled *Naobi no mitama* (The Spirit of Straightening), a general treatment of the Ancient Way. By the year 1786 he had also completed, in addition to the first volume of his *Kojiki den*, the *Tamaboko hyakushu* (One Hundred Poems on the Way) and the *Tama kushige* (Jeweled Comb Box). Therefore, it is proper to say that in 1786 he had completed the development of his thoughts on the subject of the Ancient Way. During the remaining twelve years of his life Norinaga continued, as his early-classical study matured, to turn out books on the Ancient Way; but there was almost none of the remarkable intellectual development that was seen in the declining years of Mabuchi.

Among Norinaga's works that deal with the Ancient Way I think the one which expresses his thoughts most concisely is the *Tamaboko hyakushu*. These poems are, of course, not literary gems; rather they are fragmentary statements of Norinaga's intellectual development. But if we savor these poems — using as a backdrop an over-all view of his thoughts and beliefs as revealed in other books — the general structure of his thought stands clearly revealed. This is why my treatment of his thought is centered here on these poems.

The Ancient Way, according to Norinaga, consisted in action itself, which had been maintained and transmitted by the Imperial ancestral Kami (*mioya no kami*); and although it was called a "Way," it had nothing whatsoever to do with reason or morality. Properly speaking, we should not use the word "Way." In the Age of Kami there was no word with such a meaning. In those times the word "way" was merely a path. Only for expedience is the word made to connote a "Way" of Kami.

According to Norinaga — and as we see in the following poem — the Way was created by Izanagi and Izanami through the spirit of the two life-creating Kami, Taka-mi-musubi and Kami-musubi:

Two deities,	Futabashira
The revered ancestral Kami,	mioya no kami zo
Created the Way	tamahoko no
Of this world	yo no naka no michi
Straight as a well-wrought spear.	wa hajimetamaeru.

The Way was then perfected by the Sun Goddess:

Immaculate as the sacred tree,	Tsukisakaki
Her spirit pure and clear,	itsu no mitama to
She lights the far corners	ametsuchi ni
Of Heaven and earth —	iteri tōrasu
The Great Kami of the Sun.	Hi no Ōmikami.

This Way is the way	Ametsuchi no
Of the Great Sun Kami,	kiwami miterasu
Whose radiance from above	takahikaru
Lightens the very bounds	Hi no Ōkami no
Of Heaven and earth.	michi wa kono michi.

The Way was transmitted by Imperial ancestors through successive reigns:

This Way is the way,	Takamikura
Received and transmitted	amatsu hitsugi to
By the scions of the Sun,	hi no miko no
As the Heavenly Sun Succession	uketsutaemasu

Of the throne on high.   michi wa kono michi.

And the Way was observed with due reverence by the people:

This Way is the way,	Ame no shita
Followed by day and by night	aohitokusa no
By the people beholden,	asa yoi ni
Numerous as the grass,	mikage to yosoru
In the realm below Heaven.	michi wa kono michi.

The carrying out of the Way, thought Norinaga, was originally the responsibility of the Sun-descended Emperors. The people merely followed. Because Japan was the place where the Way came into existence, it was the parent country of the world, the pre-eminent Imperial Country:

This great country   Hi no Kami no
    As the country of the
        rising sun,   moto tsu mikuni to
Of the Kami of the sun,   mikuni ha shi
    Is the eminent country, the
        parent country   momoyaso kuni no
Among the myriad countries.   hokuni oyakuni.

A central land without peer   Momokuni no
    Surrounded by the hundred countries: kuni no mahora wa
Great Yamato,   Ō-Yamato
    The land where reigns   waga ōkimi no
Our Great Ruler.   kikoshiosu kuni.

The Imperial land,   Kashikoki ya
    So sacred,   sumera mikuni wa
Is a fair land,   umashi kuni
    A land tranquil within,   urayasu no kuni
A land among lands.   kuni no maho kuni

Though the countries are numbered
   By the score,
Nowhere is there another
   That surpasses our Yamato,
The source of the sun.
	Momoyaso to
	   kuni wa aredomo
	hi no moto no
	   kore no Yamato ni
	masu kuni wa arazu.

And the fact that Japan had realized the Ancient Way, and been able to surpass the nations of the world throughout history, was symbolized most strikingly by the single-line descent of the Imperial Family through ages eternal:

Though with time
   All things change,
The reign of our Great Ruler,
   The Kami manifest,
Is everlasting.
	Mono mina wa
	   kawariyukedomo
	akitsu kami
	   waga ōkimi no
	miyo wa tokoshie.

Though kingships change
   In the many nations,
The reign of the scions
   Of the high-shining Sun
Does not change.
	Kuniguni no
	   kimi wa kawaredo
	takahikaru
	   waga hi no miko no
	miyo wa kawarazu.

Not only was this corroborated by Japan's past history, it was the eternal prescription for the future of Japan.

Foremost among the duties of the populace, in their observance of the Way, were reverence of the Imperial ancestral Kami and absolute loyalty and submission to the Emperors, the divine descendants of the Ancestral Kami. Towards those below, the rulers were to exercise Benevolence and Compassion:

These are the people of the Kami
   Who illuminate the heaven.
	Amaterasu
	   kami no mitami zo

You, who are their keeper,	mitamira o
Be not remiss	ōroka ni suna
In your keeping them.	azukareru hito.

The people, producers of goods,	Mono tsukuru
Are the treasures.	tami wa mitakara
Why do rulers harass them,	tsukurazuba
Without thinking of what will happen	ika ni semu to ka
If they do not produce?	tami kurushimuru.

As for children, they must practice ancestor worship and filial piety:

Forget not the blessings	Yoyo no oya no
Of your many forebears.	mikage wasuruna
Your many forebears are	yoyo no oya wa
The Kami of your clan,	ono ga ujikami
The Kami of your house.	ono ga ie no kami.

Your father and mother are	Chichihaha wa
The Kami of your home.	waga ie no kami
Regard them as your Kami	waga kami to
And serve them, oh children,	kokoro tsukushite
With heart-felt piety.	itsuke hito no ko.

Let wives, children, and servants be treated with Compassion and Love:

Wives, like tender grass,	Nuekusa no
Children and servants —	me ko yakko ra wa
All, cherished bestowals	sumekami no
Of the Imperial Kami:	sazukeshi takara
Hold them dear.	utsukushimi seyo.

In short, the Way was the practice of ordinary morality which we, both as a nation and as human beings, understood naturally; and these practices were seen in their perfection among the people of ancient times. In comparison with later periods, and especially with Chinese history, Japanese antiquity was an ideal period.

For they know not	Sumekami no
The Way of the Imperial Kami,	michi shiranu koso
The ranting	Kotosaegu
Men of China	Karakunibito wa
Indulge in artificial cleverness.	sakashira su nare.
Nerve and heart together	Kimomukau
Are turned to niggling wit;	kokoro sakujiri
So needlessly	nakanaka ni
Is man corrupted	Kara no oshie zo
By teachings from China.	hito ashiku suru.

To Norinaga, China was a country where a scholastic morality was expounded, but not a place where such teachings were put into practice. Therefore, in Japan as well, after Confucianism had been introduced and the hearts of men were infected by Chinese thought, the Way of the Age of Kami had declined and the true meaning of the ancient classics had become distorted. And so it was of primary importance for the clarification of the Ancient Way that Chinese thought be completely eliminated:

By the taint	Karazama no
Of the artificial cleverness	sakashiragokoro
Of Chinese ways	utsurite zo
Has the heart of mortal man	yonohito no kokoro
Been corrupted.	Ashiku narinuru.
They would be our guides —	Shirube su to
Ugly pundits	shiko no monoshiri
Who, nevertheless,	nakanaka ni
Lead men to wander	yokosa no michi ni
Down the wrong way!	hito madowasu mo.

How grievous,
    For, with their artificial cleverness,
They will distort
    And mold into Chinese thoughts
Writings of the Age of Kami.
	Sakashira ni
	    kamiyo no mifumi
	tokimagete
	    Kara no kokoro ni
	nasu ga kanashisa.

Beware of treacherous footing
    In that terrible stream—
The river of Chinese writings,
    Whose murkiness below
Veils its slippery bed.
	Shita nigoru
	    Karabumigawa wa
	toko name no
	    kashikoki kawa zo
	ashi fumuna yume.

Should you aspire
    To behold the clear mirrors,[1]
Wipe away the dust—
    The veil of Chinese doctrine
That bedims their luster.
	masokagami
	    mimu to omowaba
	Karakoto no
	    chirii kumoreri
	migakite shi yokemu.

Norinaga considered it to be a very difficult matter to rid oneself of Chinese influence:

Though he may think
    He has banished Chinese thoughts,
The heart of the man,
    Who reads Chinese
Is still Chinese.
	Karagokoro
	    nashi to omoedo
	fumi ra yomu
	    hito no kokoro wa
	nao zo Kara naru.

And he thought Chinese influences could be removed only through Ancient Learning.

    The above poems suggest that Norinaga's Ancient Way had about the same content as Mabuchi's. But pursuing the matter a bit further we see instead of a Mabuchi-like return to the philosophy of Lao-tzu, a different intellectual approach:

---

1) [The "clear mirrors" refer to the *Kojiki* and the *Nihongi*.]

KAMO MABUCHI AND MOTOORI NORINAGA

All matters pertaining
    To this mortal world
Can be known
    In the light of vestiges
Of the Age of Kami.
	Yo no naka no
	    aru omobuki wa
	nanigoto mo
	    kamiyo no ato o
	tazunete shirayu.

Norinaga's emphasis was upon a search for the "vestiges of the Age of Kami" referred to in the above poem, not on the meaning of the Age of Kami. And the vestiges of the Age of Kami were, with him, the facts about the Kami recorded in the *Kojiki*. Since the *Kojiki* contained concrete facts of the Age of Kami as reflected in the consciousness of the people of the ancient era, Norinaga set the *Kojiki* apart from such literary creations as the poetry anthologies and the prose stories called *monogatari*. And it was here that Norinaga's philological positivism was applied. His aim was to restore these facts literally. Any sign of subjective criticism he rejected as "Chinese thought." In contrast to Mabuchi, who similarly insisted on the rejection of Chinese thought yet tried to find a criterion in the ancient classics, Norinaga stuck to the facts throughout. He thought that each legend of the Age of Kami — explained just as it is by philological methods — revealed literally some aspect of the Ancient Way:

Behold the image
    Of the ancient era
In the mirror clear and pure —
    The time-honored Record
Of Ancient Matters [*Kojiki*].
	Kamitsu yo no
	    kata o yoku miyo
	isonokami
	    Furukotobumi wa
	masomi no kagami.

It is hallowed,
    The text that I read;
For it relates
    What was fully transmitted
From the Age of Kami.
	Kami no yo no
	    koto ra kotogoto
	tsutaekite
	    shiruseru mifumi
	mireba tōtoshi.

Norinaga explained the legends of the Age of Kami just as they were recorded in the *Kojiki*, without criticism or reflection — if anything, he was hostile to reflection. And he strove consistently for an objective expression of the consciousness of the ancients. The result of this effort was his *magnum opus*, the *Kojiki den*. In this study we can see a thorough execution of Keichū's objectivism and positivism. Examples of this are seen in: (1) Norinaga's taking the "birth of the land" by two Kami to mean literally that they gave birth to land; (2) his identifying the Plain of High Heaven (*takamagahara*) as the sky — not a terrestrial Imperial capital; and (3) his treating the Sun Goddess as the sun and, at the same time, as a personalized Imperial ancestral Kami.

Examples of these views are seen in the following poems in Norinaga's *Tamaboko hyakushu*. First about the birth of the land:

Though lands are many
    Under the heavens,
Only one
    Did the Kami beget:
Land of the Great Eight Isles [Japan].
	Ame no shita
	    kuni wa ōkedo
	kamurogi no
	    uminashimaseru
	Ōyashimakuni.

Then his nature-religion view of Kami:

Not always
    Will reason prevail;
For the wicked
    May be cursed or blessed —
All, the will of the Kami.
	Kotowari no
	    mama ni mo arazute
	yokosama no
	    yoki mo ashiki mo
	kami no kokoro zo.

So helpless we are,
    For designs in the heart
Of the bending Kami
    Will bring good people
	Yoki hito o
	    yo ni kurushimuru
	magatsubi no
	    kami no kokoro no

Terrible woes.   sube mo subenasa.

Even the Great Kami [Sun Goddess]   Amaterasu
    Who brightens the Heaven   Ōmikami sura
Was overawed   chihayaburu
    By the tempestuousness   kami no susabi wa
Of the violent Kami [Susa-no-o].   kashikomi mashiki.

All who are called Kami,   Kami to ieba
    You may think,   mina hitoshiku ya
Are one and the same.   omouramu
    There are some which are birds,   tori naru mo ari
And some, too, which are bugs!   mushi naru mo aru o.

Though they be lowly,   Iyashikedo
    The likes of these, too, are Kami: ikatsuchi kodama
The thunder, the wood sprite,   kitsune tora
    The fox, the tiger,   tatsu no tagui mo
And the dragon.   kami no katahashi.

He placed an absolute value on the life of this world:

What can I do   Tamakiwaru
    To an existence   futa yo wa yukanu
That will not traverse two worlds   utsusomi o
    In the life of one —   ikani seba ka mo
That I might go on without dying?   shinazute aramu.

Polluted Yomi,   Kitanakuni
    bourne of darkness —   yomi no kunibe wa
How dirty and disgusting!   inashikome
    I want to stay with this world   chi yo tokotowa ni
A thousand ages evermore!   kono yo ni mo ga mo.

And as for life after death, he thought the place where the deceased went — whether they had been good or bad in this life — was a polluted land. His primitive eschatological view did not include considerations of moral retribution.

Moreover, the following indicate a primitive religious view of evil:

Dare not defile
    The home, the person, the land;
For defilement is a taboo,
    The gravest of *tsumi*
In the eyes of the Kami.
	Ie mo mi mo
	    kuni mo kegasuna
	kegare wa shi
	    kami no imimasu
	yuyushiki tsumi o.

Take care lest
    The cooking fire be defiled;
For should the home fire
    Incur defilement,
Evils will arise.
	Kama no hi no
	    kegare yuyushi mo
	ienuchi wa
	    hi shi kegarureba
	maga okoru mono.

A fearsome thing!
    The evil of [Izanami's]
        partaking
Of repast in Yomi
    Was the beginning
Of evils that were to come.
	Anakashiko
	
	    yomotsuhegui no
	maga yori zo
	    moromoro no maga
	okori some keru.

Should you incur *tsumi*,
    Cleanse yourself
In limpid shallows.
    To the goddess, Princess
        Swift-Clear,
Swiftly go and wash it clear.
	Tsumi shi araba
	    kiyoki kawase ni
	misogi shite
	
	    Haya-aki-tsu-hime ni
	haya akirameyo.

Such expressions were not merely intended as philological clarification of the consciousness of the ancient people, they were expressions of

Norinaga's personal faith. They formed the content of his Ancient Way. Thus they thwarted a philosophical intensification of Mabuchi thought. At the same time, they appear to be useless intellectual elements for the development of such thought.

At this point we see, immediately and clearly, that there was an attitude of faith in Norinaga's antiquarianism. How was he to explain such things as mythological events and the acts of Kami recorded in the ancient Shinto classics in terms of an Ancient-Way thought based on Mabuchi's natural-philosophy world view, which held all religious faith to be superstition and which regarded human beings as the vermin of Heaven and earth? If he had lived a little longer and had really undertaken research in the Shinto classics, as he had done in the *Man'yōshū*, how would Mabuchi have looked at the mythological accounts recorded in them? Would he have seen these myths as symbols of his principles of natural philosophy, as the existing Buddhist and Confucian oriented Shintoists saw them? Or would he have searched in them for the deeds of heroes associated with the founding of the nation, as did men in the existing historical schools? Or would he have seen in them the oldest national epics before the *Man'yōshū* and rejoiced in their expression of a simple spirit, in the same way as he extolled the diction of the Great Purification liturgy for being free of heaviness? As to the first two of the above hypothetical positions, Mabuchi probably would have relapsed into the existing Chinese and Buddhist views of the Shintoists that he had rejected. With regard to the third position, he probably would not have been able to discover a foundation for the philosophical needs that led him past the *Man'yōshū*. For the Mabuchi philosophy, in entering the world of the Shinto classics, would have been doomed to separation from philology. The Shinto classics, as objects of philological study — in other words, just as they stood — did not have a character that would permit them to serve as authoritative texts for the Mabuchi philosophy. To Mabuchi the all-important fact of the " Imperial line, unbroken for ages eternal " was the pure symbolization of the ancient spirit —

everything else was quite trivial. Consequently, the various legends recorded in the Shinto classics would have been considered insignificant things which he would have eventually discarded.

Norinaga, on the other hand, believed implicitly in everything contained in the myths recorded in the Shinto classics. His agnostic mysticism supplied the epistemological foundations for his thought:

What a fool —
    He who says he knows.
Though we may plumb it,
    The reason of this world
Has no bottom.
	Shiru to yū wa
	    tare no shiremono
	hakarite mo
	    yo no kotowari wa
	sokoi naki mono.

It is the ignorance
    Of those who know not
The mysteries of this world
    That makes them deny
The presence of mysteries.
	Ayashiki o
	    araji to yu wa
	yo no naka no
	    ayashiki shiranu
	shiregokoro kamo.

There is mystery
    Between this Heaven and earth
        of ours.
Indeed, there is.
    How much more mysterious
Must the Age of Kami have been.
	Ayashiki wa
	
	    kore no ametsuchi
	ubena ubena
	    kamiyo wa koto ni
	ayashiku arikemu.

The miraculous reason
    Of this world
Is not to be known
    By us,
Who are not Kami.
	Shirayubeki
	    mono naranaku ni
	yo no naka no
	    kushiki kotowari
	kami narazu shite.

To subject this mystery to reason and speculation is nothing but the superficial Chinese approach:

How vain it is
    For the men of China
To discuss the reason of things
    When they know not the reason
Of the miraculous!
	Kusuwashiki
	    kotowari shirazute
	Karahito no
	    mono no kotowari
	toku ga hakanasa.

All who speak
    On the reason of things
After pondering thus
    And considering so
Speak Chinese.
	Hito mina no
	    mono no kotowari
	ka ni kaku ni
	    omoihakarite
	yū wa Karakoto.

And so, all doubts about the ancient legends in the Shinto classics should be cast out, and the legends believed without subjecting them to reason:

Would we know,
    No means have we
But tradition.
    Let the unknowable
Remain unknown.
	Tsutae naki
	    koto wa shirubeki
	yoshi mo nashi
	    shiraenu koto wa
	shirazute o aramu.

For everything emerged from the will of the Kami:

The original source
    Of all creation:
The creating power of
    Divine-Producing and
Exalted-August-Producing.
	Moromoro no
	    nariizuru moto wa
	Kami-musubi
	    Taka-mi-musubi no
	kami no musubi zo.

Manifest affairs
    Are willed by the Great Ruler;
Obscure, divine affairs
    Are the working of the will
	Arawa ni no
	    koto wa ōkimi
	kamigoto wa
	    Ō-kuni-nushi no

Of the Great-Land-Master.[1])　　　　kami no mikokoro.

Both good and evil	Yo no naka no
In the world.	yoki mo ashiki mo
In everything and everywhere	kotogoto ni
All come about	kami no kokoro no
By the will of Kami.	shiwaza ni zo aru.

Not always	Kotowari no
Will reason prevail;	mama ni mo arazute
For the wicked	yokozama no
May be cursed or blessed —	yoki mo ashiki mo
All, by the will of the Kami.	kami no kokoro zo.

He thought it difficult to do anything with mere human power:

How can we be	Ouke naku
So presumptuous as to challenge	hito no iyashiki
The works of the Kami	chikara mote
with the lowly strength	kami no nasu waza
Of human beings!	arasoi eme ya.

Therefore man could only revere and worship the Kami:

How futile	Ajiki naki
Is the artificial cleverness	nani no sakashira
Of those who fail to serve,	tamachihau
Of those who slight,	kami itsukazute
The propitious Kami.	ōroka ni shite.

---

1) [This refers to the compromise effected between the terrestrial Kami of Izumo and the Imperial Kami of the Plain of High Heaven. The deity Ō-kuni-nushi of Izumo yielded the sovereignty of Japan to the Sun Goddess but retained prerogatives in religious affairs. It was apparently out of this arrangement that there emerged the distinction between Earthly Kami and Heavenly Kami.]

Children all,
    Do not be artificially clever:
Assist and respect
    The workings of the Kami
Propitious to man.
	Iza kodomo
	    sakashira sezute
	tamachihau
	    kami no mishiwaza
	tasuke matsuroe.

Awe-inspiring, indeed!
    The divine affairs,
Unseen by us,
    Willed by the Kami—
Heed them with reverence.
	Me ni mienu
	    kami no kokoro no
	kamigoto wa
	    kashikoki mono zo
	ō ni na omoiso.

And one should place his absolute trust in the blessings of the Kami:

The grains that grow,
    The myriad trees and grasses—
All are blessings
    Of the Great Kami of the Sun,
Who lightens the Heaven.
	Tanatsumono
	    momo no ki kusa mo
	amaterasu
	    hi no ōkami no
	megumi ete koso.

But for the blessings
    Of the Kami
Of Heaven and earth,
    Could we live
One day, one night?
	Ametsuchi no
	    kami no megumi shi
	nakariseba
	    hitohi hitoyo mo
	arietemashi ya.

The food that sustains life,
    Our clothes, our dwelling—
They are the blessings
    Of our Ruler,
Of our Kami.
	Inochi tsugu
	    kuimono kimono
	sumu ie ra
	    kimi no megumi zo
	kami no megumi zo.

    Concerning Norinaga's religious sentiments about the " blessings of Kami" — as Ōnishi Hajime [1864–1899][1] has noted — we have, in the words of a chapter under that heading in the fourteenth scroll of the *Tama katsuma,* an expression of profound devotion that is rarely seen in the history of Japanese literature. In the concluding passage of that chapter Norinaga says:

> If we never forget that everything is the gift of the Kami, we would know as a matter of course that it is impossible not to revere the Kami. It is as if when we wanted a hundred *ryō* of gold, someone gave us ninety-nine, and we were one *ryō* short. Should we be pleased with the giver, or resentful? A person who resents the Kami as worthless because his prayer has not been answered is like someone who resents the giver of ninety-nine *ryō,* and considers him worthless. How foolish it is to forget the blessings of the ninety-nine *ryō* and to resent not receiving one more![2]

Here we see the most profound aspect of Norinaga's antiquarian thought.

On the other hand, Norinaga, like Mabuchi, often praised the Sincere Heart (*magokoro*) and rejected affectation and hypocrisy. What he meant by the Sincere Heart is indicated in these poems:

The Sincere Heart 　Is the heart that is moved When there is cause — 　Cause for joy, Cause for sadness.	Koto shi areba 　ureshi kanashi to tokidoki ni 　ugoku kokoro zo hito no magokoro.
The heart that can be moved 　Is a Sincere Heart	Ugoku koso 　hito no magokoro

---

1) [A scholar of ethics and Western philosophy whose works are collected in *Ōnishi zenshū* (Collected Works of Onishi).]
2) *Tama katsuma* [*Motoori zenshū* VII, 440.]

Those who boast
   That they cannot be moved —
Are they made of stone and wood?
	ugokazu to
	   iite hokorou
	hito wa iwaki ka.

To veil and hide
   The Sincere Heart,
To put on airs,
   To pretend —
Such are the ways of China.
	Magokoro o
	   tsutsumi kakushite
	kazaraite
	   itsuwari suru wa
	Kara no narawashi.

Do you think you can counterfeit
   The heart that feels sincerely
By learning the tricks
   Of the men of China
And putting on airs?
	Karahito no
	   shiwaza naraite
	kazaraite
	   omou magokoro
	itsuwarubeshi ya.

As we see from the above, Norinaga's emphasis upon the importance of the Sincere Heart was quite different from Mabuchi's concepts of "valor" and "manliness." Norinaga's thoughts were more humanistic; and they would have been rejected by Mabuchi as effeminate. This humanism of Norinaga was nothing but a projection of the emotionalism, discussed above, that emerged from his research in Heian literature.

Finally, there is a practical, worldly strain in Norinaga's thought:

We dare not disobey
   The edicts we receive
From time to time,
   For they are the bidding
Of the Kami.
	Tokidoki no
	   minori mo kami no
	tokidoki no
	   mikoto ni shi areba
	ika de tagawamu.

In the present world,
   Respect the edicts
	Ima no yo wa
	   ima no minori o

> Of the present.
>   Do not commit
> Offensive acts.
>
> Blessed by birth
>   In a tranquil land
> In a tranquil era.
>   My life is tranquil.
> Thus I am content.
>
> When I hear described
>   The turbulence
> Of eras past,
>   How reverent I am
> For this era of peace.
>
> May it endure
>   A myriad generations —
> That tranquility
>   Of the " Kami
> Who lightens the East " [Tokugawa
>   Ieyasu].

> kashikomi te
>   keshiki okonai
> okonau na yume.
>
> Yasukuni no
>   yasurakeki yo ni
> umareai te
>   yasukekute areba
> monoomoi mo nashi.
>
> Karigomo no
>   midarerishi sama
> kiku toki shi
>   osamareru yo wa
> tōtoku arikeri.
>
> Azuma teru
>   kami no mikoto no
> yasukuni to
>   shizume mashikeru
> miyo wa yorozuyo.

As we see from the above, Norinaga accommodated himself to the conditions of his day and even praised the military government. There are no bold reformist assertions in his writings. Although Mabuchi had the same general attitude toward the military government, and toward reform, there was a more defiant streak in his temperament. In his later writings, Mabuchi developed restorationist views which centered on the theory that the Imperial capital should be moved to Edo. But we see nothing comparable to this in Norinaga's writings. Even in political theories included in his *Hihon tamakushige* (Secret Book of the Jeweled Comb Box), where he answered questions raised by the Lord of the Province of Kii, Norinaga upheld "respect for the Kami" as the fundamental political principle; and he advocated the concept of "restoring a natural economy." We find Ancient Way views in the above theories, but these theories are always calm, restrained, conservative, and gradualistic. Norinaga's optimistic world view, which lay behind such an outlook on the current situation, was a special characteristic of his thought. It is also revealed in the poems quoted above. In one sense, this optimism was a product of his study of the nature of the ancient people. Furthermore, in his interpretation of the ancient legends — all the way from the myth about the birth of lands by the two Kami to the one about the Sun Goddess emerging from the cave — he recognized the principle that in the co-existence of good and evil the good ultimately prevailed. This lay at the foundation of his optimism. Thus in his outlook on life there was a definite buoyancy.

Even though Norinaga's Ancient Way ideas were inherited from Mabuchi, it should be clear from what has been said that they showed signs of a separate development. As a result, his Heian-Era ideas (which had emerged earlier because of the influence of Keichū) as well as positivistic tendencies (which accompanied his Heian ideas) operated rather like resistant elements in his thought — as has already been pointed out. The existence of these resistant elements has been noted merely to provide an historical explanation for the uniqueness of Norinaga's Ancient-Way thought. This is only a negative reason for pointing them out. In the final analysis, when considering the development of Mabuchi's and Norinaga's thought, we detect similarities in form, but differences in content. Norinaga, in moving to the Ancient Way from an interest in literary criticism, and Mabuchi, in moving to the Ancient Way from an interest in the *Man'yōshū*, were alike — both moved to the Ancient-Way thought from studies of Japanese poetry. On the other hand, if we look at the content of their thought, we see in Mabuchi a consistency in his idealization of a doctrine of plainness (*soboku shugi*) which resulted from his study of the *Man'yōshū* and which was expressed in the terms "naturalness" (*shizen*) and "simplicity" (*tanjun*). But in Norinaga's case we see, in the shift of his interests from Heian literature to the *Kojiki*, a change in values.

Of course, Norinaga (like Mabuchi) used the concept of "naturalness." With him the spirit of the Japanese poems, which avoided reason and revealed natural human feeling, was ultimately the spirit of the Kami Way (Shinto) of antiquity. That is, he considered poetry a bridge to the Kami Way and spoke of it as if it were something that clarified the transition for him. Nevertheless, a naturalness which has sensibility to things (*mono no aware*) for its content is not at all the same as a naturalness which has plainness for its content. As has already been pointed out, the two were never reconciled, so that the Heian and *Man'yōshū* styles in poetry stood in opposition to each other. A similar confrontation existed in the differences between Norinaga's and Mabuchi's idea of the Sincere Heart. But this situation only demonstrates more clearly the fact that in contrast to Mabuchi, Norinaga had a positivistic tendency or mentality of seeing ideology in the ancient classics, rather than trying to see the ancient classics in the context of an ideology. But this says nothing about the basis for the individuality of his antiquarian thought as a whole, which gave form to the ideas comprising this tendency or mentality.

On the other hand, a more positive reason for the preservation and development of this individuality of Norinaga's thought was *the very state of mind* at the base of his thought—one of absolute faith, uncritical and unreflective. This state of mind caused him to set forth literally the primitive features (religious and otherwise) of the *Kojiki* and, at the same time, to believe in them. The Age of Kami legends of the *Kojiki*, as myths of an ancient people, include much that is absurd and strange, juvenile and irrational. These myths had to be subjected to considerable rationalization in later ages in order to make the *Kojiki* acceptable as a classic of the Kami Way. Even the distasteful "Chinese thoughts," which Norinaga attacked, were nothing else but a result of this need for rationalization. But Norinaga rejected such rationalization as being, from a philological standpoint, forced analogies. While boldly laying bare the primitive irrationality of the Shinto classics, he approved of, and believed in, these irrationalities just as they were. Proof of irrationality, and belief in that which was irrational, ran parallel to each other — one did not infringe at all upon the other. This leads us directly to assume the existence of a state of absolute faith. Contradictions such as existed in the confrontation of literary and Ancient-Way views, or of doctrines of "Heianism" and "Nara-ism," were submerged naturally in this absolute faith; and so there was no consciousness of any contradiction.

This state of mind, of course, could not have been nurtured and acquired from philological research into the *Kojiki* or, needless to say, from Heian literature. It had no connection with — actually was just the opposite of — the natural-philosophy atheism of Mabuchi's Ancient Way. Neither does it come from Keichū's scholarship. For the origin of Norinaga's religious feelings of absolute faith, we must consider the existence of a different group of intellectual relationships — that is, a grouping made up of three intellectual movements: Dazai Learning; Suiga Shinto; and the Pure Land Sect of Buddhism.

Philological study of ancient classics — an aspect of antiquarian thought within Confucianism — was not only a historical forerunner of Norinaga's thought; it was something with which Norinaga came into contact during his stay in Kyoto. With Dazai there had been a remarkable development of faith in the Chinese Sages and in the classics which recorded their acts; and quite early Norinaga became familiar with Dazai's works.

Suiga Shinto was a powerful movement in the Shinto world during Norinaga's youth; and among the Kami books in which he, from an early age, was absorbed, there were naturally some written by members of this Suiga School — actually, it is thought that most of the books he read were of this School. Moreover, the Shintoists who were Norinaga's close relatives were members of this School. Suiga Shinto had come to have fervent religious sentiments of absolute faith in the Imperial ancestral Kami and in the Imperial Family. Of course, the Confucian analogies that had cropped up in the Suiga Shinto interpretations of the Shinto classics were rejected by Norinaga on philological grounds — actually, they became a target of his attacks. But, at the same time, there is no doubt but that he was influenced and inspired by the religious sentiments of this School.

The Pure Land Sect of Buddhism was in a special position as the religion of Norinaga's home. His father and mother, and many close relatives, were devotees of the Sect. From childhood, Norinaga had read books associated with Pure Land; he was familiar with Buddhist matters; and he was imbued with its teachings. We can assume that these Buddhist teachings, with their preaching of absolute supernatural power (*tariki*), and Buddha's blessings (*button*), were most effective in nurturing his religious sentiments and in giving form to his belief habits. Needless to say, Norinaga's beliefs were not Pure Land Sect beliefs transmitted to him unchanged. It is difficult to find, for example, any traces in his thought of the Buddhist consciousness of sin, or its pessimistic view of life. And yet, if we look through his various books, we find numerous likenesses to the Pure Land position of absolute submission and faith — as, for example, when asked whether the Kami Way included security after death, he said that insecurity meant security; or his statement that since the Kami were like puppeteers and people like puppets, men — being manipulated as the Kami willed — should entrust everything to the Kami; or his declarations on the absolute beneficence of the Kami.

When we recognize the nature of Norinaga's faith in which these three elements are fused, I think we can probably understand the special character of his thought. A powerful support for this attitude of faith was his positivistic agnosticism by which he placed man's wisdom within the limits of his senses, rejected all abstract reasoning as blind guessing, and ascribed everything else to mystery. This agnosticism also explains the unique character of his philology. In contrast to Mabuchi, who was inclined to abstract facts and to favor reason, Norinaga always adhered to facts and avoided reason. His idealism led him toward mysticism; and his mysticism was naturally bound up with faith.

Having carried the discussion thus far, we should now be able to illuminate the individuality of Norinaga as an antiquarian thinker. Compared to Mabuchi (the poet-thinker), what stands out most vividly in Norinaga is his " believing " nature. On this point, he differs not only from Mabuchi, but from all other Confucian and National Learning thinkers. On the other hand, as a thorough scholar of the ancient classics, he was a representative — even a perfecter — of the scholarly approach in the whole field of ancient thought. This was because he was more a student of Keichū than of Mabuchi. Although scholarship and faith are thought to be incompatible, in Norinaga they were strangely united — a phenomenon that I think did not occur often in the history of antiquarian thought in Tokugawa Japan. Therein lies the uniqueness of his thought.

Norinaga's thought is so unique, however, that it is frequently difficult for the superficial observer to understand him; and this induces skepticism about the sincerity of his faith. We have an example of this in Murdoch who discusses Motoori in the third volume of his recent monumental work: *A History of Japan*. Murdoch writes that it is inconceivable that an intelligent classical scholar like Norinaga could have believed, *in toto,* legendary myths which abound in the absurd and the incredible. He thinks that Norinaga was reacting against Confucianism (which was extremely popular at that time) and that, in opposing the Confucianists, he desired to make a name for himhelf in National-Learning philological study — away from the philosophical abstractions which he did not comprehend. And so, argues

Murdoch, Norinaga — in disagreeing particularly with Confucian views — turned to belief in ancient Shinto.[1] Of course, says Murdoch, Norinaga was aware, in the beginning, of this irrationality; but, deceiving himself, he boldly proclaimed such beliefs and, thanks to the psychology expressed in the proverb " even the head of a sardine can be an object of faith," he convinced others and eventually gained numerous disciples. Murdoch also expresses the opinion that Norinaga was exploiting the patriotic pride of the people. Needless to say, such views show a complete misunderstanding of Norinaga. We have only to remember how Norinaga's scholarly achievements of a life-time of study went into the foundation of his faith in the ancient Kami Way, and also how this faith in the Kami Way was sustained by his philological research in the ancient classics, especially in the *Kojiki*. We have only to note that his devout personality and great scholarship not only attracted hundreds of disciples from all over Japan while he was still living, but brought many worshippers after his death; that he was a source of tremendous inspiration in the long cultural history of the Tokugawa Era; and finally that he was even worshipped as a Kami by many of his followers, almost coming to occupy the position of a religious founder.

In considering Norinaga from the viewpoint of intellectual history, we must bear in mind that it was the special character of Norinaga's thought, with scholarship and faith so strangely fused, which precipitated the theological and religious development of Ancient-Learning Shinto; and that it was this special character of his thought which produced extremely interesting developments in the thought of his student, Hirata Atsutane [1776–1843], and in the thought of others in Hirata's school. Of course, Norinaga's Ancient-Learning Shinto was propagated in Hirata's view of Shinto, but in this propagation three distinctive developments appeared. First, in clarifying points in Norinaga's interpretations written in the first section of his " Com-

---

1) [James Murdoch: *A History of Japan* (London, 1926), III, 478–9.]

mentary on the *Kojiki,*" Hirata asserted the divinity of The-Kami-Who-Is-Master-of-the-August-Center-of-Heaven (*Ame no Mi-naka-nushi no Kami*), as a personified supreme Kami of creation that existed prior to Heaven and earth. Secondly, he recognized a world of souls which he called the "concealed world" (*yūkai*) — something different from Norinaga's Yomi. His idea of a "concealed world" was based upon the separation of powers over the concealed and the manifest referred to in the myth about Ō-kuni-nushi no Kami (the Great-Land-Master Kami), giving up his territory to the Sun Goddess — a separation in which the concealed world was assigned to Ō-kuni-nushi no Kami and the manifest world to the Heavenly Kami. In making this distinction, Hirata added moralistic and future-life dimensions to Shintoism. And so the ancient Shinto, which was a polytheistic and this-worldly religion, took on monotheistic and other-worldly characteristics. It was taught that the human world of the present was temporary and that the divine world of the future was central. In this theological development of ancient Shinto, it is to be noted that Hirata was influenced by theology that originated in books on Catholic dogma, which were then proscribed in Japan. The acceptance and application of such influence gives us some insight into Hirata's mental experience at that time. Thirdly, on the basis of the Kami-genealogy outlook of the ancient legends, Hirata united Japanese ancestor-worship around the worship of the ancestral Kami of the Imperial Family. By doing this, he made Shinto into a national, ancestral-Kami faith; and he established its rites and ceremonies.

The beginnings of Hirata's thought were of course in the thought of Norinaga. Moreover, it is clear that many Confucian elements were incorporated into Hirata's views. But Hirata regarded the Shintoism that he had formulated to be the source of all religions. He held that the Kami of Japan were world Kami and that Shinto was the basis of all religions. We see here, in form and content, an ingenious reversal of the "manifestation of original Buddhas" doctrine. But at the same time, in speaking of the Kami-descended

Emperors as rulers of the world, and of Japan as the "ancestor country" of the myriad countries, Hirata was fervently advocating his imperialistic convictions, making an adjustment to the international tension that prevailed in those closing years of the Tokugawa military government.

These developments in Hirata's Shinto were carried on — in whole or in part — by his disciples in various ways. Several notable intellectual movements have been detected, but that which manifested the greatest maturity was the thought of Nanri Yūrin [1812–1864], a Shintoist from the Province of Saga. Proceeding from Hirata's concept of "the concealed and the revealed" (*yūgen*) — or "hidden and manifest" (*inken*) — Yūrin taught that there was a spiritual dualism in everything. Explaining that there was unity in the highest spirituality — that with the Kami nature of Ame no Mi-naka-nushi no Kami there was a return to the highest *in* — he affirmed the immortaility of of spiritual reality as a manifestation of this [highest *in*]. Finally he held that although the Kami Way, or Shinto, stood in opposition to [this spiritual reality], the latter was fundamental. The essence of Shinto, he said, lay in the mind and not in words and deeds — in short, that Shinto was a doctrine of the spirit. According to Nanri's philosophy of life, the Heavenly Kami, while encompassing both good and evil in their absoluteness, were at the same time the highest good. Accordingly, while both good and evil, and fortune and misfortune, were ultimately the lot and product of man, the conscience of man was endowed with a Kami nature. By perfecting his conscience and accumulating meritorious deeds, he could bring out his Kami nature. On the one hand, a human being could commune with the Kami and become a Kami; and, on the other hand, he could bring prosperity to himself and avert disaster. But this was philosophical theory. In actuality, human beings, being intellectually and morally imperfect, could never know the impenetrable mystery (that is, the Kami will) and could hardly perform deeds that were perfectly virtuous. Therefore, Nanri taught that we are not in touch with the Kami Principle (*shinri*) through enlightenment (*godō*) alone, but must believe in, and depend on, the Kami. If a man offered his faith with utmost sincerity, the Kami would bless him. It was here that Nanri found the miraculous area of contact between man and Kami. And he proposed prayer and exorcism as ritual for that religion. Nanri's Shinto, like Hirata's, was influenced by the new Christianity that was seeping into Japan at that time.

It is clear that this sort of development within Hirata Shinto, because of its originality (it was not mere imitation) and profundity, was very important in the intellectual history of Japan. We need not point out specifically how individual elements in it stem back to Norinaga. We must only say that it resulted from internal developments of Norinaga's highly unique Ancient-Learning Shinto, and that if it had not been for Norinaga's unique brand of Shintoism, the sort of intellectual development that we see in Hirata Shintoism would not have occurred.

In the final analysis, Norinaga's Shintoism had, with its emphasis upon philological study, completely eliminated all the existing analogies applied to the ancient Shinto classics; and into this primitive form which had been thoroughly cleansed [of foreign influences], there was injected a further element of deep faith. Therefore, he was able to continue accepting this new religion by means of a state of mind which enabled him to believe in it because it was irrational. But this special balance of mind could not be passed on to Hirata, a man who did not have absolute faith. And so naturally, in him, the balance was dissolved; and along with the dissolution there could not but be intellectual development. The influence of foreign religion on his intellectual development — in contrast to the situation which prevailed in Medieval Shinto — was not simply analogy and imitation. Finally, it should be recognized as a salient fact in Japanese history that the Imperialism and Emperorism in Norinaga's thought were perfected by Hirata, and became a powerful element in the political motivation of the Meiji Restoration. This cannot be overlooked — even from the viewpoint of historical materialism.

Note: The following are important materials for the study of Norinaga as a thinker:
(1) *Shibun yōryō* (Essentials of Murasaki's Prose) [*Motoori zenshū* X, 227–322], and
   Isonokami sazamegoto (Whispered Words of the Past) [*Motoori zenshū* VI, 463–534];
      1763, age 34.
(2) *Naobi no mitama* (The Spirit of Straightening) [*Motoori zenshū* I, 1–68]; completed by 1771, age 42.
(3) *Gyojū gaigen* (Complaint on the Failure to Bridle the Chinese) [*Motoori zenshū* VI, 131–235];
      1778, age 49.
(4) *Kuzubana* (Arrowroot Blossoms) [*Motoori zenshū* V, 455–516]; 1780, age 51.
(5) *Tamaboko hyakushu* (One Hundred Poems on the Way) [*Motoori zenshū* X, 109–116],
   Tama kushige (Jeweled Comb Box) [*Motoori zenshū* VI, 1–22]; completed by 1786, age 57.
(6) *Hihon tama kushige* (Secret Book of the Jeweled Comb Box) [*Motoori zenshū* VI, 22–60];
   completed by 1787, age 58.
(7) *Omi no michi* (Way of the Subject) [*Motoori zenshū* VI, 100–3]; completed by 1800, age 71.
(8) *Suzunoya tōmon roku* (Suzunoya Dialogues) [*Motoori zenshū* VI, 104–30];
(9) Portions of the *Tama katsuma* (Jeweled Bamboo Basket) [*Motoori zenshū* VIII, 1–144].

Chapter V

Changes in Ideas about 'the Concealed and the Mysterious' in Restoration Shinto[1]

1

Shinto thought in Japan has emerged and developed *within studies and interpretations* of the Shinto classics, especially of the "Age of Kami" books of the *Kojiki* and the *Nihongi*. And just as in the history of learning in general, the history of the study of the ancient Shinto classics reached a turning point in the early part of the Tokugawa Era.

This history begins with lectures on the *Nihongi*, which can be deduced from extant fragments of the *Nihon shiki* and which were held at the Imperial Court from 721 down into the Heian Era. Then in the Kamakura Era we have the *Shaku Nihongi* (Interpretation of the *Nihongi*) by Urabe Kanekata and the *Kojiki uragaki* (Notes on the *Kojiki*) by Urabe Kanebumi, both dating from the last three decades of the thirteenth century. Somewhat later we have: the *Jinnō shōtō ki* (Record of the True Lineage of the Sacred Emperors) and the *Gengen shū* (Notes on Origins) both by Kitabatake Chikafusa [1293-1354]; the *Tōka hiden* (Secret Traditions of an Eastern House), said to be written by Kitabatake; and the *Jindai kuketsu* (Oral Traditions of the Age of Kami) by Imbe no Masamichi. And finally, there is the *Nihonshoki sanso* (Commentaries on the *Nihongi*) by Ichijō Kaneyoshi [1402-1481] which culminated the history of medieval Shinto studies. All these authors, while regarding the *Nihongi* and the *Kojiki* as Shinto classics, tried for the most part to interpret words

---
1) [First published in *Tetsugaku zasshi* (Journal of Philosophy) XXX, 342 (August, 1915) and included in *Zōtei Nihon shisō shi kenkyū, pp. 288-320.*]

in these classics in terms of the authoritative texts of various Confucian and Buddhist schools, and so on the whole their works are nothing more than reflections of the various undigested and inconsistent thought tangles in the minds of these men. Therefore, their studies — as attempts to clarify the meaning of the Shinto classics — generally fell to the level of far-fetched interpretation. However, this sort of thing was not merely characteristic of Shinto research. It was an essential by-product of the imported character of Japanese civilization and, as such, nothing but a manifestation of the heterogeneity common to cultural phenomena in Japan since antiquity.

But Tokugawa culture — the development of which began with the independence of Confucianism from Buddhism — had clearly opened a new phase in Shinto studies during the first decades of the Era. The Shinto-classic ideas of such Confucian and Shinto scholars as Hayashi Razan [1583–1657], Kumazawa Banzan [1619–1691], Watarai Nobuyoshi [1615–1690], Kikkawa Koretari [1616–1694], and Yamazaki Ansai [1618–1682] were mostly freed from Buddhist doctrinal mixtures and were associated with attempts to achieve a closer union with Confucianism.

With classical studies carried out by scholars within Confucian and National Learning schools during the Jōkyō and Genroku eras (1684–1704) — studies which were associated with a spirit of *free inquiry* — there emerged some truly scholarly research in ancient texts. Keichū's [1640–1701] study of the *Man'yōshū*, based on an investigation of the ancient language, was the starting point for later scholarly research on the Shinto classics. In the introductory volume to *Man'yō daishōki* (Commentary on the *Man'yōshū*) Keichū stated that the *Kojiki* and the *Nihongi* were not [authoritative] classics, but compilations of legend.

The first stage of Tokugawa-Era investigation of the Shinto classics was historical research, seen for the first time in this period. The *Kojiki* and the *Nihongi* — looked at from Keichū's point of view that they were not [authoritative] classics — were generally considered to be subjects for historical study. Efforts were made to clarify the history of the ancient past by interpreting these works more or less allegorically. The principal representatives of this group of scholars were Arai Hakuseki [1657–1725] — who was like Keichū in following a scholarly approach based upon interpretations of the ancient language — and Yoshimi Yukikazu [1673–1761]. Although Ise Sadatake [1715–1784] was no specialist in Shinto-classic research, he was definitely critical of the attitudes of the old Shinto scholars, claiming on the basis of research in ancient customs that Shinto was nothing more than the ceremonies of rites, prayers, and exorcism and that the Shinto classics were not [authoritative] classics but history — see his *Jindai no maki dokken* (Private Views about the Age of Kami Books [of the *Kojiki* and *Nihongi*]) and his *Shintō dokugo* (Monologue on Shinto). Because of these claims, then, he too belongs to this group and is, moreover, a forerunner of the second stage.

The second stage was philological research. Here the objective was clearly to recapture the consciousness of the early Japanese *just as it was* by treating the Shinto classics as compilations of legend which expressed the whole of early Japanese consciousness. By rejecting all allegorical interpretations, and attempting studies based on a scholarly investigation of ancient words, the scholars of this stage brought to completion the Ancient Learning which had begun with Keichū's work on the *Man'yōshū*. Foremost among them was Motoori Norinaga [1730–1801], a scholar who, with a full measure of scholarly awareness, made lasting contributions. Having been impressed by Keichū's work, he entered classical studies at an early age. Moreover, *he fully mastered the spirit of Keichū's scholarship,* and then went on to study under that ardent poet-antiquarian, Kamo Mabuchi [1697–1769], and to bring his own work to completion. Motoori's masterpiece, the *Kojiki den* (Commentary on the *Kojiki*), laid immovable foundations for the later studies of the Shinto classics. As a result of Motoori's work, the *Nihongi* — which up until that time had been the most valued of the Shinto classics — lost its place (because of its Chinese literary embellishments) to the *Kojiki,* a purer version of the ancient legends. Hirata Atsutane [1776–1843], who claimed to be the successor of Motoori after the latter's death and who founded a later Shinto school, also belonged — in the spirit of his scholarship — to this group of philologists.

The third stage of Shinto-classic research was criticism, which grew — partly from internal reasons — from the pure philological research of Motoori. Scholars adopted a critical attitude toward the Shinto classics because they felt a need to seek rationally satisfying interpretations by resolving the moral and theoretical contradictions that existed in the uncritical, devout attitude of stage-two scholars toward the Shinto classics. Even with Atsutane the trend was already discernible, but those who took a critical attitude — from the beginning and consciously — were Motoori's opponents, Fujitani Mitsue [1768–1823], and Tachibana Moribe [1781–1849].

In all these stages, research into the Shinto classics continued to be the chief concern, and the assertions of Shinto thought were its product. On the other hand, there emerged a separate group of scholars who, though equally concerned with research in the Shinto classics, did not so much strive for a philological elucidation of the words in the Shinto classics, as to try — judging at least from the results — to establish Shinto doctrines of their own on the basis of the Shinto classics. In other words, there was a fourth group, which might be called the Shintoists (*shintōka*) and which included certain followers of Hirata Atsutane — such as Satō Nobuhiro [1769–1850], Oka Kumaomi [1783–1851], Mutobe Yoshika [1798–1863], Nonoguchi Takamasa [1792–1871], Gonda Naosuke [1809–1887], and Yano Harumichi [1823–1887] — and some who belonged to other schools, such as Kubo Sueshige [1830–1886] and Suzuki Masayuki [1838–1872].

If we assume that there were elements in these traditional studies of the Shinto classics which produced, more or less spontaneously, thoughts that might be called philosophical or theological, we must not look for them in the medieval period when Shinto was mixed up with Confucian and Buddhist teachings. They are found in the Tokugawa Era, especially in the development that followed philological research — that is, in the so-called Restoration Shinto (*fukko shintō*) that is also known as Ancient-Learning Shinto (*kogaku shintō*). And among the notable elements of Shinto thought in this period the idea of "the concealed and mysterious" (*yūmei*) is one of the most important.

2

The term "concealed and mysterious" (originally just "concealed") was the opposite of "visible and open" (*kenro*). The most important reference to the latter term is in the Age of Kami book of the *Nihongi*, in the second variant of the legend about Ō-na-muchi no Kami giving his reply to the two Kami that had been dispatched by Taka-mi-musubi no Mikoto. In Taka-mi-musubi no Mikoto's original order we find these words: "*Visible and open matters* over which you have administered should now be administered by my Imperial Grandchild. [Hereafter] you are to administer *Kami matters*." Then Ō-na-muchi no Kami makes the following reply: "*Visible and open matters* which I have administered will now be administered by the Imperial Grandchild. I will retire and administer *concealed matters*.... I will withdraw and depart from here." Then the account states: "And then he received the eight-foot string of pure jewels and *hid himself* forever." The corresponding passage in the main version states only: "'If the Heavenly Grandchild uses this spear to rule the land, he will surely reign in peace. I will now retire past the eighty road-windings and *remain hidden*.' So saying, he *hid himself*."[1] Again in the *Kojiki* there is the reference: "'I will hide myself past the eighty road-windings and be in attendance. Moreover,

---

1) *Nihongi*, [*Kokushi taikei*, I, 72–3 and 64. *Kokushi taikei* will be cited hereafter as KT].

if my sons.... serve [the Heavenly Grandchild] before and behind, there will be no disobedient Kami.' (Thus he spoke and *hid himself*)."[1] Then in the congratulatory prayer offered [at the Imperial Court] by the governor of the province of Izumo, we find this phrase: ".... they conciliated and pacified the great Kami who founded the land [Ō-na-muchi no Kami] and made him *relinquish* manifest and visible matters in the Land of the Great Eight Islands."[2]

Thus a positive use of the term "concealed matters" occurs in the second variant of the *Nihongi* legend, where the term "Kami matters" is also recorded. But in the first version of the *Nihongi*, in the *Kojiki*, and in the congratulatory prayer offered by the governor of Izumo, neither "concealed matters" nor "Kami matters" appear. In these references we find — in connection with the handing over of "visible matters" to the Heavenly Grandchild — only such expressions as "hid himself" and "relinquish."

Among medieval commentators the *Nihongi* term "concealed matters" was interpreted in two ways. According to the first, "concealed matters" or "Kami matters" — by way of contrast to "visible matters," which were thought of as the duties of administering the state — were rites performed for a Kami. Such an interpretation is found in Imbe no Masamichi's *Jindai kuketsu*. The opposing view was that Kami matters meant the world of the dead, for "visible and open" matters were of man and "concealed and mysterious" matters were of Kami. Rites, according to this view, were thought of as visible and open, belonging to the affairs of man. Such an interpretation is found in Ichijō Kaneyoshi's *Nihon shoki sanso*. The former view was based purely and simply on an interpretation of words, but the second arose out of Buddhist scriptural thought. Consequently, with the second interpretation, and a further extension of it, the two [concealed and visible] spheres were considered interdependent, like day

---

1) *Kojiki*, [KT, VII, 41. "Hid himself" was placed in parentheses by Motoori to fill a lacuna in the text].
2) [*Nihon koten bungaku taikei*, I, 455.]

and night and the negative and positive principles (*Yin* and *Yang*). If a man committed an evil act in the visible sphere, the ruler would punish him. But if this happened in the "concealed and mysterious" sphere, souls of the dead (*ki*) and Kami would inflict punishment. Obtaining happiness by doing good followed the same principle. In later sections I will show that these views of Ichijō Kaneyoshi were a strong influence on ideas of "the concealed and mysterious" held by Restoration Shinto schools. But bear in mind that such ideas were not spontaneous thought with Kaneyoshi, but simply textual glosses adapted from Buddhist scripture.

3

Views about the word "concealed" which emerged in Motoori Norinaga's philological research were naturally short and simple, for his research was carried on with the purpose of recapturing the consciousness of the ancient people, just as it was, by removing Confucian and Buddhist analogies from interpretations of the Shinto classics.

He explained the *Kojiki* expression "I will hide myself and be in attendance" as signifying that even though Ō-na-muchi no Kami was departing the visible world for Yomi, he intended to serve the descendants of the Heavenly Kami and protect them from afar. He concluded that the *Nihongi* statement "I will administer concealed matters" was implied in "be in attendance." And so he held that "visible and open" matters referred to the government of the Imperial Court and to the way in which men should conduct themselves in this world, whereas "concealed matters" meant "Kami matters"— things which could not be seen by the eye or attributed to the acts of men, but were performed by Kami. Nevertheless, since everything in the world took place at the will of the Kami, even "visible matters" were fundamentally within this category; but the term "Kami matters," he concluded, was used provisionally to distinguish specifically invisible occurrences from the acts of men.

However, the source of Kami matters, that is, of the "concealed and the mysterious," was ultimately nothing else but Yomi which was, like the "root country" (*ne no kuni* or *ne no katasukuni*), a polluted underworld — a dark land where people went after death regardless of whether they were of low or high class, good or bad. This was not a pretentious interpretation that made Yomi a hell which contrasted with a Heaven. Death was something to be grieved and hated, and because Yomi was the land of the dead, it was — in contrast to this world — an evil place. But if we look at the legends of the Age of Kami, we find that in the beginning Izanami and Izanagi were separated — one going to the visible world and one to Yomi; that their offspring, the Sun Goddess and Susa-no-o no Kami, also separated; and finally that the children of the Sun Goddess and Susa-no-o no Kami were, in turn, separated. This meant that a confrontation existed between the visible and the concealed; there was an alternation of good and bad fortune, but good fortune was destined to prevail. Nevertheless, matters of this sort were basically Kami matters and beyond human ken.

In short, it was Motoori's view that "concealed and mysterious" was Yomi — the land where people went after death — and that "concealed matters" belonged to Yomi and were mysterious Kami matters which could not be seen. Chamberlain, in the introduction to his translation of the *Kojiki* (pp. 56–57), has pointed out inconsistencies in the *Kojiki* references to Yomi. For example, Yomi is depicted as a part of the real world or, although belonging to heaven, as having conditions that in every way are like those of this world; or it is shown as a polluted place of residence for the deceased that exists outside the real world, and in this connection is represented as a place where only the dead go; but again as a place where people can go even before death.[1] Of course, Motoori, without probing very deeply, admits everything as fact that existed in the consciousness of

---

1) [*Ko-ji-ki or Records of Ancient Matters* (2nd ed., Kobe; 1932), lxiv–lxv.]

the ancient people; and he makes his explanations in terms of the text itself. Whenever he encounters a problem, he treats it as something transcending human understanding, and considers that the real significance of ancient legend consists in precisely this sort of unaccountable matter. Knox, in his *The Development of Religion in Japan* (1907), criticized the ancient classics in these terms: " Nothing was unnatural, for nothing was natural."[1] He was here unconsciously taking the same position as Norinaga. Possibly it was for this reason that Norinaga could not come to terms with the fact that in his concept of Yomi there were two logically incompatible natures — the evilness of Yomi as the land of the dead and source of misfortune, and the divinity of Yomi as the root of concealed matters, that is, of Kami matters.

But with Norinaga philology *was* the Ancient Way. That is, it was his philosophy and his religion. The recapturing of the belief of the ancient people meant belief in that belief. As a philologist, he fully appreciated the sense of August Böeckh's " cognition of cognitions." While he learned to understand as the ancients understood, he also came to philosophize as the ancients philosophized. Cognition of cognitions became belief in cognitions. For him the Ancient Way was the way *which was not a way*, and the *Kojiki* was the *classic which was not a classic*. [That is, they were absolute and not comparable with things normally classed as " Ways " or " classics."]

It was probably for this reason that the concept of Yomi, as discussed above, became Norinaga's concept, and part of his religious thought. Since man, according to Norinaga, always went to the polluted land of Yomi when he died, death was a misfortune. Such ideas as retribution after death were rejected by him as academic questions for which there was no corroborative evidence in the ancient legends. And when his disciples asked him how to prepare for life and death, he answered that in Shinto there were no references to peace

---

1) [*The Development of Religion in Japan* (New York and London; 1907), 17–19.]

of mind (*anshin*) like those found in Confucianism and Buddhism, and that this, after all, was peace of mind. However, in his heart he embraced the idea of benefaction and the peace of mind of absolute trust, which were completely absent in the religious feelings of the ancients. It should be noted that this absolute trust — which was an ingredient of the Taoist concept of " the natural way," learned from Kamo Mabuchi — was rooted in the pious and absolute belief in supernatural [saving] power (*tariki*) of Pure Land Buddhism, not a little of which he had obtained in his own upbringing. But it should also be noted that this irrational faith contained, on the one hand, nationalistic thought of reverence for things ancient and, on the other, thought that was sensualistic and agnostic. Furthermore, this faith supported his uncritical attitude toward ancient tradition, which has been mentioned above. While this faith enabled him in truth to perfect a philological attitude in his study, it added a piously religious character to his Ancient Way and was the source of the religious character of later Restoration Shinto. Finally, it should be pointed out that the true religious character in Norinaga's Shinto thought did not exist in his Shinto, but belonged to the Buddhist faith which he had rejected.[1]

4

It has become clear to me, in reading the works of Hirata Atsutane, that in the spirit of his scholarship he was not only Norinaga's truest successor but even made some improvements on Norinaga's approach. So I cannot help but be impressed with the spirit of Norinaga's scholarship as well as with the earlier Ancient Learning approach of Keichū and Mabuchi, which had even made a sectarian personality like Atsutane into a searcher for truth and enabled him to become what he was. Atsutane's *Koshi seibun* (A Composition of Ancient History) — in

---

1) I have gone into this, in detail, in *Motoori Norinaga*, published in 1911.

which he synthesized selections from the *Nihongi,* the *Kojiki,* the Shinto liturgies, the ancient provincial gazeteers (*fudoki*), the *Kogo shūi* (Gleanings from Ancient Stories), and even the *Kujiki* (Chronicle of Ancient Matters) which, in spite of its being rejected by Norinaga, he thought should be used even though it was a forgery — as well as his *Koshiden* (Commentary on " A Composition of Ancient History ") and *Koshichō* (Evidence about "A Composition of Ancient History"), in which he interpreted and glossed these sources, are great works that deserve to be ranked, philologically, with the *Kojiki den* (Commentary on the *Kojiki*) by Norinaga.

Atsutane also resembled Norinaga in the fact that his philological study of antiquity was at the same time the Ancient Way itself. But, as to personality, he was never a gentle scholar like Motoori. Not only was he more accomplished in Confucian and Buddhist learning, but he also had a smattering of Dutch and Biblical learning. Within him there was a fierce hostility toward all foreign ideologies and, moreover, he had *no intellectual hide-outs* like Norinaga's belief in otherworldly power [of salvation]. Possibly it was in this connection that his fond desire to establish a Shinto based upon the old traditions and to stand up against all foreign teachings compelled him as a matter of course to enter into the ancient consciousness which he was trying to propagate, and to some extent did propagate. It is for this reason that he wrote the somewhat subjective adaptation of the ancient classics which we see in the *Koshi seibun,* and the subjective, theoretical interpretation which we see in the *Koshiden.* (However, it should be noted that the degree of [subjectivity and theory] in both books was *relatively slight,* and that his attitude was *not destructive* [of contemporary society]. This was because he was a student of Norinaga.) But there are two points about the *Koshiden* which should be noted. The first is his further development of the argument in the *Sandaikō* (Three Great Ideas) — by his senior among the followers of Norinaga, Hattori Nakatsune [1757–1824] — and his being influenced, it seems to me, by the Old Testament and having Genesis-like ideas about creation, in the sense of asserting the existence of a Kami before there was a Heaven or an earth. And the second point is his concept of the "concealed and mysterious." The two problems of Restoration Shinto, cosmogony and eschatology, were emphasized for the first time by Atsutane, and are discussed particularly in *Tama no mihashira* (True Pillar of the Soul).

Atsutane had been very critical of Norinaga for being too severe in pointing out the shortcomings of the *Nihongi* and for excessive zeal in demonstrating the virtues of the *Kojiki*. Unlike Norinaga, who in his rewriting of the Age of Kami book in *Kamiyo no masagoto* (True Words of the Age of Kami), relied principally on the *Kojiki* text and merely appended the second variant of the *Nihongi*, Atsutane took the latter for the 123rd section of his *Koshi seibun* and added the following italicized words: " Visible and *clear* matters which I have administered will now be administered by the Imperial Grandchild. I will retire and administer concealed and *mysterious* matters." He equated " visible and clear matters " with "manifest matters," giving to the term the Japanese reading *araha goto* (open matters) and equated " concealed and mysterious matters " with Kami matters, giving to the term the reading *kakuri goto* (hidden matters). (Norinaga had read the latter as *kamigoto*.) In interpretations given in this section of the *Koshi seibun*, Atsutane quoted the following statement from Ichijō Kaneyoshi's *Nihon shoki sanso*: " Visible matters are of the way of man and concealed matters of the way of Kami." He held that while Kaneyoshi's interpretation was written in Chinese, it made sense, and concluded that " concealed matters " were not Kami matters associated with the process of creation but were matters pertaining to the supreme authority which resided over the spirits of both Kami and men who had passed through this world and gone to the " concealed world."

Atsutane, as a student of Norinaga, did not interpret " concealed and mysterious " as a hell that stands in opposition to Heaven. On the other hand, he could not identify it with Yomi as Norinaga had done. There were two reasons for this. In the first place, his rejection of Norinaga's view was based upon his theory — which lay at the heart of his doctrine — about the creation of Heaven and earth. According to Atsutane, Yomi was the moon, in contrast to Heaven or the sun, which was separated from the earth and, after creation, became completely severed from the earth. It was a "bottom country" (*sokotsukuni*) which, by comparison with the earth, was made of turbid elements. As to the land where souls must go after death, that was something quite different. The second reason why Atsutane rejected Norinaga's view of Yomi was that the idea of souls going after death to a polluted land called Yomi did not satisfy the spiritual needs which he required of Shinto. Consequently, he took the position that this view came from a tradition with foreign admixture and had no basis in the pure traditions of antiquity. He held that the *Kojiki* legend of Izanami's passage to Yomi referred to a time before the country of the moon had been separated from the earth. She went there in her mortal body, not as a soul after death. On this point both the *Kojiki* and *Nihongi* traditions were incorrect, he maintained, and the tradition to accept was the one incorporated in the Shinto liturgy of the Fire-Pacifying Festival (*Ho-shizume no matsuri*).[1] He considered Norinaga's view of Yomi, which disregarded this tradition, as wrong.

And so with Atsutane "the concealed and the mysterious" was now clearly *a world of souls after death*. And matters of "death" and "souls" were somewhat more lucidly thought out than was the case with Norinaga. He thought of life as the emergence of a man in the world through the creativity (*musubi*) of the Kami, endowed with a "heart-soul" (*shinkon*) and four elements (wind, fire, water, and earth) that were each controlled by a Kami. The most important element of life was wind: that is, the breath which stemmed from the exhalation of Izanagi.[2] Life (*iki*) was after all breathing (*iki*); and it was the cessation of breathing that constituted death. A soul

---

1) [Cf., Philippi: *Norito*, 51–52.]
2) [Izanagi exhaled and produced the wind Kami. See *Nihongi*, KT, I, 13.]

was a kind of "spirit-air" (*reiki*), capable of such miraculous action as appearing in dreams, attaching itself to plants and animals, and becoming a "word-spirit" (*kotodama*) that bespoke good fortune. Even though the form returned to the ground after death, the soul was not extinguished. It went to "the concealed and mysterious" where it served Ōkuni-nushi no Kami,[1] received orders from this Kami, and protected its descendants and relatives. Furthermore, as these ideas about life after death, or "the world to come" (*raise*), were given definite form by Atsutane, there developed of necessity an insistence on the concept of retribution which appeared in the interpretations of Kaneyoshi's *Nihon shoki sanso*. That is, the retribution of good and evil was not necessarily fair in this life, but that was because this world was a *place where the Kami tested us,* and the final rewards and punishments would be found in the "concealed and mysterious" world. It followed, then, that the present world was rather a *temporary world* and the important world was that of the "concealed and mysterious." In other words, the good and evil fortunes of this life were temporary and those in the world of the "concealed and mysterious" were true. If we acted prudently, fearing only the Kami and healing our conscience — without being misled by the temporary good and evil fortunes of this life, and without being moved to no purpose by the praise and censure of other people — and if we followed the Kami Way (Shinto) and acted virtuously in this life, then we would receive the *true blessings of the fundamental world* of the "concealed and mysterious."

Thus there was a change in the character of Ō-kuni-nushi no Kami who, with Norinaga, was the Kami that ruled over Yomi, the source of evil. Now he became a Kami who ruled over the fundamental world, in contrast to this world. But for Atsutane, who had never discarded spiritualization, this world of the "concealed and mysterious" was thought of as having, in part, a material quality. That is, he did think of the realm of the dead as being a place apart from and outside

---

1) [Same as Ō-no-machi no Kami.]

of this visible world. The Kami held court everywhere, right inside the visible world, and administered "concealed matters." Their main court was in the Great Shrine of Izumo. Nevertheless, there was a strict separation between the visible and the concealed. The concealed world could not be seen from the visible, but the visible could be seen from the concealed — just as a dark place cannot be seen from a lighted place, whereas the lighted can be seen from the dark. The land of the dead, however, was not necessarily dark. In it as well were all the concerns associated with clothing, food and shelter — it was in every respect just like the world of the living. The soul of every individual after death had a definite abode which it chose — for example, it might settle on top of the grave and there come under the control of the "concealed and mysterious." And so he earnestly believed that when he himself died, he would go to the neighborhood of Norinaga's grave on Mt. Yamamuro, where he would serve the master's soul, carry on studies with him, and cultivate the Ancient Way forever. He, who had missed the fact that the true source of Norinaga's "peace of mind" was elsewhere, believed that in his closing years Norinaga had become aware of the fallacy of his views on Yomi as far as the destination of souls was concerned, and by way of proof took literally the lines in Norinaga's death poem: "in Yamamuro I shall lodge for a thousand years," and held that Norinaga himself believed his soul would dwell at the graveside on this mountain.

5

The scholarly theories of Tachibana Moribe — a representative figure of the group that took a critical attitude toward the study of the Shinto classics — arose from a clear consciousness of the fundamental contradictions that were inherent in Norinaga's view of the Shinto classics. Moribe's *Nan Kojiki den* (Criticism of [Norinaga's] *Kojiki den*), which is a point-by-point criticism of the views included in the first volume of the *Kojiki den,* and his *Itsu no chiwaki* (Awesome Way-

Clearing), in which he expounded a general view of the Shinto classics and attempted to interpret the Age-of-Kami book of the *Nihongi*, were — together with other studies he made — very rich and clearsighted works.

Moribe, who as author of the three *Senkaku*[1] (Selections of Stylistic Forms) was skilled in the rhetorical study of ancient literature, attempted much the same sort of rhetorical analysis of the Shinto classics; and he accomplished research that was more advanced than that of Norinaga or Atsutane. What is most worthy of attention in Moribe is the fact that his view of the Shinto classics forms the basis of his research. He maintained that the most distinguishing characteristic of the extant classics was their "old-word style" — that is, they had a legendary content; and it was this feature that made them valuable. (But the basic reason for their value was not that they were ancient traditions which reflected the consciousness of ancient people, or that they were unlike the writings of the "original-word style" which deviated from exact truth and were amplified by empty falsehood.[2] They were valuable because they contained *considerable historical evidence*. Moribe's approach was, in this respect, at odds with the traditionalism of Norinaga.) Thus, Moribe claimed that various nursery-tale (*yōgo*) and fable (*danji*) elements were mixed up with the basic traditions of the classics. He said that if the fable elements were analyzed, they would be found to contain things which had been

---

1) [The three Senkaku were the *Chōka senkaku* and *Tanka senkaku* for poetry, and the *Bunshō senkaku* for prose.]

2) [The terms "old-word style" (*kyūjiburi*) and "original-word style" (*honjiburi*) were coined with reference to the decree of Emperor Temmu ordering the compilation of the *Kojiki*, which is quoted in the preface to that work. As translated by Chamberlain, the pertinent passages are: "I hear that the chronicles of the emperors and likewise the *original words* in the possession of the various families deviate from exact truth, and are *mostly amplified by empty falsehoods*. .... So now I desire to have the chronicles of the emperors selected and recorded, and the *old words* examined and ascertained, falsehoods being erased and truth determined, in order to transmit [the latter] to after ages." *Ko-ji-ki or Records of Ancient Matters*, 10–11. Italics added.]

intentionally added at the time of narration, injections of old tales (*mukashibanashi*), and representations of the Kami as behaving like ordinary men. The essence of the Shinto classics could be grasped only when these extraneous elements had been eliminated and when the true meaning of the allegories had been made clear. In general, he thought that the passages which dealt with such subjects as the appearance of the Heavenly and Earthly Kami, the origin of the three Imperial Regalia, the Imperial line of descent from the sun, the great shrines and provincial shrines — those subjects which were left after the various extraneous elements had been eliminated — provided the overall pattern of the Shinto classics. Within these passages were contained: a morality and philosophy which constituted "an honest doctrine" or reverence for the Imperial Family; loyalty of ministers and subjects to the Emperor; social order; and miracles of Kami and spirits. It was these passages which made up the tradition of the ancient people and became, as a matter of course, the fountainhead of their education and culture. Therefore, Moribe concluded, the followers of Confucianism and Buddhism (who said that there was no Way in the ancient period) and Norinaga (who admitted this but argued that the very absence of a [formal] Way contributed to the Great Way) were equally wrong.

In this way the nonsensical elements in the classics, which were all tolerated by Norinaga were either eliminated as children's tales and fables, or, in the case of irrational and unintelligible statements about the Kami, explained as allegory. Thus the numerous contradictions, inconsistencies, and irrationalities in the Shinto classics were removed, for with Moribe the content of the classics was not merely ordinary historical evidence. It was also a revelation of strange and miraculous philosophical principles. And what he emphasized as the fundamental principle of the philosophy contained in the classics was his doctrine of "the visible and the concealed." At this point his view of the classics moves, in a single leap, from the sphere of philology to the field of Shinto theology.

Moribe divided all phenomena into the visible and the concealed. His interpretation of the visible as being the entire phenomenal world of men which could be seen was like that of previous scholars. He divided up the concealed, which stood in opposition to the visible, into *Heaven* and *Yomi*. Neither could be seen by the human eye. The two worlds of Heaven and Yomi adjoined each other, but basically they were one and the same, belonging to the concealed, except that Kami were associated with Heaven and souls of the dead with Yomi. The Kami that ruled over Yomi were Izanami no Mikoto, Susa-no-o no Mikoto, Ō-na-muchi no Kami [also called Ō-kuni-nushi no Kami] and Kotoshiro-nushi no Kami. As for Yomi's being considered a polluted place, he thought that Norinaga had made a mistake in interpreting fable as fact, being misled by the phrase " maggots were swarming and [she was] rotting "[1] in that section of the *Kojiki* dealing with Izanami's departure to Yomi. He said that there were examples in the ancient traditions which indicated that both good and bad fortune came from Yomi. Furthermore, he took the position that Heaven and Yomi were not necessarily located outside this world. They were near enough to envelop the human body, but were not felt, and were distant enough to fill the universe, but were not seen. He thought of the world of the visible and the concealed as a duality — like day and night, and man and woman — that were mutually dependent. Consequently, everything in this world came into existence in accord with the plans of the concealed and mysterious Kami, and ups and downs, misfortunes and good fortunes, and blessings and punishments of this world, all emerged from unseen shades. To him the relationship between the visible and the concealed was very close — not being able to see the concealed world from the visible, but seeing the visible from the concealed, was like the inside and outside of a bamboo blind. But human intelligence was limited and man was naturally unable to

---

1) [KTK VII, 11–12. As translated by Basil Hall Chamberlain, *Translation of 'Ko-ji-ki,' or 'Records of Ancient Matters'* (Kobe, Japan; 1932), 142.]

understand the mystery of the "concealed and the mysterious," since he was permitted only that which fell within the range of his thought, strength, vision, hearing, and experience. The Kami matters of the concealed and mysterious were something he must hold in *awe*. Furthermore, such matters as life and death, the origin of souls, and the places where souls go after death were of course managed by the Kami and were not within the bounds of human understanding. For the human mind was originally a loan from the world of the concealed and the mysterious. Thus Moribe's theorizing went no deeper in answering questions which would naturally occur, such as the difference between Kami and souls of the dead, the nature of souls, and what happens after death. For him the descent of the Imperial Grandchild from Heaven was an allegory of Kami emergence from the "concealed and mysterious" to the "visible and clear," and the concealment of Ō-kuni-nushi no Kami "beyond the eighty road-windings" meant that he left the "visible and clear" to enter "the concealed and the mysterious." These facts, together with the fact that the two Kami— [Izanagi and Izanami] who became the parents of the universe— passed between the "concealed" and the "visible," stemmed back to a simple philosophical principle that ran through the Shinto classics.

In some respects Moribe's thought was similar to that of Norinaga, and in other respects to that of Atsutane. At these points of similarity there is no doubt but that Moribe was influenced by these two men. But if we disregard these side-issues and think of that which is basic, it becomes clear that his concept of the concealed and the mysterious, being coupled with the results of research in the Shinto classics from an entirely different point of departure, was essentially independent and original. A characteristic of his thought—which deserves particular attention—is that he distinguished the concealed and mysterious from the concept of death, and contrasting Heaven and Yomi, included them both within the concealed and mysterious. His explanation of the concealed and mysterious, inasmuch as it was based solely on a critical interpretation of the ancient legends, or inasmuch as it was not restricted by the literal meaning of the ancient legends, was the plainest and most highly developed philosophical thought down to that time. And to this extent he was extremely far removed from the consciousness of the ancients, which had become the object of philological study.

6

As the Shintoism of the Ancient-Learning School took on a deeper religious coloration among the followers of Hirata Atsutane, thoughts about " the concealed and the mysterious," along with theories about the creation of Heaven and earth, received the greatest emphasis in their arguments; and earlier thought was either carried on and blended, or refined and deepened.

In general, Satō Nobuhiro and Nonoguchi Takamasa, men who devoted their energies to theories of creation, belonged — along with Mutobe Yoshika, Oka Kumaomi, Kubo Sueshige, Gonda Naosuke, and Yano Harumichi — to the group that inherited the thought of Hirata Atsutane. But the one who was the clearest in his exposition of the theory of the concealed and the mysterious was Yoshika, the author of *Ken'yū-jun kōron* (Thought and Theory about the Relationship between the Visible and the Concealed).

Atsutane's theory about the form of the soul had not yet been clearly developed, but with Yoshika it was essentially a hidden offshoot of the creative Kami. In man, the soul occupied a vacant place in the brain and was usually not visible, but at times it would assume a form that was not different from that of the mortal body. At other times, however, the spirit left the body and would then be seen in such forms as white Ether (*ki*) or red Ether during the day, or as a bright red gleam during the night. Gonda Naosuke, who came from a medical family, stated that the soul was fire ether and resided in the breast. He considered the Western idea that it resided in the brain to be mistaken.

As to the nature of the "concealed world" where souls dwelled after death, Satō Nobuhiro in his *Tenchi yōzō kaiku ron* (On the Creation and Evolution of Heaven and Earth) explained it as a world of "fragrantly enveloping Ether" without form, content, or odor, and which existed between Heaven and earth. And Mutobe Yoshika and Yano Harumichi [the latter in his *Yaso no kumade* (Eighty Road-Windings)] went on to explain the organization of the world. They described a single great system consisting of a "concealed rule" with headquarters at the Great Shrine of Izumo and branches in the tutelary (*ubusuna*) shrines of each area, which exercised such powers as superintending and controlling "concealed matters" of the human mind, ascertaining the motivation of good and evil and right and wrong, and also governing the life spans of human beings. The "concealed world" was provided with everything as in the real world — from a political organization to a social system which included such things as food, clothing, and shelter. Moreover, the "concealed world" was not only more broad and deep than the real world but also more tenuous and subtle, beyond the reach of human intelligence, so that once human beings had entered that world, they flew about freely, having discarded the shackles of the body.

Such views do not go beyond a refinement of Atsutane's theories. On the other hand, there is evidence of remarkable intellectual advance in the views of these men about the *destination* of souls in the concealed world, which came as a natural conclusion to the idea of retribution. They thought that Norinaga's view that the souls of both the good and the bad went to Yomi was, as Atsutane argued, a fallacy. But they also thought that Atsutane's theory, which recognized no distinctions within the concealed world, and left the soul at the graveside, did not go far enough. Some of them, like Atsutane, identified Heaven and Yomi with the sun and the moon, and thought of the concealed world as something entirely different from either. They affirmed the existence of both a world of a Kami order and a world for evildoers within the concealed world, and made a distinction between where good and evil souls went after death.[1] Certain writers (such as Oka Kumaomi in his *Chiyo no sumika*, or The Eternal Abode) attempted to blend Norinaga's views with those of Atsutane by stating that regardless of good or evil, a " basic soul " went to Yomi via the root country (*ne no kuni*), while another remained on earth for a long period and then entered the " world of the concealed and mysterious."[2] But others (such as Yano Harumichi in his *Yaso no kumade* and Kubo Sueshige in his *Itsu no kuchitsuge*) distinguished separate worlds within " the concealed world ": a Kami world (*shinkai*), a sylph world (*senkai*), and a ghost world (*yōkikai*). The Kami world belonged to the Plain of High Heaven and was under the control of the correct Kami. The ghost world belonged to Yomi and was a place where Buddhas and ghosts resided. Good souls went to the former and evil ones to the latter. Still other writers (such as Gonda Naosuke in his *Nagoshinoya ikō*, or Extant Manuscripts of Naosuke) took a slightly different line, maintaining that good persons went to a Kami world and the bad to a demon world (*makai*), but the very good went to the Plain of High Heaven and the very bad to Yomi. In this way different men had their own views about the relationship between the Plain of High Heaven, Yomi, and

---

1) Yoshika's view, however, held that the expression "Kami-rising" (*kamuagari*) —applied to noble persons in the Shinto classics—was an honorific, while the expression "going to Yomi"—used for subjects and commoners—was humble. Therefore, the terms were not taken literally. Arakida Hisaoi [1746–1804] had already pointed out, in his *Nihongi uta no kai* (Interpretation of the *Nihongi* Songs), that both views concerning the destination of souls after death—whether they ascended to heaven or went to Yomi—existed in antiquity; and Ban Nobutomo [1775–1846] later made the same point. Mutobe Yoshika's argument was mainly directed against what had been written by Ban Nobutomo in his *Takahashi ujibumi kōchū* (Commentary on the 'Document of the Takahashi Clan'). [An historical account said to have been writen in about 789 by an official of the Imperial Household Ministry.]

2) [This is similar to an early Chinese belief that man was endowed with two souls: a spiritual soul (*hun*) that returned to the sky, and an animal soul (*p'o*) that returned to the ground.]

the "concealed world." But while they differed from each other, they did not identify the essence of the concealed and mysterious world as simply a polluted underground world. They thought of it as being parallel, but superior, to this world and as a world which, in comparison to this temporary world of preparation, was true and permanent. At the same time they always considered the superior quality of that concealed and mysterious world in this-worldly terms. (For example, in describing conditions in the invisible world, men such as Gonda Naosuke said that they were far superior to those of the visible world. Everything there was clean and beautiful: there was no darkness like the nights in this world, no dampness when it rained, no coldness when clothes were not worn, no hunger when food was not eaten; whatever one thought of occurred; whatever one desired was provided; and there was no physical strain when one walked far or climbed high. The freedom of such a world was surely no different from conditions in the Kami age.) Such views were an elaboration of Hirata Atsutane's beliefs.

On the other hand, as the world of the concealed and the mysterious began to acquire a superiority over the world of the living, the divinity of Ō-kuni-nushi no Kami, who presided over the concealed and mysterious world, came to be essentially higher than that of the this-worldly Kami. Grace (*onrai*) of the creative spirit (*musubi*) or divine compassion (*mi-utsukushimi*), that is, Benevolence and Compassion, became the main purpose of "concealed rule" and were thought of in contradistinction to the virtues of *loyalty and sincerity* in men of the mortal world. And so there was a tendency for the Kami of the concealed world to become the principal object of religious belief with these men, and for the divine significance of the visible Kami to remain theoretically undeveloped.

Finally, a scholar in this group who deserves special attention because of the thoroughness and clarity of his thought is *Suzuki Masayuki,* the author of *Tsukisakaki* (Sacred Cleyera Tree). Concerning the relationship between the concealed and the visible he held, first of all, that all creatures of Heaven and on earth were born in the concealed world and then brought to perfection in the visible. In comparing Kami with men, he said that the activity of Kami was concealed and the actions of men were visible. As to the Kami themselves, their actions were manifest and their minds concealed. And in comparing mind with soul, the former was visible and the latter concealed. Among men, too, there was the same [dualism] in everything. Thus he explained all creation in terms of a *dualistic relationship* between the concealed and the visible — the noumenon was concealed and the phenomenon was visible. He held that the assignment of exclusive control over concealed matters to Ō-kuni nushi no Kami was an erroneous view dating from Norinaga. The deity in charge of concealed matters was none other than the supreme master of creation: *Ame no Mi-naka-nushi no Kami* (The Kami Master of the Center of Heaven) who had existed in space since before the creation of Heaven and earth. All things — beginning with the two original Kami: Taka-mi-musubi no Kami (The High Sacred Creating Kami) and Kami-musubi no Kami (The Sacred Creating Kami) — were the divine work of this Kami, but his works were not referred to in the ancient classics because he entrusted visible matters to the two Creating Kami and he himself handled concealed matters. In discussing souls, Masayuki separated mind from soul. The mind lived and died in the visible world, and the soul was indestructible in the concealed. The mind was a product of the soul, and the soul was *nothing but Kami*. The spirituality of the soul was truly inscrutable: one wondered whether it had form, and it seemed to have none; one wondered whether it had no form, and found that it definitely had one. As to *birth*, he thought of the souls of the father and mother as coalescing, and through a secret function of the souls, bringing about the visible result, the producing of a body; while *death* resulted from the cessation of the soul's operation followed by the degeneration of form. As to *where the soul went* after death, like Hirata Atsutane, he recognized Heaven and Yomi as completely *separate* from the concealed world, and equated heaven with the sun and Yomi with the moon. Heaven he thought of as a fiery land produced by the mysterious actions of the two Creator Kami, as the place where the descendants of the various Kami, beginning with the Heavenly Kami, handled the administration of creation — it was the central land for the creation of all lands in all ages. Yomi he depicted as the land of the polluted moon, the place where evil Kami gathered. Then he explained that the souls of men, after death, went to Heaven or Yomi, depending on whether they were good or bad. He maintained that the interpretations of Norinaga and Atsutane had not been complete and were at variance with ancient tradition. He found evidence in the ancient traditions for the existence of three types of souls: those that stayed in this world; those that went to and from Heaven dispensing good fortune; and those that went back and forth between this world and Yomi dispensing bad fortune. In this way the world of the concealed and mysterious, in Masayuki's thought, was *completely* separated from the destination of souls and was conceived of as a divine world existence, in contradistinction to the phenomenal world. Ame no Mi-naka-nushi no Kami, as the master of the concealed world, was thought of as *the highest Kami* who controlled the visible world as well.

These scholars also made several not-insignificant contributions through their philological research in the ancient classics. When they interpreted the Shinto classics, they did not neglect to verify their theories on the basis of specific legends. For example, in his *Michi no hitokoto* (A Word about the Way) Mutobe Yoshika took issue with Tachibana Moribe's critical attitude and went so far as to say that Moribe had made his interpretations carelessly by picking over the revered legends of antiquity for whatever suited his sly purpose. Moreover, when we consider this issue against the background of their outlook on Shinto, we find that the philological spirit of the revered Norinaga was being respected only *formally,* and that their interpretations were in each case dictated by the requirements of their thought — limited of course by the ancient traditions. As Motoori Ōhira [1756–1833] pointed out in the supplement to his *Kogaku yō* (Essentials of Ancient Learning), from the point of view of Norinaga's scholarship, such things as the cosmogony of the *Sandaikō* (Three Great Ideas) [by Hattori Nakatsune] and the eschatology of the *Tama no mihashira* (True Pillar of the Soul) [by Hirata Atsutane] were superfluous. This trend was especially strong in their development of creation theories and in their exposition of a physics in imitation of Dutch Learning (*rangagu*). Satō Nobuhiro and Nonoguchi Takamasa even described the Shinto classics as "*the original books of physics*" — as in Takamasa's *Shinkō shinshaku* (New Interpretations of the True Message). With these men we even see a reappearance of medieval distortions and an arrival, unknowingly and unconsciously, at positions that were contrary to the original spirit of Ancient Learning. But it should be noted that the underlying cause of this trend actually lay within the scholarship of Norinaga himself; that is, it lay within *the psychological abnormality of equating objective research with subjective faith,* in which Norinaga could maintain a *psychological balance* because of his believing attitude, but which gradually broke down with Atsutane, who was more clearly a founder of a sect of Shinto. To put it objectively, it lay in Norinaga's very concept of *the Way which is not a Way* and *the classic which is not a classic.*[1]

7

In essence, Norinaga's simple and clear concept of Yomi — based upon ancient tradition — gradually took on theological significance and eventually developed into otherworldly thought that was associated with retributive ideas. Moreover, the foregoing development which created an intellectual content involving a noumenal and Kami world

---

1) [See p. 178 above.]

went beyond the possibilities of philological research; though from another point of view, it was a development of Shinto thought within philological limitations. In the development there was some stimulation and influence from Indian religion and other foreign ideologies. ("Indian religion" is not the Hinduism of today, but a generic term including Brahmanism and Buddhism. It is used later on in this paper in the same sense.) But since it was rooted in the purified consciousness of Ancient Learning which rose in a spirit of liberation from Buddho-Confucian admixtures, it was certainly not pure imitation. The fact that whenever there were similarities in their opinions with Indian or other foreign thought, these scholars normally argued that they were transmitting a fragment of Japanese tradition, bespeaks — from one point of view — a conviction on their part that their ideas were more or less spontaneous. In this sense, their views of the concealed and mysterious had a certain *vitality* as both theological thought and religious belief. Thought about "the concealed and the mysterious" was rather like an *illegitimate child* of Tokugawa-era philology. Although not legitimate, it was real.

I am inclined to think that the thought process that has been dealt with here probably is, to some extent, a universal phenomenon common to all early stages of religious history. I can recognize one parallel in the development of psyche and afterworld beliefs in ancient Greece, a parallel which I feel is rather significant.

In ancient Greece materialist views prevailed, from the beginning, over spiritual life. Before the time of Plato there was no concept in philosophy, let alone in general religious consciousness, of a spirit, in the strict sense, which was independent of the body. But already there were ideas which admitted of *a twofold life,* a life of the body and a life of the mind; and with the development of these ideas there arose eventually a clear concept of "spirit." This was the concept, held by most Greeks, of a tiny ethereal psyche (or daemon) — that is, a soul which existed apart from the body. The idea of a secret and dark world where the psyche went to dwell — sometimes conceived of as underground, and sometimes as an aerial existence — as well as the idea that men lived on after entering this world after death and exerted an influence on the mortal world — are all thoughts seen in Shintoism. This afterworld was the Hades of Homer and was nothing more or less than Yomi. But in Homer there was as yet no eschatological conception — all men were thought to go to Hades regardless of what good and bad actions they had committed in life. It was not until the Eleusinian mysteries in the 7th century B.C., that the problem of eschatology appeared, and retribution in the two worlds of Eysium and Tartarus after death was preached. This development resembles the mutation of the concept of the concealed and the mysterious that took place from Norinaga to Atsutane and his followers. Then with further development the cult of Dionysius — with Orphic and Pythagorean thoughts — became popular in Greece in the last half of the 7th century B.C. These became fused with the eschatological outlook of the Eleusian cult and transformed the old ideas of the psyche and afterworld. Psyche was no longer a reflection of the self, an after ego, but a *higher* self; and the afterworld was not simply a reflection of this world, but *a transcendent world.* After death the psyche now entered the transcendent world to receive eternal life. Atsutane and the scholars who followed him had a comparable idea in regarding the afterworld as the " true world." And also comparable to the Greek conception of the moral world as an episode of the external world were the ideas of a *temporary world* and a *place for testing* held by Atsutane and his successors. The idea of transmigration, seen in Pythagoras, was not definitely approved by Hirata and his followers, who had learned about it from their study of " Indian religion "; but they did show a rather sympathetic attitude. Just as Greek eschatological thought did not emerge from the pure worship of the Olympian gods, but from the Egyptian beliefs in Demeter and Dionysius, so in Shinto the eschatological thought of Atsutane was influenced, through the interpretations of Kaneyoshi's *Nihon shoki sanso,* by Indian thought.

On the other hand, such highly developed ideas as a "spirit" that was *directly opposed* to the body and an afterworld *directly opposed* to the moral world — which arose from ecstatic states produced by drunkenness and esceticism among the devotees of Dionysus as well as in Orphism and Pythagoreanism — were never attained by Shintoists. And, likewise, the Shintoists were, of course, completely ignorant of such philosophical concepts as the pantheism which Xenophanes, in a separate intellectual development, added to the above ideas and which contained the religious idea of an afterworld. The thought of these Shintoists was far removed from any perception of a spiritual world. The principal cause for this was that there was no *philosophy* in these men. In individual theories, where Shintoists of the Hirata School applied their knowledge of Dutch Learning, there are many elements reminiscent of the physical theories of ancient Greek philosophers. It excites a certain interest to note that in their writings (as astrologers, of course) the name of Pythagoras has been handed down. But most of these theories are distortions of passages in the Shinto classics based on Western physical theories, and not original philosophy. The second cause [of this lack of attention to the spirit] is that they could never disassociate their thought from this world. Consequently, the ascetic thought in "Indian religion" — comparable to the Pythagorean teachings in the history of ancient Greek thought — was, for them, simply *knowledge* and never became a sustenance for their ideas about the concealed and mysterious. Actually it was usual for them to accentuate the very opposite of ascetic thought as the principal characteristic of their Shintoism. Being consistently absorbed in this worldly thought — an interest they shared with the ancient Greeks — they could not but think of the blessings of the concealed and mysterious world as being, in the final analysis, a reflection of this-worldly blessings. Their ideal descriptions of this-worldly happenings for the concealed world are to be understood *literally*. The world of the concealed and mysterious became for them a higher world morally, but it could not become a higher world philosophically.

Their creation of the concept of an external world from the concealed and mysterious was not a qualitative transformation as in the case of the Greeks. But if among these Shinto scholars there was even a slight tendency toward this sort of development, it deserves close attention. If we detect in Moribe a tendency to see a *different* kind of world that is not this-worldly, based on theories about Yomi but free of eschatology, it is actually in Suzuki Masayuki that we find the beginnings of a transformation which deserves further attention. Moribe never got beyond the materialistic conception of a " fragrantly enveloping ether" without form or content. But Masayuki's idea of the concealed, together with his conception of the soul as distinct from the mind and identified with Kami, and his recognition of an absolute Kami in Ame no Mi-naka-nushi, constitute something much more philosophical and spiritual. His reinterpretation of the theory of Heaven and Yomi as destinations for souls bears a resemblance to Plato's view of Hades and Elysium (as a world beyond the stars), in which there were vestiges of the Eleusinian cult. I have been in touch with [the works of] Inō Hidenori who was born in the Shimofusa area. He died in 1871 when he was only 35.[1] We do not know much about his life; and not many of the books he wrote are extant. It is regrettable that more cannot be said here about this noteworthy scholar.

One other important quality that runs through the thought of these Restoration Shintoists is noteworthy: *patriotic faith* centered on the state and in the " fatherland Kami." This faith, together with the concept of *blessing*, which stemmed from their Buddhist faith, as well as feelings of *awe and respect*, which accompanied their ideas of the concealed world, formed an important ingredient of their belief, and in particular, made up the *psychological core* of their thought as a whole. It began with the formation, under the stimulus of

---

1) [This statement does not tally with the birth and death dates of Inō Hidenori given in either the *Dai jinmei jiten* or the *Nihon rekishi daijiten*: 1805–1877.]

current events, of an ever more marked *national self consciousness* after the emergence of Ancient Learning within National Learning, and in later times became an ever more powerful and exciting conviction. It was their firm belief that the ancient traditions of Japan were the oldest and purest in the world, that Japan — with such ancient traditions and a glorious history — was destined, having the best people in the universe, to develop more and more and eventually to become the universal country. But it should be noted that the thoughts of these scholars, particularly those within the Dutch group of the Hirata School (see, for example, the *Michi no hitokoto* of Mutobe Yoshika), were certainly not perversely anti-foreign. Their nationalism not only included respect for the past, but was something very *progressive*. If we assume that Xenophanes came to have doubts about the gods of his fatherland after witnessing the decline of his country, and eventually found an asylum for his faith not in Homer's world of anthropomorphic and conceptualized deities but in an absolute afterworld, a world of an unchanging and everlasting god, then we must admit that there was good reason for the this-worldliness of the ideas of the concealed and mysterious held by these Shinto scholars, for they lived at the beginning of a new national awakening in Japan at the close of the Tokugawa Era and were representative figures of " revere-the-Emperor " thought, which motivated this awakening.

July, 1915

Notes

(1) The idea of "concealed sound" (*yūon*) is of interest as a by-product of the concept of the "concealed and mysterious," which we find in Restoration Shinto. Having studied under Hori Hidenari [1819–1887], and carrying on Hirata Atsutane's theory of "creation phonetics" as set forth in his *Koshi honji kyō* (Canon of the Original Words in Ancient History), Ochiai Naobumi [1840–1891] attempted to present an original view and explained "concealed sound" (as learned from Hidenari) in his book *Kojiki betsuden* (Another Commentary on the *Kojiki*) —the manuscript has a preface by

Hori Hidenari dated the 2nd month of 1864. In a chapter on "The Concealed Sounds: *a, i, u, e,* and *o*" he writes: "The term 'concealed sound' refers to what are popularly called the final vowels of syllables, that is, to the prolongation of vowels as when syllables like *ka, ki, sa, shi* are pronounced *kaa, kii, saa, shii*. The popular view that such prolongations are the manifest sounds *a, i, u, e, o* is mistaken. Even these manifest sounds, when they are prolonged into *aa, ii, uu, ee, oo,* cease to be manifest and revert to concealed sounds. (This is the same principle by which human life of the manifest is short and reverts quickly to the concealed, while the Kami life of the concealed is long. The fifty manifest sounds are like the human body, and the five concealed sounds like the human soul. Consequently, there is not a single one of the fifty manifest sounds which does not have a concealed sound within it.) Therefore, if we concentrate, we can always hear two sounds in every syllable—such as *aa* for *a*. The concealed sounds are what Master Nonoguchi referred to as *a, i, u, e, o*. Before the creation of Heaven and earth, they neither "were" nor "were not," but pervaded the great void omnipresently. The creative Kami blended the elements of the five ethers with the fifty elements and created the celestial bodies as well as the globe and all things on it. That is why, of all the sounds, the concealed sounds are most notable."

(2) This article—written earlier than any other article in this volume—was almost the first one I ever wrote, and it therefore includes several points which as a result of subsequent research, could have been enlarged upon. In this connection, I would like to refer the reader particularly to the next article in this volume (on Hirata Atsutane), to the next two, and to the preceding one on Tachibana Moribe.[1] I hope that the reader will take the trouble to read them.

---

1) [The four recommended articles are: (1) *Hirata Atsutane no shingaku ni okeru Yasokyō no eikyō* (Christian Influence on the Theology of Hirata Atsutane), *Zōtei Nihon shisōshi kenkyū*, 321–36; (2) *Nanri Yūrin no shintō shisō* (Shinto Thought of Nanri Yūrin), *ibid.,* 337–65; (3) *Nōson no unda ichi kokugakusha Suzuki Masayuki* (Suzuki Masayuki, a National Learning Scholar who was produced by an Agricultural Village), *ibid.,* 366–90; and (4) *Tachibana Moribe no gakusetsu* (Theories of Tachibana Moribe), *ibid.,* 275–87.]

Chapter VI

Hirata Shinto and the Ideological Control of the Meiji Restoration — Down to the Time of the Official Recognition of Religious Freedom[1]

Of course there was more than one facet to the intellectual motivation for the Meiji restoration of Imperial rule, but National Learning — and especially Hirata Learning — was without doubt the most important. Of special importance was the direct and indirect participation in the intellectual movements of the new period — sometimes through recommendations and sometimes by oral presentation — of those followers who gathered around Hirata Kanetane [1799–1880] in Kyoto during the preparatory period beginning in the early 1860's. A well-known example of such activity was that of Tamamatsu Misao [1810–1872], a student of Ōkuni Takamasa [1792–1871] who assisted Iwakura Tomomi in various ways and who advocated the restoration of Jimmu's Imperial rule. In the 7th month of 1867, Hirata Kanetane was also asked by the Iwakura group for his views about the current situation; and in the secret memorial which he submitted he recommended, first of all, the revival of the Department of Shinto Affairs (*jingikan*). As to the pressing problem of Buddhism, he wrote that the government should avoid direct attacks and should, instead, work toward the self-destruction of Buddhism by taking such steps as removing it from the ceremonies of the Imperial Court. In the 12th month of the same year, a policy of " unity of worship and administration " (*saisei ittchi*), centered on Shintoism, was set forth in detail in Yano

---

1) [First published in *Tetsugaku oyobi shūkyō to sono rekishi* (Philosophy and Religion, and their History) in September of 1938 and included in *Zoku Nihon shisō shi kenkyū*, 333–56.]

Harumichi's [1823–1887] *Kenkin sengo*. In this same month the restoration of Imperial rule was proclaimed; and in the second month of 1868 the Office of Shinto Affairs (*jingi jimukyoku*) was established. A proclamation issued by the Council of State (*dajōkan*) on the 13th day of the 3rd month stated:

> Whereas the restoration of Imperial rule is founded upon the achievements initiated by Emperor Jimmu, and whereas the nation is being restored to a polity of general renewal and unity of worship and administration, it is ordered that, first of all, the Department of Shinto Affairs shall be revived, and further that rites and sacrifices shall thereafter be performed.

In a communication from the Office of Shinto Affairs to the Shinto shrines of the country, it was stated: "Whereas at present Imperial rule is being restored, and the nation cleansed of old abuses, it is ordered that at large and small shrines in the various provinces those 'intendants' who wear Buddhist garb, and those persons called 'shrine monks' and the like, shall return to secular life." Here we see already the adoption of a new indoctrination policy in which Buddhism is replaced by Shintoism as the state religion. The Charter Oath, in which the policies of the "renovation" were declared, was actually issued on the day following the above-mentioned proclamation of the Council of State. At last, therefore, we have "Restoration Shinto prescribed as the religion of the Imperial Country." The separation of Shinto and Buddhism led to the development of a movement to "abolish Buddhism and destroy the Buddhist icons." In July of the following year (1869), after the Office of Shinto Affairs had been replaced by the Department of Shinto Affairs, the Board of Shinto Missionaries (*senkyō-shi*) was established and attached to the Department of Shinto Affairs (*jingikan*). Here we have the beginning of the period of the Department (or Ministry) of Shinto Affairs — and the Board of Shinto Missionaries — that continued on until March of 1872.

This was the first period of early-Meiji Shinto indoctrination, and a flourishing one.

The so-called Board of Shinto Missionaries was established for the principal purpose of indoctrinating Christians, who were showing signs of becoming active again in the Kyushu area. Through this effort the government planned, along with abolishing Buddhism, to check the spread of Christianity. For this purpose the Great Teaching (*daikyō*) or the Great Way of Kami (*Kannagara no daidō*) was propagated. First, the Imperial Edict establishing the Pacifying Festival (*chinsai*) was issued on the 3rd day of the 1st month of 1870; and this was followed by an Imperial proclamation, and then an Imperial Edict, on the propagation of the Great Teaching. Shinto missionary offices were set up in the capital and in local areas, particularly at Nagasaki. The persons responsible for affairs at these offices were principally Hirata Shintoists under Fukuda Bisei [1831–1907], Vice Minister of Shinto Affairs and Assistant Director of the Board of Shinto Missionaries. Their teachings were those of Hirata Shinto.

But when the Ministry of Shinto Affairs (it was changed from a Department to a Ministry in August of 1871) was abolished in March of 1872, the Board of Shinto Missionaries was also abolished. With this development we enter the second period of indoctrination — lasting until May of 1875 — which might be called the period of the Ministry of Religion (*kyōbushō*), Office of Religious Instruction (*kyōdōshoku*), and the Great Teaching Institute (*daikyō-in*). The difference between this period and the earlier one was that the Buddhist priests, who had been excluded from the indoctrination of the Christians during the first period, now participated with the Shintoists in the government's indoctrination program; so that now the Board of Shinto Missionaries became the Office of Religious Instruction. These changes were made because the Buddhists would not put up with being excluded from their old work of indoctrinating the people, and also the Shinto missionary program had not really been effective. There were continuous activities and petitions by the Buddhists; and this could not be disregarded by the authorities. Nevertheless, the Shinto orientation of the Great Teaching could, of course, not be altered by these developments, and so it became necessary to set up guiding principles for an instruction that was to be carried out by both Shintoists and Buddhists all over the country. Consequently, the Ministry of Religion formulated the Three Principles of Instruction (*sanjō kyōken*), proclaimed on April 28, 1872:

Principle 1. Compliance with the spirit of reverence for Kami and love of country.

Principle 2. Clarification of 'the principle of Heaven and the Way of man.'

Principle 3. Exalting the Emperor and obeying the Imperial Court.

Shinto and Buddhist priests were appointed assistant Instructor-Rectifiers (*kyōsei*) and placed in charge of Offices of Religious Instruction. Not only Konoe Tadafusa [1838–1873], Director of Rites of the Ise Shrine, and Senge Takatomi [1845–1917], Great Shrine Magistrate (*daigūji*) of Izumo, but as many as twenty-one Buddhist priests were selected for appointments as Instructor-Rectifiers, including Kōson of the Hongan-ji and Kōshō of the Eastern Hongan-ji. But at this time the Buddhists proposed that they should set up a special organ for training the officials of Religious Instruction of their own sects. Representatives of each Buddhist sect petitioned for this right, and the request was granted. In February of 1873 the proposal was acted upon. However, the authorities included Shinto priests as well as Buddhists and made the new organ an educational institution for all the officials of Religious Instruction. Consequently, the organ was essentially Shinto. It was called the Great Teaching Institute (*daikyōin*) and was first set up in Kōjimachi of Tokyo, but later moved to the Zōjō-ji temple in Shiba of Tokyo. Middle Teaching Institutes (*chūkyō-in*) and Small Teaching Institutes (*shōkyō-in*) were set up locally. Certain shrines and temples were recognized as Small Teaching Institutes.

HIRATA SHINTO AND THE IDEOLOGICAL CONTROL

The "eleven themes" and the "seventeen themes" were drawn up for the training of the officials of Religious Instruction and, at the same time, to provide standard topics for sermons. The "eleven themes," proclaimed by the Ministry of Shinto Affairs, embodied the tenets of Hirata Shinto:

(1) Kami virtue and Imperial favor;
(2) Immortality of the human soul;
(3) Creativity of the Heavenly Kami;
(4) Difference between the worlds of the visible and the concealed;
(5) Love of country;
(6) Kami worship;
(7) Pacification of souls;
(8) Lord and vassal;
(9) Father and son;
(10) Husband and wife; and
(11) Great Purification.

The "seventeen themes" established by the Great Teaching Institute were:

(1) Imperial Country and Nation Body;
(2) Renewal of Imperial rule;
(3) Immutability of the Way;
(4) Adjusting organizations to the situation of the day;
(5) Difference between man and animals;
(6) The necessity to teach;
(7) The necessity to learn;
(8) Intercourse with foreign countries;
(9) Rights and duties;
(10) The use of minds and bodies;
(11) Various types of political institutions;
(12) Civilization and enlightenment;
(13) Development of law;
(14) National and civil law;

(15) Rich nation, strong army;
(16) Taxation, and labor levies; and
(17) Production and control of goods.

These themes encompassed the "civilization and enlightenment" (*bunmei kaika*) knowledge of that day; and it should be noted that absolutely no Buddhism was included.

The Buddhist priests, in applying themselves to instruction in accordance with the Three Principles of Instruction and the two sets of themes, could not but attempt to harmonize their own beliefs with Shinto by resorting to a "manifestation of the original Buddhas" type of Shinto-Buddhist fusion, or by striving to revive the Shinto of Prince Shōtoku, or by playing up the concept of the "fundamentality of the king's law in secular affairs."[1] Nevertheless, it was natural that they should have been deeply pained by having to expound on "reverence for Kami," with the service of Buddha placed in a secondary position. Actually no conformity between the sermons of the Buddhists and those of the Shintoists could be detected, and because of this the priests were subjected to popular ridicule by contemporaries. Therefore, quite early the view was voiced by the powerful Shin Sect that they should be freed of Shinto domination and permitted to apply themselves independently to the work of indoctrination. Such views led to the Great Teaching secession movement which had already begun to develop late in 1872. Finally, in May of 1875, when the time was ripe, joint propagation by the Shintoists and Buddhists was discontinued. This marks the end of the second period. It also marks roughly the end of the policy of Shinto indoctrination adopted in 1868.

In the third period there was, with the abolition of the Great Teaching Institute, independent propagation by the various Buddhist sects. Within the highly fragmented Shinto world obstructions to control began to emerge. While associated originally with Hirata

---

1) [Buddhist equivalent of "Render unto Caesar that which is Caesar's."]

Shinto, there was the separate [Hirata] Kanetane School, the Ōkuni [Takamasa] School, and the Great Shrine [of Izumo] School — also the Ise School. In addition, Shinto included the Kurozumi Sect and other founder-sects. Although the Office of Shinto Affairs (*Shintō jimu kyoku*), accompanied by the Shinto Great Teaching Institute (*Shintō daikyō-in*), had been established, and various people were appointed to head the sections — first three and then four — of the Shinto Office of Religious Instruction, the objectives were not fully realized. Beginning with the Kurozumi and Shūsei sects, one founder-sect after another acquired its independence. In the meantime the Ministry of Religion was abolished, the Office of Shinto Affairs was transferred to the Ministry of Home Affairs (January, 1877), and the practice of Shinto priests serving as officials of Religious Instruction was discontinued (January, 1882). In 1888 the Tenrikyō church was founded — it became an independent sect in 1908. Thus this policy of indoctrination was gradually liquidated.

The history of the above three periods, when seen from the point of view of the original plan for Shinto control, was nothing but a gradual progression to failure — in short, it can only be termed a history of defeat. The admission of Buddhist officials of Religious Instruction which aimed — with a thorough-going anti-Buddhism — at a Shinto-centered indoctrination constituted the first compromise. Even though the first of the Three Principles of Instruction was "reverence for Kami," and even though there were no Buddhist elements in the two sets of themes, the fact that the program had to rely so early on Buddhism for indoctrinational strength indicated that the original ideal could not be upheld. The later secession of various Buddhist sects certainly shook the foundations of control; and the separatist movement within Shintoism, which was even a greater blow, led finally to a division between Founder Shinto and Shrine-Shinto.

Why was it that Shinto indoctrination, in spite of its association with the great reform movement known as the "Restoration of Imperial rule," ended so soon? There were various internal and external reasons. The first external reason is that this indoctrination policy was not at all compatible with the requisites of national strength — requisites which were at that time epitomized in the slogan "civilization and enlightenment." This can be seen in the views of Fukuzawa Yukichi [1834–1901], a representative scholar of the enlightenment at that time, particularly in his *Bunmei ron no gairyaku* (Outline of Civilization Theory) — written in 1875, shortly before the prohibition, by the Ministry of Religion, against joint propagation by Buddhists and Shintoists, and published in the following year. The gist of this book is that Japan, from the point of view of civilization, does not measure up to the West, and that the Japanese had better plan, in the face of this new trend, to perfect national independence by learning about Western civilization. He explained the need to "eliminate infatuation with the shackles of ancient tradition" and by throwing off these shackles "to advance to a condition of emotional and intellectual vigor, to uphold national prestige through the intellectual power of the whole country, and to establish the foundations of the Nation Body." Western civilization was "the one thing that will strengthen our Nation Body and further glorify our Imperial line." Having taken the position that "Japan should definitely adopt Western civilization," he said that Shintoism — like Confucianism and Christianity — was not at all adequate for sustaining the human heart. Of Shinto in particular he maintained that one could hardly credit it with having yet developed a doctrinal structure:

> Although we occasionally hear the word 'Shinto' these days, it is only an insignificant movement trying to make headway by taking advantage of the influence of the Imperial Family at the time of the government's reforms. Being only a temporary, fortuitous thing, it should not be recognized as having an established doctrine.

Although Fukuzawa displayed the same un-religious attitude toward all faiths, his espousal of Western civilization may be said to have increased respect for Christianity, or at least to have contributed to the correction of the view that it was a perverted faith. On the other hand, he was contemptuous of Shinto. Such an attitude definitely reflected the spirit of the times, when the national policy was to " open the country" (*kaikoku*). The policy of Shinto indoctrination was hardly compatible with these currents.

The second important reason for the failure of the policy of Shinto indoctrination was the immaturity of Shinto. Even in such a situation, if there had been greater doctrinal and religious maturity in Shinto, most likely the policy of ideological control would not have failed so completely and quickly. The Hirata Shinto had developed originally out of Motoori's Ancient-Learning Shinto, and it was moving toward the formulation of a theology. Among the adherents of Hirata Shinto there were various efforts; and some notable development was made in individual speculation. But these were immature efforts. This was particularly true of those made by Hirata Atsutane. That is, he was very strong in his spirit of Emperorism, and in his fervor for the restoration of Imperial rule; but because of an immaturity of religious thought he necessarily failed to establish full control over Shinto itself — which has an essentially complex historical make-up — much less to establish absolute control over foreign, or of course Buddhist, beliefs. This immaturity was an advantage for the Buddhists as well as a cause of dissension within Shintoism itself.

I would like to consider three areas of this dissension. First, there was the doctrinal question about Creator Kami in the Age-of-Kami traditions. At the beginning of the Age-of-Kami books, in both the *Kojiki* and the *Nihongi*, there are myths about the beginnings of Heaven and earth. Interpreting these myths in accordance with the *Kojiki* version, Motoori read the introductory phrase as *ametsuchi no hajime no toki* (at the time of the beginning of Heaven and earth); and he ventured to interpret this phrase as meaning that Ame no Mi-naka-nushi no Kami and the two Kami under him had existed, before Heaven and earth, as Creator Kami. This interpretation — which of course had not yet been fully grounded by Motoori in a textual criticism of the *Kojiki* — was developed theologically by Hirata. In the *Koshi seibun* (A Composition of Ancient History) he stated that these three Kami had existed before "the birth of Heaven and earth" and that they had created Heaven and earth. Of course Hirata's view was accepted after the Department of Shinto Affairs was set up in 1869. Thus the first article of the five-article "Regulations on the Compilation of Religious Books," issued by the Great Teaching Institute in July of 1873, reads:

> That portion of the *Kojiki* dealing with the first seven generations of Kami, and the Age-of-Kami book of the *Nihongi* down to the phrase: "Kami were born in Heaven and earth", enable us to understand clearly the Kami Principle of the creation of Heaven and earth and the evolution of the myriad things. Since they are the foundation stones of the fundamental doctrine of the Imperial Way, not one word is to be deleted from, or added to, those passages.[1]

This implied that the first three Kami, beginning with Ame no Minaka-nushi no Kami, were the creators of Heaven and earth and were responsible for the evolution of the myriad things. And such works as *Shinkyō yōshi ryakkai* (Brief Explanation of the Essentials of Kami Doctrine) written jointly by Konoe Tadafusa and Senge Takatomi and published in 1873, and the *Sanjō taii* (Outline of the Meaning of the Three Principles of Instruction) written by Yano Harumichi and published in 1875, were inherited from — with respect to their conception of Kami as rulers and creators — Hirata theology. But on this point such writings were quickly attacked by the Buddhists, for

---

[1] Cited in Tokushige Asakichi: *Ishin seiji shūkyō shi kenkyū* (Study of the Political and Religious History of the Restoration), published in February of 1935.

the Buddhists taught that the life of Heaven and earth was fundamentally a matter of karma, and therefore the Shinto creation doctrine was heresy. They maintained that the *Kojiki* text, which the Shintoists took as their authority, was obscure from the beginning. The Buddhists felt that such creation doctrines had really begun with their enemy, Hirata Atsutane, who had spouted violent anti-Buddhist words; and they also felt that these doctrines clearly smacked of Christianity, a heretical faith.

The Christian views of Hirata are scattered throughout such writings as *Tama no mihashira* (True Pillar of the Soul), the *Kodō taii* (Outline of the Ancient Way), and the *Ibuki oroshi* (Wind of Atsutane). Because he referred to Adam and Eve and went along with the Copernican theory, he was charged with "uniting Kami and the barbarians." He was also severly criticized for his creation doctrine. The more severe attacks on Hirata are found in : (1) "Questions and Answers on Identifying Heresy" (*Ketsuja mondō*) in the first issue of *Kōdō sōsho* (Collection of Studies on the Way) (1870); (2) *Shingaku benkō* (Definition of Kami Learning) by Sasaki Yūchō, printed in 1870 and issued in 1874; (3) *Jūichi kendai roku hyō* (Criticism of the Eleven Themes) printed in 1874, by Sasaki Yūchō; (4) *Wayō shinden* (Divine Myths in Japan and the West) of 1875, also by Sasaki; and (5) *Sanjō bengi* (Analysis of the Three Principles of Instruction) by Shimaji Mokurai included in the *Hōshi sōdan* (1874–75).

Among these Sasaki Yūchō argued as follows: In reading the opening phrase of the *Kojiki,* 天地初發之時, as *ametsuchi hajime no toki* (in the beginning of Heaven and earth), Motoori avoided the meaning "creation," but the interpretation of 發 as "beginning" was hardly correct. That this word simply meant "parting" was proved by a phrase in the preface to the *Kojiki* which reads: "the Heaven and earth first parted and the three Kami initiated creation." Likewise, in the oracle of the Moon Kami, recorded in the Emperor Kenzō section of the *Nihongi,* there is the phrase that Taka-mi-musubi no

Kami "molded Heaven and earth." This, according to Sasaki, should be understood simply as "molding and hardening" and did not support the Shinto assertion that Heaven and earth were created. To have construed such passages to mean that Kami existed before Heaven and earth came into being and then created Heaven and earth was, in short, a misconception which Hirata inherited from Motoori and allowed to grow as a result of being influenced by Christianity. It was definitely not the true meaning of the ancient traditions. The traditions of Japan did not reveal a first creation by a creator, but rather a cycle of birth resulting from prior causes, as taught in Buddhism. Such was Sasaki's line of attack.

We cannot yet definitely deny the validity of the Motoori view, based on the opening phrases of the *Kojiki,* that there was here something different from the Chinese-like views of creation. But even if ideas about a Creator Kami had been held by the ancient Japanese, we have to admit that they were as yet quite nebulous. Consequently, there is plenty of room for skepticism about such interpretations. Attacks that took advantage of this situation as well as those which were pressed in terms of "uniting Kami and barbarians," really hit home. Thus it can not be denied that the Shintoists were shaken. According to the *Criticism of the Eleven Themes,* the word "Heaven" was purposely omitted in the proclamation issued by the Great Teaching Institute in July of 1873, at the time of the festival of the four Kami (the three Creator Kami and the Sun Goddess). The statement concerning Kami creation read "creating the great earth", instead of "creating Heaven and earth." Also, the first (1873) edition of the *Sanjō engi* (Expatiation on the Three Principles of Instruction) by Tanaka Yoritsune [1836–1897] carried the words "molding Heaven and earth," but in the second edition these were deleted and the preface contained the following: "The expression 'Izanagi and Izanami, great Kami who are Heavenly ancestors and creators' shows that the word 'creation' was applied to these two Kami who are associated principally with earth." In short, this indicates that in the creation theology of Hirata Shinto — which was advancing even as far as Watanabe Ikarimaro's[1] position that "the doctrine of the true lord of Heaven means the doctrine of Ame no Mi-naka-nushi no Kami" — it was impossible to maintain internal controls. This was because of the immaturity of their theology, which was constricted by studies of the ancient classics.

The second point of attack was on the conception of the afterworld, another important aspect of Hirata Shinto. It is in thought about the "concealed and the mysterious" that the afterworld teachings of Hirata Shinto, which had developed theologically under the influence of Christianity, constitute (along with the Creator Kami doctrine) a most prominent feature of this school. Therefore, Article 3 of the above-mentioned "Regulations on the Compilation of Religious Books" reads: "Yomi means the world of the moon. *Yomi kōshō* (Study of Yomi) as well as the teachings of Motoori and Hirata shall be authoritative." Article 5 states: "Ideas about where souls go after death are to be based upon the theory of retribution for good and evil." Similarly, in *Kyōsho henshū taii* (Important Points for Compiling Religious Books) it is stated:

> Our souls are made by the Great Kami of Creativity [Taka-mi-musubi and Kami-musubi] through the creative and transforming powers of the great Kami Ame no Mi-naka-nushi. They begin but do not end, they are eternal and indestructible. Therefore the true principle of "concealed rule" shall be made manifest: that even though the returns of good and evil may be avoided in this life, they are inevitable after death.

Regarding the destination of souls, this work says that "the problem of retribution for good and evil is to be in accord with views expressed in the *Yaso no kumade* (Eighty Road-Windings) and in the preface of

---

1) [See Chapter II for comments on Ikarimaro's theology.]

Maki-bashira (True-Wood Pillar), [both by Yano Harumichi]." And " since there is nothing for apprehending the essentials of the ' concealed rule' which does not pertain to the divine virtue of the ruling Kami [Ame no Mi-naka-nushi], the content of the religious books must also develop this principle fully."

However, numerous difficulties were inherent in such statements. In the first place, everything was to be in accord with the explanations of Motoori and Hirata, but of course the explanations of these two men were not always in agreement. The same was true even within the Hirata School, where — quite early — there was debate among adherents about such questions as whether the land of Yomi was a terrestrial or lunar land. Or: if there were two Yomi, to which Yomi would the souls of evil men go after death? The theory of retribution for good and evil, which was treated as orthodoxy, had been adopted in 1872–73 by the Great Teaching Institute as a guiding principle, and was a summation of views included in the above-mentioned *Study of Yomi* (written by Yano Harumichi) and elsewhere. The explanations were chiefly about judgment in the next life, and in them there was a tendency to consider afterworld teachings as the essence of Shinto. They led naturally to a recognition of the superiority of Ō-kuni-nushi no Kami, the ruler of " concealed matters," over other Kami, and, consequently, included elements that raised serious questions about the relationship between Ōkuni-nushi no Kami and the three Creator Kami. It was at this point that Hirata Shinto had been definitely influenced by Christianity. But some influences may have come unconsciously from Buddhism. There were no outright attacks from the Buddhists of the sort seen previously, possibly because there was some doctrinal agreement and the Buddhists saw nothing that could be opposed.

On the other hand, these questions really did arouse controversy and contention within Shinto itself. The problem of the location of Yomi was set aside for a time and the most violent struggle was over the theological position of Ō-kuni-nushi no Kami. That is, the question was: what Kami should be worshipped in the shrine of the Office of Shinto Affairs. In 1873, when the Great Teaching Institute was set up in Shiba, the three Creator Kami and the Sun Goddess were worshipped there; but then the shrine was moved to Hibiya in 1875. Later on a new shrine was built and the question arose at the time of the ceremony for the removal of this shrine in April of 1880. Senge Takatomi and his group advocated that Ō-kuni-nushi no Kami be worshipped along with the three Creator Kami and the Sun Goddess, because Ō-kuni-nushi no Kami not only presided over the "concealed rule" of the earth and ruled over the various Kami under Heaven, but was also the great Kami who passed judgment on the souls of men after death. In opposition were Tanaka Yoritsune [1836–1897] and others who represented the position of the Ise Shrine. Senge Takatomi's view had been presented three different times — in May and July of 1878 and again in January of 1880. He stated that not worshipping Ō-kuni-nushi no Kami along with the three Creator Kami and the Sun Goddess was a "great doctrinal flaw". He wanted, by worshipping all five Kami, to fully carry out the will of the Heavenly Kami who had produced that which people were to rely upon while living, as well as after death. In this way Senge wished to rectify the foundations of the Shinto creed. Kubo Sueshige [1830–1886], Yano Harumichi, and many other influential adherents of the Hirata School supported this position; but Tanaka Yoritsune and his group never gave a clear endorsement. The upshot of the difficulty was that Tanaka Yoritsune — in a statement dated June 7. 1880 — expressed the opinion that since the Kami [currently] worshipped in this shrine constituted the "great source" of the Kami Way and the origin of the fundamental teaching, for the eternal good of the empire one could not but regard with deep concern the question of adding another Kami for worship. It would not do, he maintained, to make rash changes in the worship of the four Kami established when the shrine was founded, and for that reason he was opposed to adding Ō-kuni-nushi no Kami for worship. Furthermore, in his statement he referred to Jesus, implying that Ō-kuni-nushi no Kami was an imitation of Jesus; and in rejecting the idea of worshipping Ō-kuni-nushi no Kami with the three Creator Kami and the Sun Goddess, he said: " I am convinced the shrine of our central headquarters certainly should not have its present structure altered." Senge Takatomi also replied to this statement.[1] Another example of the opposition viewpoint is Ochiai Naoaki's [1852–1934] *Shintō yōshō ben* (Criticism of the *Shintō yōshō*), directed at Senge Takatomi's *Shintō yōshō* (Essentials of Shinto) written in July of 1880. In the preface to this work, written by Miwata Takafusa, we read: " I have recently heard that the Great Instructor-Rectifyer Senge claims that the foundations of our theology are infirm because Ō-kuni-nushi no Kami has not been included among the Kami worshipped in the shrine of the Office of Shinto Affairs. My general impression is that this is nothing more than a self-serving argument." In the main text of the book, the *Essentials of Shinto* is criticized for placing Ō-kuni-nushi no Kami on a par with the Sun Goddess and for tending to credit the former with the power of creation. It went on to say that since the book had Ō-kuni-nushi no Kami presiding over souls before and after death, this meant that Ō-kuni-nushi no Kami was in charge of the souls of the Heavenly and all other Kami. By implication, according to Ochiai, there was even the impropriety of having the souls of Emperors receive punishments and rewards from Ō-kuni-nushi no Kami. Moreover, Tokoyo Nagatane, who had originally been in agreement with Senge Takatomi, now claimed to have recognized his mistake and wrote that the theory which had Ō-kuni-nushi no Kami presiding over the " concealed and mysterious " and judging souls had no basis whatever in ancient tradition, but was something concocted by recent scholars. And he expressed his opposition to the views presented in Hirata's *Koshi den*.[2]

---

1) The *Shinden saishin ron* (Debate on the Kami Worshipped in the Shrine of the Office of Shinto Affairs) in the Gyokuroku collection of the Mukyū kai Bunko is a very important source for this affair.
2) *Obama no agetsurai*, written in 1880.

The controversy, however, was finally resolved by Imperial intercession. In January of 1881 it was decided that the Kami and imperial spirits enshrined in the Imperial Palace would be worshipped from afar in the shrine of the Office of Shinto Affairs. But the conflict of views that had swirled about this problem was not simply a power struggle. As pointed out above, it arose out of the doctrines of Hirata Shinto. And even though there was now a practical solution to the question about which Kami were to be worshipped at the central shrines, the theological confrontation was of course left unresolved. One result of the conflict was that the Senge School immediately established its independence, as the Great-Shrine Teaching (*Taishakyō*), and formulated its own doctrine.

The third cause of dissension among the Shintoists was a natural incompatibility — outside the realm of theological questions — between conservative and progressive tendencies. A very progressive quality is notable among such Hirata Shintoists as Hirata Atsutane and Ōkuni Takamasa. The so-called "proponents of civilization and enlightenment" included Meiji Shinto scholars influenced by this progressive bent, and these progressive Shintoists were aligned against the conservative restorationists. This situation is already evident in the Imperial Pronouncement issued at the time of the propagation of the Great Teaching. In the section dealing with the responsibilities of the Board of Shinto Missionaries, there is the statement that Missionary duties rest "primarily upon the great will of the Imperial ancestor, Emperor [Jimmu], who ruled over the founding of the state at the Kashiwara Palace..... These offices have been established, and officers appointed, in accordance with the Imperial will, which seeks through the great achievements of the Emperor [Sujin] who ruled the world from the Mizugaki Palace, to restore and rectify the confused minds of the Imperial subjects and to subdue them to single-mindedness." But Kubo Sueshige [1830–1886], in discussing this part of the Pronouncement in his officially authorized commentary,[1] makes the point

---

1) *Taikyō sempu shōsho semmyō kai* (Interpretation of the Imperial Pronouncement and Imperial Edict on the Propagation of the Great Teaching), published by the Great Teaching Institute.

that Emperor Sujin's performance of rites to the Kami of Heaven and earth was the first achievement of Imperial efforts in religious indoctrination. More specifically:

> In these times, too, it is the Imperial will to revere the Kami of Heaven and earth and to project the radiance of Imperial prestige overseas by adopting the standards of Emperor Sujin's reign. Therefore, as the Emperor establishes relations overseas, foreign people flock to our shores in vast numbers. Each nation brings to his attention its civilization and enlightenment and offers him its marvelous machines and exquisite skills. By building railroads and telegraph lines, he improves the communication facilities. By opening up iron foundries and shipyards, he builds useful machinery and increases the profits of transportation. By strengthening his military and naval forces, he defends the county against uprisings by vicious groups. By establishing centers for relief and land reclamation, he gives industries to the people. He accepts the learning of all countries and disseminates the world's knowledge. And most important of all, by setting up the Board of Shinto Missionaries, he spreads indoctrination far and wide. All these things are done in accordance with the political structure of Emperor Sujin. What a noble and beloved reign this is!.... But there are undiscerning fellows who apparently believe that the restoration of the Imperial rule of Emperor Jimmu means following the customs of antiquity and copying the systems of the ancient past in everything that is done. Now Emperor Jimmu pacified the country by raising an armada such as had never been seen or heard of before. Emperor Sujin learned things that had never been heard of in that day. He even took a census of the people and levied taxes and corvées; but not one person voiced a complaint. Therefore, the great Imperial reign of the present is based on the outstanding achievements of the courts of Kashiwara and Mizugaki, but it makes dispositions to suit the times, so that neither in acts nor in things does it imitate the ancient past. Let no one be mistaken in this conception!

Here was an assertion of civilization and enlightenment which was clearly incompatible with the simple conservatism of the slogan "unity of worship and administration."

A representative figure of such progressivism in Shinto was Fukuba Bisei [1831–1907], a man who — as the Assistant Director of the Board of Shinto Missionaries — commanded real power in those days. He was a student of Ōkuni and a very clear-sighted man. Showing great concern for the welfare of Christians, he dedicated himself to preserving their lives. In an address which he made on November 1, 1873 — on the occasion of the first commemoration ceremony in Tokyo honoring "the three great men of National Learning" — he said that if these three men had been born during the reign of Emperor Meiji,

They would have exerted themselves in every deed, and not only would their expositions have been even more brilliant, but they would have been broad-minded in rejecting perverted doctrines; so that many things would have been explained to us with perfect clarity: not only the facts of Emperor Jimmu's reign, but also such things as how ably Emperor Kaika established organizations; how majestically Emperor Sujin held sway; how willingly Emperor Ōjin accepted foreign books; how foreigners came over one after another to enlighten our land; and how the followers of Kūkai and Dengyō gave utility and a better life to our people. And they would have pointed out that the Buddhist terms "Heaven" and "hell" as well as such words as "paradise" and "inferno" are but alternate appellations for "Plain of High Heaven" and "Yomi." So that the ancient traditions of all the nations on earth would have been regarded as variants of our own Kami traditions. And we would have shone forth in glittering lucidity and we would have achieved the very height of well-being. Thinking of what would have been, I find myself even more inspired by my recollections of these great men.

Fukuba went on to say that in exerting ourselves in the present age of a new dawn — without hesitation or delay — on the tasks of enlightenment, each of us is acting in accordance with the spirit of the great National Learning scholars. Here we see a train of thought akin to the interpretation of the Imperial Edict given above. This sort of progressivism could not but cause conflict with many conservatives, the so-called "undiscerning gentlemen." When Fukuba was given an additional position — which was his principal one — on the Board of Shinto Missionaries, he expressed the view — concerning the responsibilities of the Board of Shinto Missionaries — that useful foreign ideas should be adopted, and willingly mastered. For, he said, Japan has a Nation Body that is not against reform, since the country has the tradition of an unbroken Imperial line. Nevertheless, he went on, there are few people today who understand this, and many have the absurd fear that if numerous new things are constantly introduced from abroad, our customs will be destroyed. In May of 1872 he started a controversy in the Department of Shinto Affairs, and found himself in the minority, his views unacceptable. Consequently, he was relieved of his offices in both the Department of Shinto Affairs and the Board of Shinto Missionaries. His dismissal coincided roughly with the abolition of the Ministry of Shinto Affairs. The net effect was the first serious setback for the religious-indoctrination movement. It goes without saying that the removal of such influential persons from the movement greatly diminished the strength of Shinto.

The third and most basic reason for the failure of the religious-indoctrination movement was the unreasonableness of giving priority to attempts to establish political control over religious matters. That such a policy can not succeed has been demonstrated in both ancient and modern history — the Christian question in the early years of Meiji demonstrated this once more. While the Meiji control policy did not of course lead to the kind of persecution that had been inflicted upon the Christians by the Tokugawa Shogunate, it was carried out with even greater coercive power. Even so, it could only end in failure. Control in this case did not merely constitute a negative regulation of the various religions, but a positive substitution of Shinto for other religions. This Shinto clearly made the claims of a religion. As explained above, it not only expounded, as a theology, an afterlife faith, but taught repentance and the remission of sins through Great Purification and Great Exorcism rites. Clearly it carried religious elements. And in this connection Shinto could not but be related to Buddhist and Christian beliefs. Attempting to impose Shinto by the use of politial authority was clearly interfering with belief, and it cannot be denied that there existed here a confusion of politics and religion. Therefore, even though the Shin Sect, for example, took the position that it should not oppose the policy, since it was based upon orders from the Imperial Court (it was Imperial law), and even though it tried to justify its approval, arguing from the position that " Imperial law is basic," it was utterly impossible for it to say that these Shinto rites — carried out for souls in the next life and for the prevention of misfortune — did not belong to those heretical acts and practices eschewed by the Shin Sect. An eminent priest of the Pure Land Sect, Fukuda Gyōkai [1806–1888], wrote in his book *Sanjō no guben* (Humble Appraisal of the Three Principles of Instruction) that it was impossible for him, a person who had chanted the name of Buddha for seventy or eighty years, to suddenly change his ways because of some governmental order, to give up chanting the name of Buddha and speak only of " reverence for the Kami and love of the country," and to preach that it did not matter whether people go to paradise or not. Moreover, objections against the irrationality, on this point, of the policy of religious indoctrination were already being voiced by pioneers whose position was based on a clear awareness of the issue. All of these men were Western educated. The first of these was Nakamura Masanao [1832–1891]. He returned to Japan from England in 1868, moved to Shizuoka, and became a professor in the Shizuoka Center for Learning (*gakumonjo*). In August of 1871 he wrote,[1] in reply to a question raised by Mita Hōkō (the man in

---

1) In July of that year he had published his *Saikoku risshi hen* (Biographies of Self-Made Men in Western Countries) [a translation of Samuel Smile's *Self Help*]. Cf., Tokushige, *op. cit.*

charge of the Shizuoka *han* Office of the Board of Shinto Missionaries) : "I am unhappy about the phrase 'one path for government and religion.' Government is one thing, and religion another; and they should be kept apart. The phrase is Chinese, not European." Furthermore, with regard to the *Kojiki* and the *Nihongi* — the classics of the Shintoists — he said: "One glance arouses skepticism and disbelief"; and he also remarked that he could not but have doubts as to whether there really was a Great Way of the state.

The second man in the group was Mori Arinori [1847–1889] who wrote *Religious Freedom of Japan* in November of 1872, while he was studying in the United States. Putting his remarks in the form of a memorial to Prince Sanjō, he stated that among the cultured peoples of the world freedom of conscience, and especially freedom of religion, were not merely a human right, but the most fundamental requisite of human progress. Mori stated that government should not interfere with the freedom of belief, and that it was unreasonable to oppose the introduction of Christianity into Japan on the ground that it was subversive. He also criticized the religious-indoctrination policy of that day and said that the government could never win the confidence of the people by doing such things as setting up a special ministry for the administration of religious matters. Any move like forcing a fusion of Shinto and Buddhism, and imposing a manufactured religion on the people, would of course end in failure. Not only that, it would lead to nothing more than disregard of freedom of conscience, and crushing the human soul. This plan of the government, he said, could only be called something absolutely incomprehensible.

Finally, sharper and more concrete criticisms emerged from the Buddhists, who suffered the most, since they were actually the ones being brought under control. The defensive movement of the Buddhists had naturally persisted, under different forms, ever since the 1868 movement to "abolish Buddhism and destroy the Buddhist icons." The government, too, found it very difficult to deal with this Buddhism which had had the tradition and history of being a state religion. After the practice of selecting Buddhist priests as Religious Instructors had been initiated, it was necessary, more and more often, for the government to assume a compromising attitude. Nevertheless, it was difficult for the Buddhist priests to put up with such political control.

The person who dared to lodge protests in behalf of Buddhism was Shimaji Mokurai [1838–1911], the principal defender. He was one of the new intellectuals of the Buddhist world of that day, belonging to the Hongan-ji School of the Shin Sect. Even the establishment of the Ministry of Religions during the summer of 1871 stemmed from a proposal made by him. In December of 1872, after he had gone on a trip to Europe, he submitted a petition that the Great Teaching Institute be divided; and he spoke in behalf of the proposal. His statements were very detailed. In this respect he advanced one step farther than his two predecessors. In general outline, he took the position that government and religion were different and should never be confused. Government dealt with the affairs of man and was limited to the control of bodies of people within its political boundaries; its objective was to bring advantages to the individual and security to the state. On the other hand, religion dealt with divine matters and concerned itself with the control of the minds of people; its purpose was philanthropy, benevolence and affection. Although there was an international law, it was only by having this joined with religious law that the hearts of the people could be regulated, and their base made firm, peace maintained, and civilization developed. Only when religion and government complemented each other could a nation become a nation and a man become a man; only then were there wealth and strength, culture and enlightenment. The frequent religious and political mistakes in China and Japan had been due to a confusion of government and religion. In ancient times this had been true in Europe, too, but it was not true in modern times. He noted, nevertheless, that the directives handed down by the Ministry of Religion violated that principle. In the Three Principles of Instruction, for example, the first article referred to " reverence of Kami and love of country "; but " reverence of Kami " belonged to religion and " love of country " to government. Failure to revere the Kami did not imply failure to love one's country. If the authors of the article meant the myths of a single country by this reference to Kami, then their position was primitive, as far as religion was concerned. If they conceived of a single Kami (god) for all countries, then they were taking a position taught by Christianity, but in no way equal to that religion. In the second article of the Three Principles of Instruction, he went on, the phrase " the principle of heaven and the way of man " only referred to the substance (principle) of religion; it could not be identified directly with religion. Religion was a composite of reverence (faith), emotion (means) and substance. Discarding reverence and emotion, and taking only the substance did not make a religion. Not to mention the fact that the concept of " the principle of heaven and the way of man " altered (in extension) with the times and (in depth) according to one's erudition. It was simply too abstract. If religion and government were made to complement each other, there would be adjustments to the times and to one's scholarship; and " the principle of Heaven and the way of man " would be attained spontaneously. As to the phrase " exalting the Emperor and obeying the Imperial Court " in the third article of the Three Principles of Instruction, " exalting the Emperor " referred to the Nation Body, not to religion, and " obeying the Imperial Court " was proper to dictatorship, not to a constitutional structure. It goes without saying, he added, that we should respect the Nation Body; but with regard to government, " there will be errors in public debate from time to time " and so we should not make public debate into a religion." He went on to say:

> In considering the contents of the ministerial promulgations, I wonder if they have not arisen from fears that the Nation Body might be altered. If this is really so, and we strive to achieve such an objective by such means, not only will religion become ineffective, but the desired objective will not be realized. The reason why I deplore this greatly and feel impelled to submit my humble views is

that no one can be forced to accept a religion. How can anyone who has not submitted to a creed with his heart follow it or believe in it? If he cannot believe in a religion, he will certainly have contempt for it. And if this is so, I fear that it will affect the stability of the nation, which has been unparalleled and unshakeable fo myriad ages. If the administrators adopt good laws and use these to bring about the fortification of the Nation Body, without any relationship to religion, who then could possibly develop feelings of disrespect? This matter has been unbearably painful to me. It is something which involves the Nation Body. Having reflected deeply, and picked up evidence in various contries of Europe, I have arrived at these definite, firm views.

In this document Shimaji also noted that the European newspapers had reported a plan by the Japanese government to manufacture a new religion, and were critical of it. He wrote: " Now I realize that those reports were true. How well we deserve the scorn of the Europeans! For a religion is created by gods, not by men. How can it be something like organizations and laws, which are decided by public debate and then announced? The success of the movement to divide the Great Teaching Institute, continued after Shimaji's return to Japan in July of 1873, was a direct result of Shimaji's petition.

The failure of this religious-indoctrination policy was certainly associated with the trend toward official recognition of the principle of religious freedom, which soon came to be pressed. The beginning of the trend dates back to the removal of the posters banning Christianity (the " perverted faith "), which was the target of the state's missionary program. The ban was lifted on February 21, 1873 — the date by the new calendar adopted on January 1st of that year. (By the old calendar the date was the 3rd day of the 12th month of 1872.) The ban was lifted because protests had been made by various foreign countries and especially because criticism had been reported by the Iwakura Mission, despatched to Europe and America. By this time the religious indoctrination policy had entered its second stage, discussed above. By 1874 Nishi Amane's [1829–1897] *Kyōmon ron* (Discussion of Religious Sects) had appeared; and with subsequent changes in the situation, the idea of recognizing the principle of religious freedom gained momentum in spite of a strict enforcement of the religious-indoctrination policy. Finally, article 28 of the constitution, promulgated on February 11, 1889, stipulated: "Japanese subjects shall, within limits not prejudicial to peace and order, and not antagonistic to their duties as subjects, enjoy freedom of religious belief."[1] Itō Hirobumi's *Teikoku kempō gige* (Commentaries on the Constitution of the Empire of Japan), in referring to this article, sets forth the history of the adoption of the principle of religious freedom in European countries:

> The principle of religious freedom can be regarded as a glorious fruit of modern civilization. The task of extending truth and the freedom of conscience — the most cherished ideals of mankind — has passed through centuries of darkness and obscurity and is now lifted to light. Freedom of conscience, something which exists within man, is of course outside the sphere of interference by national laws. The forcing of a special belief by the adoption of a state religion constitutes an obstruction to the natural intellectual progress of man, and to the competitive development of science and the arts. Therefore, no country should have the function or right to suppress religious belief through the exercise of political authority.

And he concluded: "This article does indeed follow the policy laid down since the Meiji Renovation and opens a broad highway toward the spiritual rights of the individual." With the adoption of the constitution, then, we can say that the indoctrination policy, insofar as it concerned religion, was definitely liquidated. In the Imperial Rescript

---

1) [As translated in Ito Hirobumi, *Commentaries on the Constitution of the Empire of Japan*, translated by Ito Miyoji (Tokyo, 1889).]

on Education, issued in 1890, education was completely divorced from religion.[1]

We cannot say that the religious indoctrination movement of Meiji produced absolutely no results. Contributions in the area of popular moral awakening, for example, are not unworthy of attention. But that is a separate problem. Only one more word should be added: it was certainly unfortunate for Hirata Shinto that it received such official recognition, and was protected politically. Because of this protection, the sort of philosophical and religious development that had occurred, to some degree, among its adherents could not develop fully and was broken off.

May, 1938.

---

1) As early as May of 1874 "a distinction between education and religion" had been made.

Chapter VII

Separation of State and Religion in Shinto: Its Historical Significance[1]

1

The directive of the Supreme Commander of the Allied Powers — dated 15 December 1945 and entitled " The Abolition of Governmental Sponsorship, Support, Perpetuation, Control, and Dissemination of State Shinto " — may be said to have done two things: First, it deprived Shrine Shinto[2] of all the national, political, economic, and educational prerogatives it had hitherto enjoyed; and, secondly, it liberated the Japanese people from all external coercion from Shrine Shinto. Its impact on Japan has certainly not been insignificant: those persons associated with Shrine Shinto have been shocked and distressed; and the effect, as far as Shrine Shinto is concerned, has been clearly revolutionary. But if we look at the matter historically, we will see that this is not the first time the Japanese have had such an experience. Furthermore, what we see today is not difficult to understand. Since the directive is to some extent consistent with precedent, it should not prove to be hopelessly disheartening to Shrine Shinto. I would like to amplify these points.

Editorial comments about the directive note the frequent use of the phrase " separation of worship and administration." But I feel that this phrase is somewhat inappropriate and carries with it a

---

1) [Published in *Asahi Hyōron* (March 1, 1946).]
2) [The SCAP directive preferred the term "State Shinto" which was explained as referring to "that branch of Shinto (*Kokka Shinto* or *Jinja Shinto*) which by official acts of the Japanese Government has been differentiated from the religion of Sect Shinto (*Shūha Shintō* or *Kyōha Shintō*) ...." *Political Reorientation of Japan* (SCAP; Washington, D. C.), II, 468.]

misconception. For it presupposes a unity of worship and government. While "unity of worship and administration" was one of the slogans pushed vigorously during the war, strictly speaking, such unity never existed.

"Unity of worship and administration" properly refers to an ancient form of government, a form that was common to various peoples and one in which religious ceremony was equated with government. This meant that all administration was conducted in accordance with a devine will that was determined ritually. In Japan, for example, when the two Kami, Izanagi and Izanami, were giving birth to the country, they learned — through divination with oracular bones — that the female Kami's having spoken first induced an ill-fated result. Then they knew this was because they had acted against the will of the Heavenly Kami and were able to consummate the matter by reversing the order of speaking. Also, there is the case of Empress Jingū's carrying out the subjugation of Silla in accordance with the Kami will of the Sun Goddess, who was manifested in the Empress.

But later there was historical development and cultural diversification, and it was natural and inevitable that unity of worship and administration could not be perpetuated. In our country the trend toward separation appeared early in history. The following significant events occurred during the reign of Emperor Sujin [who probably reigned in about the fifth century A.D.]: the Kami shrine was separated from the Emperor's palace; the Sword and Mirror, which had been enshrined in the palace, were taken away; and Imperial princesses were appointed especially to take charge of worship. From that time onward we note gradual cultural development in various areas [of Japanese life]. It goes without saying that, as a modern state, Japan is now completely disassociated from unity of worship and administration in this sense. Whether the Emperor is conducting the ceremony of honoring the four directions, as the first act of government at the beginning of a new year; whether he is carrying out administration with a just heart, in communion with the deities and embodying the will of the ancestral Kami of the state; or whether the high officials are applying themselves to their governmental responsibilities with a Kami-serving attitude of selflessness and reverence — such activities certainly cannot be identified with unity of worship and administration.

Nevertheless, the term has been carelessly misused. As a result of its being propagandized so much, there is a mystic quality about the politics of Japan that is inscrutable to the outsider. And I think it cannot be denied that there exists a strong impression that all our extreme nationalism, with its threat to the outside world, is deeply rooted in this concept of "unity of worship and administration." It is clear that the major responsibility for this rests with Shrine Shinto. Be that as it may, in the light of the foregoing I will use the term "separation of state and religion" and avoid using "separation of worship and administration."

2

To begin with, the sort of experience we are having now is certainly nothing new in the history of Shinto. We had such an experience about fifty years ago, at the beginning of the Meiji Era.

It is not at all rare in the religious history of either the Orient or the Occident for a religion to receive the support of the state, and to develop because of this support. Actually in ancient and medieval times this was rather the rule. In our country Shinto, along with Buddhism, enjoyed the support of the state from very early times. And especially since Shinto was the indigenous religion and the religion of the Imperial Court, the fact of state support was prominent and has continued on down to the present. However, no matter how much support is given by the government, we cannot say, simply because of this support, that there is unity of state and religion. To be able to say this, there must be the will to impose Shintoism on the people as the national religion, and there must be regulations in the various areas of national life which embody this will, directly or indirectly.

SEPARATION OF STATE AND RELIGION

It is not until the Meiji Era that we find, for the first time, a clear case of putting such a policy into effect. As early as 1867 the Hirata School of Shinto, which provided the chief intellectual motivation for the restoration of Imperial rule and prided itself in this role, sent a memorial to the authorities advocating revival of the Department of Shinto Affairs, and carrying out a politico-economic policy of "unity of worship and administration" centering in Shinto. At the time of the Restoration these proposals were adopted and, at first, an Office of Shinto Affairs was established. But at length, Restoration Shinto was prescribed as the religion of the Imperial Country. Then followed a clear distinction between Kami and Buddha through an elimination of Buddhist admixtures dating back to medieval times; and a violent anti-Buddhist movement swept the entire country. Immediately afterward a Department of Shinto Affairs was set up in place of the Office of Shinto Affairs. Missionaries were attached to the Department of Shinto Affairs in an attempt to check Christianity, which, toward the end of the Tokugawa Era, had shown signs of coming to life in the Kyushu area. For this purpose the Great Teaching, or Great Way of Kannagara, was proclaimed; and Imperial Edicts and Imperial Pronouncements were issued. This first period of the Department of Shinto Affairs, or the period of Shinto missionaries, lasted until March of 1872.

The second period, which might be called the period of the Ministry of Religion, Office of Religious Instruction, and Great Teaching Institute continued on until May of 1875. When the Department of Shinto Affairs was abolished and replaced by the Ministry of Religion, an Office of Religious Instruction was set up to replace the Board of Shinto Missionaries. Buddhist priests, who had been excluded from the indoctrination of the Christians, now participated prominently in the government's indoctrination movement. But of course the Buddhist priests could not alter the Shinto orientation of the Great Teaching. The Ministry of Religion adopted these three principles as a basis of religious instruction: (1) "reverence for Kami and love of country"; (2) "the principle of heaven and the Way of man"; and (3) "exalt the Emperor and obey the Imperial Court." Furthermore, a Great Teaching Institute was set up in the capital, and Middle and Small Teaching Institutes were established in local areas to serve as educational organs for officials of Religious Instruction. In these Institutes attempts were made, principally through the use of Shintoism, to control the indoctrination of both Buddhists and Shintoists. But of course the Buddhists were not able to put up with this situation for long, and quite early a separatist movement arose among them. It had already begun to develop late in 1872; and in May of 1875, when the time was right, joint propagation by Buddhists and Shintoists was abolished. Therefore, this second period saw the ascendancy of Buddhism, and the retreat of Shintoism.

In the third period, the Great, Middle and Small Teaching Institutes were abolished; independent missionary work by the various Buddhist sects was permitted; internal dissension developed within Shintoism; and, importantly, various Founder Shinto sects acquired independence. In the meantime, the Ministry of Religion was abolished and in January of 1877 the Office of Shinto Affairs was transferred to the Ministry of Internal Affairs, retaining control of only what was left of the official Shinto program. Furthermore, in 1888 the Tenrikyō Sect was established from within Shinto. Under such circumstances the government's policy of controlling religious education was destined to collapse almost completely. Thus the movement to make Restoration Shinto the national religion, in spite of initial enthusiasm and loud cries of encouragement, ended in failure after only a few years of activity.

Why did this happen? Such a policy of religious education was not compatible with the practical requirements of a nation that had adopted the slogan: "civilization and enlightenment," and from the beginning was nothing more than a futile assertion of a group of conservatives. It was almost entirely ignored by intelligent leaders in and out of government, and by the intellectual class generally.

Then there was the inner immaturity of Shinto itself and especially the theoretical poverty that had made Shinto absolutely unable to compete with Buddhism and Christianity as a religion. And finally political control of these advanced religions was fundamentally irrational. The above points, especially the last one, was debated spiritedly among Buddhists, Christians, and the new intellectuals of the day. Representative figures in the debate were Shimaji Mokurai [1838–1911], Nakamura Masanao [1832–1891], and Mori Arinori [1847–1889]. In November of 1872 Mori, who was then studying in the United States, wrote a book entitled *Religious Freedom of Japan*. Putting his remarks in the form of a memorial to Prince Sanjō, he stated that the freedom of belief was a right to which cultured peoples were entitled. He criticized, and absolutely opposed, the recent scheme of the Japanese government to unite Shintoism and Buddhism by force, and to press upon the people a " manufactured religion." That the Japanese government was scheming to manufacture a religion was what Europeans and Americans were saying, at the time, about the Meiji government's religious education program. These charges induced a reconsideration of the question by the authorities; and recognition of freedom of religious belief, a general trend of the day, was demanded more and more. Finally, religious freedom was stipulated in Article 28 of the constitution, promulgated in 1889. There was no mistaking the intent of the introductory clause of Article 28: " Japanese subjects shall, within limits not prejudicial to peace and order, and not antagonistic to their duties as subjects .... " And the closing words of the Article, " .... enjoy freedom of religious belief," implied that there would be no compulsion to accept any particular religious belief. Therefore, it recognized the freedom to believe in any religion, even Christianity. Consequently, it must be said that the Article was a complete rejection of the political elements of Shinto. And this view is not in conflict with the explanations made by Itô Hirobumi [1841–1909] in his *Commentary on the Constitution*. If this view is correct, we must conclude that removing the political prerogatives of Shinto — the intent of the present directive — had, in theory, been previously experienced by our people.

Finally, it should be noted that the most powerful factor in the Japanese recognition of the principle of religious freedom was really the violent criticism which was directed by Europeans and Americans at the Japanese government's attitude toward Christianity. This was something which Ambassador Iwakura and his party keenly sensed during their travels abroad in the early years of Meiji. The power of foreign countries was as compelling then as now.

3

Why is it, in spite of what has been said above, that our government and people are now unable to recall, generally or clearly, an experience which is similar to receiving the present directive? It is my view that in spite of the fact that religious freedom was stipulated by the constitution in principle, it can hardly be said that a complete separation of state and religion was achieved in practice. More particularly, the position of Shrine Shinto as a state religion was not liquidated. Rather, Shrine Shinto expanded and prospered in the developments of the half century that followed.

The character of Shrine Shinto as a state religion is seen formally in its institutions and substantively in its doctrines. The Shrine system was designed — along lines as prescribed in the *Engishiki* — as early as 1871. In classifying the shrines, a distinction was made between official shrines (*kanpeisha* and *kokuheisha*[1]) and miscellaneous shrines. All shrines of the entire country, large or small, were made into public institutions to be officially administered; and at the same time a system of shrine officials was instituted. Although the

---

1) [The *kanpeisha*, as defined in the *Engishiki*, were shrines that received offerings directly from the Department of Shinto Rites; whereas the *kokuheisha* were shrines that received offerings from the provincial governor (*kunizukasa*).]

Department of Shinto Affairs was subsequently abolished, and the initial plan was curtailed, one result of separating the shrines from religion was that the position of the shrines was assured under national law. This was made increasingly clear in 1900 when the Bureau of Shinto Shrines (*jinja kyoku*) was made the most important bureau in the Ministry of Internal Affairs, and even clearer in 1940 when the Shinto Affairs Chamber (*jingiin*) was made an extraordinary bureau of the Ministry of Internal Affairs. I remember that this was connected with outcries for a revival of the Ministry of Shinto Affairs.

On the other hand, the problem of the relationship between Shrines and religion — that is, the question as to whether or not Shrine Shinto was or was not a religion — began to be debated as early as 1887; and the debate became more heated in the Taisho Era (1912–1925). This was because the existence of religious elements in Shrine Shinto was clearly a fact that could not be denied. Therefore, even among the adherents of Shrine Shinto, there were not a few who boldly affirmed that Shrine Shinto was a religion. In general, the latter were familiar with Western religions. But there were also persons who took the opposite position. They contended that there were elements in ancient Shinto, expounded in Shrine Shinto, which definitely could not be measured in terms of foreign concepts of religion; that Shrine Shinto was focused upon rites which antedated religion, and as such should be considered the original pattern of the national spirit, a pattern that predated all such cultural diversification as is represented in the terms " moral," " political," etc. From this point of view they took the line that Shrine Shinto was not a religion. And the views of these people provided a convenient rationale for the government's administration of Shrine Shinto — their views were designated a school that was differentiated from the " Western school." This interpretation was at least valid to the extent that the proponents were aware that Shrine Shinto was identified with the essential character of ancient Shinto. But the subsequent attitude of the proponents of Shrine Shinto and of the government were absolutely contrary to such a view of Shrine

Shinto. Instead, the Shrine rites were regarded as state functions, as the foundation of popular education, and as an obligation of students — views which suggest that Shrine Shinto was thought of in terms of the enforcement of belief. At the same time, Kami-Country Imperialism — which emerged out of the dogmas and beliefs of Shrine Shinto — was advocated more and more. Beginning, in particular, with the period after 1894-95 — at a time of startling Japanese overseas expansion — there was an upsurge of this Imperialism. Of necessity, it now received more and more emphasis; and it took the form of a creed of "loyalty to the Emperor and love of country" (*chūkun aikoku*). After 1904–05 there was still another spurt of development in this Imperialism. Once again this was regarded in foreign countries as " manufacturing a new religion." A particularly illuminating opinion appeared in a pamphlet, *The Invention of a New Religion* (London, 1912), written by Professor B. H. Chamberlain, an English Japanologist who had just returned to Europe after having lived in Japan many years. It created a great stir at the time. In this pamphlet Professor Chamberlain wrote that the creed of " loyalty to the Emperor and love of country," the spiritual basis of Japan of that day, was the product of efforts made by the Meiji bureaucrats to manufacture a new religion for political purposes. He said that it had no popular or historical roots. At the same time, he spoke of its amazing success. These views of Professor Chamberlain are rather extreme, and I find it difficult to agree with them completely. I have discussed them before, however, and so it is not necessary to deal with them here. We should note, nevertheless, that there were elements in Shrine Shinto that provided ample ground for such views as those expressed by Professor Chamberlain.

After that, and in connection with the extension of the national power of Japan, Shrines were established abroad. For example, in 1925 the Korean Shrine (*Chōsen jingū*) — where the Sun Goddess and Emperor Meiji were both enshrined — was erected. In 1936 and 1937 a number of smaller national shrines (*kokuhei shōsha*) — where the principal Kami was the Sun Goddess — were established in Korea. Then in 1938 the Kwantung Shrine (*Kantō jinja*) — enshrining the Sun Goddess and Emperor Meiji — was built in Port Arthur; in 1940 the South Seas Shrine (*Nanyō Jinja*) — where the Sun Goddess was enshrined — was erected; and in that same year the National Founding Shrine (*Kenkoku Shinbyō*) — honoring the Sun Goddess — was established in the Imperial palace at Changchun. It is thought that the creation of these various shrines outside Japan startled foreign countries. And at the same time various slogans, which were certainly not used in their classical sense, were recklessly and excessively propagandized as the situation seemed to dictate. Consequently, there was sufficient reason for people in foreign countries to sense, more and more, the increasingly aggressive intent of Shrine Shinto, and to consider it a danger. Furthermore, in recent years the authorities had ordered the Christian churches of the country to perform certain Shrine Shinto ceremonies as a prerequisite to their receiving equal treatment with other officially recognized religious sects; and this certainly could not but be considered as pressure against Christianity. With the culmination of these developments, promotion of Shrine Shinto was tantamount to state enforcement of a kind of supra-religious cult. Since it was an ultramilitaristic faith that completely disregarded the principle of religious freedom guaranteed by the constitution, the conclusion emerged that Shrine Shinto was extremely dangerous, that it provided the intellectual basis for Japan's militaristic world agression, and that unless Shrine Shinto was rooted out, the task of making Japan a peaceful nation would be absolutely impossible. The better we know this historical background, the better we can understand why [people should have arrived at such a conclusion].

Thirdly, let us consider whether the fate that has befallen Shrine Shinto at this time is something to be utterly pessimistic about or whether it ought to be regarded as unimportant for this religion. Certainly the removal of all state prerogatives was a heavy blow for Shrine Shinto. Nevertheless, from one point of view, this was a just and inevitable retribution. Ancient Shinto, from which Shrine Shinto was derived, was the primitive, indigenous religion of the Japanese people. Its special character was rooted in the cheerful and refreshing qualities of the bright and pure heart, as is symbolized in the plain and unadorned beauty of shrine architecture. Its rites were exceedingly simple. The essence of its life was that it did not embody any pretentious dogmas, propaganda, or pedantry. This was what was meant by the term the "Way of *Kannagara.*" In this circumstance there existed some justification for the above-mentioned view that Shrine Shinto was not a religion. And so ancient Shinto was remote from the modern use of such terms as "the whole world under one roof" (*hakkō ichiu*); and it was not responsible for such extreme actions as the coercion of belief. If those in Shrine Shinto had been fully aware of the original character of Shinto, and had not erred by going beyond their political and other secular prerogatives, I think that they might have been able to avoid the sort of thing that has now happened. But Shrine Shinto moved in exactly the opposite direction. Being complacent about the state privileges which had been given to them, and completely forgetting the failures that they had experienced at the beginning of Meiji, the proponents of Shrine Shinto did almost no reflecting and, with the outbreak of hostilities, associated themselves with political power. Seeking mutual advantage, they cried out for a revival of the Department of Shinto Affairs and succeeded in obtaining at least the establishment of the Shinto Affairs Chamber. For these reasons, the impression was given that it was Shrine Shinto which provided the intellectual impetus for militarism and expansionism. And there is no doubt but that this was due also to their being oblivious to religious piety. The present blow, then, is nothing but retribution for such errors and failures.

If the above is true, let us inquire about the presence of militarism and expansionism in the doctrines embraced by Shrine Shinto. The December 15 directive, particularly in Article 2,[1] deals with the area of

---

1) [*Political Reorientation of Japan*, II, 467–9.]

thought. Shrine Shinto, by this directive, was to be divested of militaristic and ultranationalistic elements. Militaristic and ultranationalistic ideology was defined as embracing those theories which advocate or justify a mission on the part of Japan to extend its rule over other nations and peoples. Four examples were given: (1) The doctrine that the Emperor of Japan is superior to the heads of other states because of ancestry, descent or special origin; (2) The doctrine that the people of Japan are superior to the people of other lands because of ancestry, descent, or special origin; (3) The doctrine that the islands of Japan are superior to other lands because of divine or special origin; and (4) Any other doctrine which tends to delude the Japanese people into embarking upon wars of aggression or to glorify the use of force as an instrument for the settlement of disputes with other peoples.

It has already been pointed out that Shrine Shinto doctrines should be considered extensions of ancient Shinto thought. More precisely, however, these doctrines should be identified with Restoration Shinto doctrines of the latter half of the Tokugawa Era: the Shinto of Motoori Norinaga and Hirata Atsutane. The proponents of Shrine Shinto during and after the Meiji Era were generally associated with Restoration Shinto and were steeped in its teachings. Restoration Shinto was, correctly speaking, Ancient-Learning Shinto. It was based upon philological studies of the ancient Japanese classics, studies that had as their objective the recognition and revival of ancient thoughts. In short, it aimed for a true revelation of the reality of ancient Shinto. But it could not help but be affected, to some extent, by the character of the age and by the personalities of its thinkers and scholars who lived in the feudal period of the Tokugawa. And so, although we speak of " the Restoration Shinto of Motoori and Hirata," there are salient differences which do not permit us to treat the two men as if they were identical. The just and upright scholarship of Motoori Shinto — which was praised unstintingly by Professor Chamberlain and by other scholars of Europe and America, and which contributed greatly to their study of ancient Shinto — was widely understood and appreciated by the Japanese intellectual class. Or at least it could have been understood with appropriate explanations. Kami-Country thought, referred in (1), (2) and (3) above as ultranationalism, was of course something proclaimed in Motoori Shinto. But such thought originated in the Age of Kami legends which are presented, in typical form, in the *Kojiki*. In exalting the Emperor, this thought represented him as a descendant of the Sun Goddess, the greatest natural deity of the universe, and also held the Emperor to be the center of a state composed of land and people. Hence it was nothing but the germinating of a state ideology in the consciousness of the ancient Japanese. Such ideas naturally took shape in their consciousness as they attempted to build a new state in the land of " the eight great islands." They were not at all a result of oppression or coercion from the outside. Some may argue that these ideas are inadequate as an expression of race consciousness. But it is a common feature of ancient periods for one part of the people — those who belong to a nobility of some sort — to participate exclusively in the culture. Democratic culture of the twentieth century does not apply to antiquity; only the nobility represented the race. Others take the position that the Age of Kami legends of the *Kojiki* and the *Nihongi* which embody this sort of thought are not really so old, but were composed by political authors of the Imperial Court in an effort to unite the will of the people after the Japanese state had been founded. This view has been seen frequently in recent years, but it is just a hypothesis, a daring criticism of the traditional view. We should not hastily accept it as scientific. At any rate, judging from the over-all character of the legends of the *Kojiki* and the *Nihongi*, it is clear that no militaristic or ultranationalistic intent existed in the Kami-Country idea discussed above. It is obvious that the myths of Japanese antiquity, when compared to those of other countries, are rather rich in pacific elements, and that they do not include any accounts of gory murders or violent wars. Even in the introduction to Professor Chamberlain's famous English translation of the *Kojiki*, nothing of this sort is pointed out. Such Kami-Country thought was, after all, a product of poetic sentiments with which the plain, simple people of ancient times expressed unsophisticated praise of their country — it did not contain any malicious intent that should be guarded against. Consequently, such thoughts as outlined in (4) above are not found in ancient Shinto.

What has been said above about ancient Shinto is generally true also of Motoori Shinto. Of course Motoori was full of patriotic ardor, and when aroused by certain people of his day who were excessively deficient in their national consciousness or racial pride, he would often express a righteous indignation; but needless to say, there was no militarism or expansionism in the thought of this man who, living his entire life in peaceful Matsuzaka, devoted himself wholly to his profession as a scholar.

With Hirata the situation is somewhat different. It was already near the end of the Tokugawa Era; the dawn of a new Japan was imminent; and everything was more tense. Also the personality of Hirata differed from that of Motoori — Hirata was more political-minded, ambitious and passionate. And so we cannot deny that there was a more radical quality in the intellectual tendencies of Hirata Shinto. But Hirata Shinto also attempted to integrate Chinese, Indian, and other ancient myths around the Japanese legends, and it had a tendency toward grandiose visions, such as in its ancient historiography which could not possibly have been perfected. Either it was treated with a smile or it was worthy of some humor; but it certainly did not have enough practicality to make it deserving of international apprehension. The same is true of the students of the Hirata school. Even Satō Nobuhiro was not fundamentally different. If we think about this point, the cause and effect will appear to be just the reverse: instead of the doctrines and thought of Shrine Shinto causing the Imperialism and expansionism of the politicians and the military, it was rather Imperialism and expansionism that enhanced the doctrine of Shrine Shinto. (It would not be an exaggeration to say that the politicians and military men of our country have been all but uneducated and unconcerned with respect to the doctrines of Shrine Shinto, or the ancient classics that embody these doctrines.) But in this enhancement, the words and conduct of the polemicists of Shrine Shinto, who were puffed up by special privileges and were taking advantage of the current situation, played an important part. Consequently, we must say that something like the present directive was inevitable.

In thinking back over these developments, I conclude that this recent affair should be considered propitious for Shrine Shinto. For Shrine Shinto will be divested, for the first time, of those secular rights which it has long possessed, and now, existing as a pure religious sect like other sects, it should move on toward spiritual growth. It might be able, in a Motoori-like purity, to arouse anew the spirit of Ancient Shinto. Or perhaps it will be able to give more maturity to those notable attempts to develop Sect Shinto made by Hirata and his students. Hereafter the proponents of Shrine Shinto may rouse themselves from their long-standing hothouse torpor, deepen their faith, refine their theology, carry out the intent of their predecessors (Motoori and Hirata), and really make a contribution to the indoctrination of a new Japan. If such comes to pass, I will be happy should the few studies that I have attempted to carry out in this area during past years — studies which have been almost wholly ignored by these proponents of Shrine Shinto — prove to have some justification for existence.

Chapter VIII

On Methods of Research in Japanese Intellectual History[1]

Scholarship is a creation of the individual. Strictly speaking, therefore, research methods must be devised by the individual researcher, for no method can be prescribed that will be valid for all. This point was made by Motoori Norinaga [1730–1801] in his *Uiyamabumi* (First Tramp in the Mountains), a distinguished book in which he applied his mature knowledge to the writing of a guide for those entering Ancient Learning: He said:

> In the long run the essential thing in scholarship is simply to work hard for many years without tiring or slackening off. Any method of research is all right and so you should not concern yourself with method. No matter how good the method is, there is no achievement when you are lazy and do not apply yourself. Achievement may also vary according to talent, but it is difficult to do anything about talent, since this is determined by birth. Nevertheless, it is generally the case that even a man without talent obtains results proportional to his effort. Even the man who begins his study late in life will be unexpectedly successful if he is diligent. Surprisingly, there are persons without leisure who achieve more than those with leisure. Therefore, do not be discouraged and give up, even if you are poor in talent, have started late in life, or have no leisure. In any case, you should understand that you will achieve something provided only that you work hard. Discouragement is a great obstacle to learning.[2]

---

1) [First published in Vol. 1 No. 5 of *Nihon seishin bunka* (Japanese Spirit and Culture) in June of 1934 and included in *Zoku Nihon shisō shi kenkyū*, 25–48.]
2) [*Motoori Norinaga zenshū* IX, 480.]

I feel that these words of the great master deserve close attention.

The futility of trying to learn to swim without entering the water, referred to as "swimming on the floor," applies equally to study. Therefore, for the purposes of scholarship, it will never do, needless to say, to place such an overemphasis on research method. If this is true of methods of empirical research, how much truer it is for theoretical methodology. Certainly the practicing researcher, no matter what his field of learning, does not necessarily have to be a methodological theorist. Instead of hesitating in awe of the latter's theories, he should consider it his duty to devote himself, in his empirical work, to supplying source material for the benefit of methodology.

And yet we cannot deny that an understanding of research methods, particularly that which rises out of the scholar's practical experience, is both necessary and helpful for the researcher. It is obviously better to have a guide than to be without one when proceeding through the broad fields and deep recesses of scholarship. This was also touched upon by Motoori in the book mentioned above:

> The one who aspires to, and embarks upon, learning.... goes to a knowledgeable person and inquires about which of the various lines of study to begin with, and asks what books the initiate should read. This is the normal, and absolutely right procedure. I want a researcher to start by taking the right problem and the right method and by making proper preparations, from the beginning, for avoiding sidetracks, speeding up the work, and maximizing results. While expending the same amount of energy, one will succeed or fail depending on the line and method of study followed.[1]

Then Motoori goes on to comment about practical research methods. What I set forth below is essentially nothing more than an attempt, from a similar point of view, to supply — for the reference of those

---

1) [*Motoori Norinaga zenshū* IX. 479.]

who wish to enter this field — a few points I have learned in my work.

A decision about how to carry on research in a particular field of scholarship must be based upon a correct understanding of the nature of that field. This is especially important in what may be termed a new field: Japanese intellectual history. What is called "intellectual history" belongs, in one sense, to cultural history. Recently the term "cultural history" has gained wide currency, even in the field of Japanese history; but it frequently appears to be thought of simply in contradistinction to political history. But these two types of history are certainly not mutually exclusive. As soon as history becomes something more than a simple chronological record, and is concerned with the description of the internal meaning of historical evidence, it necessarily deals with some cultural phenomenon. History does not exist apart from culture. Even politics, being one aspect of culture, is encompassed in history as a cultural phenomenon. General or political history is definitely not at odds with the concept of cultural history. And yet general history, especially in Japan, customarily leans toward that which is political, slighting or neglecting other important areas of culture. In reaction to this kind of history — that is, in the attempt to view history from a different position, in other words, from a standpoint, originating in history, which treats culture in a more relevant sense — we can find the advocacy of what is called "cultural history." The fact that emphasis is placed on such areas as religion, scholarship, art, and morals — rather than on politics and military affairs — presupposes a culturalism at the base of this historical outlook. "Culturalism" is a point of view that places a great deal of value on spiritual or inner culture as opposed to material or external civilization. In short, it is the history dealing with cultural products *per se,* from the standpoint of this culturalism, which we term "cultural history"; and historical research in this area has always been grossly neglected as far as Japanese history is concerned. In dealing with the various areas of "cultural products," or cultural properties, special aspects of cultural history — such as religious history, ethical history, and art history—have come into being. Likewise, since culture is also best manifested, and its unique qualities best demonstrated, in particular countries — because each country is a unique cultural entity — various national cultural histories have appeared. Furthermore, there have emerged broad concepts of Oriental cultural history, Western cultural history, and the like; and by a fusion of these two types of cultural history we have such fields as Japanese ethical history and Oriental religious history.

In cultural history there are two possible ways of dealing with what is called culture: looking at it as phenomena, or as consciousness. Phenomena are materializations of consciousness, and consciousness is reflection on phenomena. Fundamentally both are united as culture, but it is a true character of culture that the two develop interdependently — sometimes one before the other, and sometimes side by side. When the development of culture is seen principally in the area of consciousness, we have intellectual history. And in the process of the development of consciousness, learning — which begins with simple thought — culminates in philosophy. For this reason, perhaps, the history of thought can include, in a broad sense, not only the histories of the various fields of learning but even the history of philosophy, which is the synthesis of them all. However, now that the history of various types of learning, and of general philosophy, has been broken up into various specialized fields of study, what is called "intellectual history" should have a *raison d'être* as history that stands apart from the history of philosophy or the history of learning, and precedes them. Thus, in contrast to theological history and the history of ethics, we have the history of religious thought and the history of ethical thought; and in contrast to the history of philosophy, we have the history of philosophical thought. In short, intellectual history is concerned with the consciousness side of culture and is, moreover, anterior to the history of learning or the history of philosophy in their strict sense.

Having arrived at such a concept of intellectual history, we can think of it as being comparatively more suitable — that is, having more *raison d'être* — in Japan, where the separate fields of learning and philosophy have not yet been independently developed, than in the West, where these fields are already well developed. Even in the West we see more *raison d'être* for intellectual history the farther back in history we look. But in Japan, where true scholarly re-cognition and construction had not yet occurred before the introduction of Western culture, treating the consciousness side of culture as intellectual history is particularly appropriate. In this way intellectual history has developed its own unique significance. On the other hand, if we try to apply various existing academic concepts — and to understand existing thoughts through forced abstraction, classification, systematization, and comprehension — then we may, because of this, miss the true meaning of traditional thought. For these reasons, we can say that Japanese intellectual history, or the history of thought, is not merely possible, but appropriate. And yet, even though such study is theoretically possible and appropriate, we face many practical difficulties in carrying out this kind of historical study. One matter which should be given very serious consideration is the diffuse quality of Japanese intellectual history.

In general, Japanese intellectual history in ancient times was a history of the introduction of Confucian and Buddhist thought and, in modern times, a history of the introduction of Western thought — a conflux of almost all the world's intellectual currents. This is a historical characteristic of Japan, an insular country. It is therefore proper to say that the content of Japanese intellectual history is, in one sense, made up of the various strains of Chinese, Indian and Western thought. But if this were the whole truth, Japanese intellectual history would be nothing more than a miniature copy of the intellectual history of the world — nothing but an extension of the history of Confucian, Buddhist, or Western thought. And I fear that such a situation would make it not merely extremely difficult but quite impossible to really establish Japanese intellectual history, for who would dare to devote himself to the historical study of all Oriental and Occidental thought? Furthermore, if Japanese thought was simply a confluence of various thoughts which had originated in other countries of culture, it would have no *raison d'être* except as an extension of the history of Chinese Confucianism, Indian or Chinese Buddhism, or Western philosophy in Japan; and there would be no need for an independent intellectual history of Japan. We have to search for that which will extricate Japanese intellectual history from this situation and which will provide it with an independent justification for existence. In doing this, I think there is no alternative but to concentrate on those qualities which, in some sense, are uniquely Japanese. The goal of Japanese intellectual history, then, should be to investigate that which has given rise to a certain Japaneseness, while foreign thoughts were absorbed and made structural elements of Japanese thought. This should bring us to the sphere of Japanese intellectual history, to the area limited by that which is Japanese, or has been Japanicized — to the study of the history of Confucianism, Buddhism and philosophy that is something more than a mere extension of the history of Confucianism in China, the history of Buddhism in China and India, and the history of philosophy in the West. In this way I think we can properly define the scope of research in Japanese intellectual history.

Having established the general meaning of intellectual history, and thus of Japanese intellectual history, we must then identify the position which this study holds within the established fields of scholarship. In a word, the problem is: specifically, to which of the already established fields is it close, or to which does it belong? The principal objects of research in intellectual history are of course written records. Research in thought cannot be carried on without them. At this point we cannot but mention philology, which has existed and developed since ancient times and which has become established as a separate field of study. Philology became established as a discipline in the German scholarly world during the latter part of the eighteenth, and the first part of the nineteenth, century. Its academic significance was clearly expressed in a dictum of its representative figure, August Böckh [1785–1868], as " the cognition of the products of the human spirit, that is, of cognitions."[1] In other words, it is the aim of philology to perceive the content of ancient written records, or thought, through exegetical and critical formal linguistic research. Cognition in philology — in spite of the fact that it ranges over the entire field of human consciousness — is different from that of philosophy and other disciplines because it is always concerned with re-cognition. Philology acquires its academic uniqueness from the fact that its re-cognition, or revival of cognition, is created objectively, never subjectively. Historically, philology was the classical study of Greece and Rome. Its nature then can be equated precisely with the academic nature of intellectual history in the sense that the subject of philological research was the whole of ancient thought before there was any modern specialization.

In Japan, Ancient Learning or National Learning (*kokugaku*) — which was similar to Western philology — was developed independently and organized superbly. The perfecter of this Ancient Learning was Motoori, who paralleled Böckh. The National Learning of Motoori was philological study that attempted to clarify ancient words and texts, and to elucidate ancient ideas and feelings. In his *Uiyamabumi*, quoted above, Motoori defined his study as follows: "Ancient Learning is a study in which, using only ancient texts, one investigates their origins and elucidates in detail things of the ancient age, without regard to anything written in later periods,"[2] What he did — with this understanding of his study and through research into the *Kojiki* (Record of Ancient Matters) and the *Genji monogatari* (Tale of Genji), classics of the Nara [710–784] and Heian [784–1160] eras — was philology in the fullest sense. Beginning with formal linguistic research into the ancient classics, he moved on to a clarification of the

---

1) [*Encyklopädie und Methodologie der Philologischen Wissenschaften* (Leipzig, 1886), 10.]
2) [*Motoori Norinaga zenshū* IX, 491.]

thought of the eras covered in these classics. In almost the same sense that Western philology managed on the whole to be the intellectual history of antiquity, National Learning became the intellectual history of our Nara and Heian eras. National Learning is therefore roughly equivalent to "the intellectual history of Japanese antiquity."

Nevertheless, it does not necessarily follow that existing National Learning, as it was, can ever constitute a history of Japanese thought. In this respect it is similar to Western philology, which likewise could not of itself become a history of ancient thought in the West. National Learning is even farther removed from the history of thought. More precisely, we cannot say that National Learning in its original form is, as yet, a history of Japanese thought, despite the fact that it can provide the foundations for such a history. It would seem that because of the nature of both Western philology and National Learning a given classic, or else individuals or periods represented by a classic, were seen, in a sense, as finished units. They tended to be treated rather superficially and were not fully viewed in terms of their phases of internal development. Consequently, the elucidation of intellectual development in relationships between one classic and another, or in internal relationships within a single classic, remained inadequate. But with a full re-cognition of the historical character of culture, and the realization of the meaning of historiography — which is a study of culture, the achievements of philology — which is also a study of culture — should logically have removed this inadequacy. Actually, Western philology developed in this direction after Böckh and witnessed the emergence of various branches of historical study as well as the establishment of a history of philosophy and the history of other fields of learning. Of course, along with this development, and as a result of academic specialization, the broad history of thought tended to yield ground to these specialized historical studies; but, at least in the case of the study of antiquity, the history of philosophy — which can almost be called intellectual history — became established as the highest historical study. But this sort of scholarly development had not yet occurred in our National Learning. Because of this, there is far more justification than in the case of Western philology for saying that National Learning was not yet intellectual history. Furthermore, since both Western philology and National Learning generally limited their sphere of research to antiqunity, and were not concerned with later periods, they were incomplete as historiography. To have become complete, it would have been necessary to extend study to other periods. In this connection, Böckh avoided "classical studies," the traditional term for philology, and maintained that the object of philology was the cognition of cognitions throughout all periods not merely in antiquity but in medieval and modern times as well. However, as I have already said, with the approach of modern times in the West, such an objective became difficult academically to achieve; and because of this, various sorts of academic specialization were inevitable. But in the case of National Learning, such an extension of interests to other periods was theoretically appropriate and practically possible. Nevertheless, Motoori — and most of his later students — did virtually nothing to extend the area of National Learning research. From the beginning the sphere of Motoori's research was limited to the period down to Heian. We might even say that he was too proud to carry on research in the classics of the medieval and post-medieval periods. It can be said that there was roughly the same tendency among later National Learning scholars as well.

And so it ought to be clear now that National Learning, as philology, comes closest to the history of Japanese thought and at the same time forms a basis for it; and it should also be clear in what ways it needs to be perfected as a history of Japanese thought. In short, when National Learning is perfected as a historical study of culture, then we will have Japanese intellectual history.

Proceeding from this consideration of the idea of "Japanese intellectual history" — particularly from a consideration of its concrete academic position — we can now examine methods of carrying on research in this new field of learning. There are two major stages to such research: the philological, and the historical. But before this there is the preparatory spade-work, as it were, of assembling, arranging, and delimiting the research materials. When we turn to the research itself, we must first determine the research topic and then look for materials that are pertinent to that topic. And at the same time we must delimit the material on the basis of the topic. It should be noted at this point that, as a principle of delimitation, it is necessary to inquire broadly and extensively without excessive attention to the nominal, or superficial qualities of the documents. As I have already pointed out, since history in our country had not yet been affected by the specialization of thought and learning, if historical materials are limited with excessive attention to their nominal value, one would be apt to overlook substantively important material. For example, if one used only the so-called didactic books as material for research, his history of Japanese ethical thought, or Japanese educational thought, would be sadly lacking in substance. In literature which is not tabbed as didactic we often find rather better material for research in ethical and educational thought. And the farther back in history we go for the subjects of our research, the truer this is. For example, in carrying on research in the Nara or pre-Nara eras, the *Kojiki,* the *Nihongi* (Chronicles of Japan), and the *Man' yōshū* (Anthology of a Myriad Leaves) must be used as historical material, regardless of where the problem lies.

Therefore, as a practical precaution in " delimiting " materials, it is safer, first, to discard that which is insignificant, rather than to pick out that which seems to be important. For assistance in this work, bibliographies, bibliographical commentaries, and chronological tables are references that will provide bibliographical information. And one should utilize source series, collected works, and source encyclopedias, all of which contain materials that already have been assembled and delimited. And so our preliminary gathering and delimiting of material can be carried out by utilizing the materials which are available in the source series and the like, but in pressing on with the research there must be a more purposeful arrangement of these materials by the researcher. In historical research it is generally best to have as much historical material as possible, but certainly research can be carried out before the gathering of materials has been completed. While history is, in a way, an inductive study, it is definitely not statistical. Ultimately, the materials must be kept or discarded — the gathering of materials, after all, is for this purpose. One should not be content with merely striving aimlessly to collect materials. Therefore, while it is certainly necessary to keep looking for new material, it is also necessary constantly to attempt evaluations and to make selections. In arranging the materials, with the above points in mind, it is convenient to divide the materials roughly, according to the research topic, into important and supporting materials. For such arrangement the bibliographical commentaries and indices will of course be useful, but they should not be used with the assumption that they are always reliable, because of occasional errors in these reference works which must be guarded against, and because compilers do not always have the same points of view as the researcher. Strictly speaking, the individuality of the researcher will already be coming into play, even in the "preparatory examination of tools," and so one must be sure to work cautiously.

The "philological stage" of the approach to intellectual history can be subdivided into two types of effort: textual criticism, and interpretation and comprehension. Textual criticism elucidates the nature and determines the significance of a given source through a consideration of such problems as its authenticity in whole or in part, the time and place of composition, and authorship. By means of this preparatory process an academic guarantee is given to the materials which are being arranged. Generally, materials published in the source serials and collected works should have been subjected to this criticism, but actually many of them have not. This is especially true of manuscripts and copies. Therefore, many materials cannot be used until they have been individually processed. There was a time when textual criticism and investigation, because of their importance, were considered to be the whole of philology. But we should not overstate their importance. It should not be forgotten that textual criticism and investigation are merely ancillary to both philology and history. Even their important "basic" significance is, after all, ancillary, not fundamental. Especially in the case of intellectual history, which deals with meaning and content, there is almost no *raison d'être* for mere textual criticism. Persons who putter around aimlessly in textual criticism get lost in dead-end streets. There are various areas of textual criticism, ranging from the grammatical area — in which each character is compared and corrected — to the problem of identifying the material as a whole; but ultimately the purpose is to determine the authenticity of the material. We should bear in mind, especially in intellectual history, that apart from considerations of authenticity, there exists the problem of importance. Just because a document is a forgery does not mean that it is valueless, for as a forgery it may have historical significance.

In carrying on research in intellectual history it is of vital importance that the materials be assigned chronological order. There will be varying degrees of complexity, depending on whether the materials are the writings of an individual or of many individuals, but the assignment of chronological order is always essential. Furthermore, items within a single document, whether by one or several authors, must be dated. For purposes of research in intellectual history, (which is devoted to the clarification of the development of thought,) the assignment of chronological order may be said to be almost a fundamental pre-condition.

The second phase of philological method of study — the one that follows textual criticism, and which is in fact interdependently associated with it — is interpretation and comprehension. This involves understanding correctly the meaning of the materials, separately and in linkage. It is identified with the term "exegesis and annotation" (*kunko chūshaku*). Interpretation and comprehension is a single process, beginning with the meaning of each word and culminating in their meaning as a whole; but a necessary condition, throughout, is that the materials at hand be interpreted *as they are,* with the objective comprehension suggested by that academic quality of "re-cognition" in philology — that is without the injection of the interpreter's subjective feelings. This is what Motoori had in mind in constantly emphasizing the importance of rejecting Chinese and Buddhist ideas and beliefs when interpreting the Japanese classics.

Interpretation and comprehension begin with the clarification of the meaning of words and phrases, which are the constituents of source material. And since these meanings are determined inductively from numerous examples, they can be established only on a grammatical basis. Along with a knowledge of grammar as a whole, it is essential to have a knowledge of the special grammar of the document at hand. Furthermore, the interpretation of the meaning of these words and phrases will be complete only when these words and phrases have been considered separately and in combination with each other, and analytically and synthetically. Thus interpretation, in the initial stages of interpreting words, already involves more than a mere grammatical knowledge.

Then we move on to comprehension, which comes by looking at the source materials, either partially or entirely, as a single thought unit and by understanding their meaning from a more composite point of view. It may be said that while interpretation aims at perceiving ideas, comprehension aims at perceiving thought. At this point, since it is necessary, in some cases, for the interpreter even to conceptualize in order to "re-cognize," other thoughts — even thoughts that are not expressed at all clearly or consciously in the documents — he will often have to have greater power of imagination and insight in comprehension than in interpretation. Not only is it possible to grasp the meaning of the whole without understanding individually difficult words and phrases, but concern about difficult words and phrases may at times prevent one from understanding the main ideas and beliefs of the classics. Even though one does not understand the meaning of 莫甞圓隣, this will not prevent him from comprehending the *Man'yōshū*. As Motoori said in his *Tama katsuma* (Jeweled Bamboo Basket), probing into the derivation of words, and into the meaning of those words that are specialized and obscure, is not the first principle for reading the ancient classics. But this does not justify arbitrariness on the part of the interpreter. There are two objective conditions which operate to prevent the subjective action of the interpreter from tending toward arbitrariness in his attempt to comprehend, and which will not permit distorted interpretations or forced analogies: the meaning of the words and phrases; and the individuality and chronology of the sources. We certainly cannot overlook these.

To summarize, the first, or philological, stage of the research method of intellectual history consists in interpreting correctly a given set of source materials in their correct form and correct filiation, and then in the re-cognition of the thoughts contained in the documents.

Then comes the second, or historical, stage. This second stage is the unfolding, or completion, of the first stage, just as philology should lead to history. Here the question of historical structure arises. To begin with, intellectual history emerges in the thought relationships among different sets of data. But in order to be made into history these relationships have to be subjected to selection and development. It has already been pointed out that history involves selection, not including all the data; and selection means the choosing and rejecting of data — from the value position of the historian, and with stress upon one essential problem. For example, when dealing with the history of ethical thought in the Nara Era, selection of data found in such classics as the *Kojiki* and the *Nihongi* is carried out from the "moral-thought" position and in accordance with the value of the data for understanding the problem. Here one should be careful to avoid confusions with moral judgment. Of course one cannot elucidate the moral-value relationships except on a foundation of moral judgment, but the moral judgment must always be internalized as history — it must not transcend it. Selection must be accomplished from this position. Therefore, only when all data are properly selected, separately and in groups, can they acquire, objectively, a historical quality and, at the same time, can history, subjectively and in accord with the data, begin to take on structure.

The concept of development is associated with perfecting the nascent historical structure — the chronological unfolding of value relationships. This does not mean lineal progression, but rather a process of advance toward an ultimate ideal. Development is produced by two conditions: one internal, and the other, external. Internally, development in based upon the logical or psychological causes of thought. Externally, it comes from the influence of environment, and of other thought. When we come to elucidating this sort of development in the material we have selected, we clarify that thought process which is constantly developing throughout the various relationships and which moves toward the ultimate value or ideal. Here we have intellectual history. But at this point we must admit that there is considerable room for the subjective activity of the researcher. That is, there are many cases in which " development " must be conceived by the researcher. History is not at all like a vein of ore in the ground waiting to be dug out. This quality of history becomes more pronounced as we move from the particular to the general; and that is why history resembles, in a sense, artistic creation.

Now we can realize how important it is for the historian to have broad vision and a liberal education. The researcher in history must never be content with investigating only narrow problems. Furthermore, history insofar as it is history, must fulfill the requirement that it be objectively sound. If you should ask where we will find that objective quality which will give credence to the subjective nature of the historical structure, I would say that it is found in such things as the rightness of the interpretations applied to each observed datum, and the rightness of the temporal sequence detected in the data relationships. One must always avoid distorting interpretations of the source material, or disregarding such facts as the temporal order and the presence or absence of relationships between documents.

Verbalizing such a historical structure is historical writing. And now we come to that which has been called "Japanese intellectual history." Historical writing, as an external manifestation of the historical structure, must always conform to, and not disturb, the conditions and nature of the above-described historical structure. Needless to say, literary and rhetorical qualities are needed insofar as historical writing is composition; but academic quality should not be impaired by literary embellishment. Other important points are: in citing references do not be satisfied with "secondary references" to original sources; strive for chronological accuracy; be careful not to let the use of modern terms cause you to distort your interpretations of the individuality and periodicity of the ideas and thoughts being treated; be careful, in the organizations of thoughts and ideas, not to lapse into unreasonable formalization; and do not confuse historical description with your own criticism.

The various stages of the research method described above are actually intertwined in a single process of research, but for the sake of clarity they have been discussed sequentially. Finally, I will deal directly with the application of this method of research.

In all instances one begins with a careful reading of the sources considered to be important for the research topic, using reliable texts which have been subjected to textual criticism by previous scholars, and following authorative annotations. But in this reading one should not be shackled, at first, to reading specifically for one's own research, but should attempt to comprehend the source itself. Later on, the source should be read a second and a third time with one's research topic in mind. But for research in intellectual history, naturally the principal matter is intellectual comprehension. Therefore, we should avoid being excessively preoccupied with the details of textual verification and annotation. But this certainly does not mean that it is all right to read carelessly. In the second or third reading, one should focus his entire scholarly effort on the intellectual comprehension of the data in the light of one's own research topic, while at the same time attempting various approaches, such as: compiling indices; trying to make summaries; drawing comparisons with other books, or with other parts of the same book; and consulting the research of others. As we refine these approaches, a way ahead — from a condition of groping in the dark — will gradually appear; and in time, by some enlightenment of our own, we will be able to make assumptions about the crux of the problem, that is, about that which is essential. If we can conceive of what might be considered a central idea, then we will proceed from that idea, testing it in other situations and investigating its validity in the documents at hand. If, as a result, other ideas — and relationships between these ideas — can be considered naturally, and explained, with this central idea as the focal point, we will be able to verify the accuracy of what we have conceived. If, on the other hand, some inconsistencies and irrationalities arise, we must turn back and make a fresh start. By going back over the above procedures time after time, we will succeed eventually in obtaining a firm hold on a central idea. If, as a result of careful research in important data, we are able to gain one true hold, we will have obtained an idea that will be equally true for other data. Then all sorts of secondary sources, and newly discovered sources, will support — from various positions — this central idea. It is usual at this point for even forgeries and unauthenticated works to have utility, according to their characteristics. If by narrowing these relationships, we can apply them to a given section of text, and so make sound choices, then by correctly understanding the key part of one section, we can arrive at an accurate understanding of the whole.

Since the building of a historical structure depends on the introduction of developmental order into the process of interpreting sources for their intellectual content, this process will be carried out first of all with reference to filiation of texts whose sequence has been established by critical theories that have stood the test of time. In the case of those sources for which the temporal position is not clear, we begin first with the relationships among textual groups, and then move on later to the problem of the temporal sequence within each group. What has been said above also applies to the important matter of making comparisons with historical developments in other periods and countries, and also to the matter of grasping and verifying — while following the above procedures — that which is crucial. Thus intellectual history is established when it is made clear by a true understanding of authentic data how various ideas and thoughts have developed from internal or external causes under the unifying force of a central idea or thought.

At this point one must be careful about drawing analogies from the history of foreign thought or philosophy. These should of course be consulted, but they should not cause us to overlook historical uniqueness. It should be borne in mind that it is the responsibility of history to recognize that while the thought development of man is, in one sense, controlled by stereotyped principles, it has, on the other hand, aspects which are unique. It is also the responsibility of history to recognize the manifestations of this uniqueness in peoples as well as in individuals.

Ultimately, then, the most important thing in research, practically speaking, is that we read and consider the principal sources carefully. Broadening the search for materials and making new discoveries should be carried out on such a foundation.

Let us give some thought to the common pitfalls of research historians. First, there is the antiquarian habit. Since historians with such a habit are interested in the past, they fall into the habit of valuing something simply because it is old. But the reason why the past has value is that in some way it has, or can have, an effect upon the present. It cannot be denied that antiquarianism has made contributions to history, but antiquarianism must not be confused with [historical] scholarship. When historical material has been discovered, that material — even when it has scholarly value — is not academically significant simply because of the search or the discovery. It should be the responsibility of the historian to make use of the material and to discover the value which derives from its meaning. Only when this is done can the work be called [historical] scholarship. This is why the discovery of heretofore unknown supplementary sources cannot, in many cases, be a primary concern.

The second pitfall is the digging habit. Since history requires the clarification of facts, the habit is common. But it should be noted that the clarification of fact is ultimately for the purpose of bringing out meaning. For this reason, the habit of simply digging up facts which are not useful in extracting meaning, and which will never have such utility, is likewise not a primary concern of history as scholarship. But persons are easily caught in such pitfalls, after all, because they do not really understand what scholarship is. A true understanding of scholarship is achieved through philosophical refinement. Philosophical training is important for scholars, and equally so for researchers in Japanese intellectual history. Of course philosophical refinement is indispensable for other reasons, particularly when the object is intellectual research.

In closing, I strongly urge that researchers in Japanese intellectual history read carefully *Uiyamabumi,* the book which I cited at the beginning of this study. It does not deal directly with Japanese intellectual history, but since National Learning has a close relationship to intellectual history, the book is an excellent guide for research in Japanese intellectual history. What is especially revealed is the breadth and thoroughness of Motoori's scholarly manner; and the book also indicates well the high road of scholarship. Therefore, it will do much to enlighten the scholar. Furthermore, it will supply concrete information about each ancient classic which should be read in a study of Japanese intellectual history — at least within the limits of antiquity. In addition, there is the old *Kokushigaku no shiori* (Guide to the Study of Japanese History) by Konakamura Kiyonori (1821–1895),[1] which includes concise comments about the principal source books in Japanese intellectual history. I will omit here a detailed discussion of other books of this type.

In the above I have written down an outline of methods of research in Japanese intellectual history. It is my opinion that the " history of the Japanese spirit " is not absolutely identical with Japanese intellectual history. In the final analysis, the former is really the history of the most essential part of the latter. Thus, what has been written here might be thought to apply to methods of research in " the history of the Japanese spirit."

---

1) [A National Learning scholar—a specialist in ancient institutional history who did much to promote the study of early Japanese history in the Meiji Era [1868–1912] both as a teacher and as a compiler of source materials.]

INDEX

Note: The title of book and the Japanese technical and special terms appear in italics

A

Agatai School (*Agataigaku* 縣居學) 110
Agatai shūgen roku 縣居集言錄 (Collected Utterances of Agatai) by Kamo Mabuchi 122, 127, 131
Age of Kami (*kamiyo* 神代) 9, 12–4, 24–6, 29, 38, 45, 53–4, 73–4, 91, 96, 120, 123, 133, 135, 142, 147–50, 154, 162, 170, 175, 178, 186, 211, 242
Ahakihara 阿波岐原 24, 30
ai 愛 (See Love)
Akahito 赤人 116
akaki kokoro 明き心 (bright heart) 31, 42
Akiyama no Shitabi-otoko 秋山之下氷壯夫 69
Ama-terasu Ō-mi-kami 天照大神 (See Sun Goddess)
Ame no Mi-naka-nushi kō 天之御中主考 (Study of Ame no Mi-naka-nushi no Kami) by Watanabe Ikaimaro 21
Ame no Mi-naka-nushi no Kami 天之御中主神 (Kami Master of the Center of Heaven) 7, 18–9, 21, 167–8, 194–5, 200, 211–2, 215–6
Anaho 穴穗 Prince 66
Analects (*Lun-yü* 論語) 79, 99, 100, 105
ancestor worship 44, 55, 68, 146, 167
Ancient Learning (*kogaku* 古學) 9, 72, 79–80, 87–8, 90, 101–2, 109–10, 166, 169, 197, 201, 245, 251

i

INDEX

Ancient Learning Shinto (*kogaku shintō* 古學神道) 4–5, 9, 16–8, 28–9, 43, 45, 166, 169, 175, 190, 211, 241
Ancient-Meaning School (*kogigaku* 古義學) 79, 88, 98–101, 104, 107
Ancient-rhetoric School (*kobunjigaku* 古文辭學) 79, 88
Ancient Way (*kodō* 古道) 4–5, 28, 43, 54, 73, 82–3, 91–2, 118–9, 126–8, 136, 141–2, 145, 147–8, 153, 161, 163, 179–80, 185
antiquarianism 73, 95–169, 262
araburu 荒ぶる (rough) 58
araburu Kami 荒神 (rough Kami) 57
arahitogami 現人神 (manifest Kami) 14–5
Arai Hakuseki 新井白石 [1657–1725] 15, 173
aru 顯る (manifest) 22
ashi 惡 (bad) 22, 58, 155

B

Ban Nobutomo 伴信友 [1775–1846] 86
Bendōsho 辨道書 (Definition of the Way) by Dazai Jun 4
Benevolence (*jin* 仁) 40, 100, 102, 122, 125, 145, 193
Board of Shinto Missionaries (*senkyō-shi* 宣敎使) 204–5, 219–22
Boeckh, August [1785–1868] 77, 179, 251–2
Book of Mencius (*Meng-tzu* 孟子) 79, 99, 100–2, 105
Buddhism: moral influence 37–42, affect on Keichū 72, 80; rejection, 89–90, 97–100; persecution, 204–7, 232–3
Buddhistic Shinto 6–8, 15–6, 18, 25–7, 32–4
Bun'i kō 文意考 (Study of Textual Criticism) by Kamo Mabuchi 110, 130
bummei kaika 文明開化 (civilization and enlightenment) 207–8, 234
Bummei ron no gairyaku 文明論之槪略 (Outline of

INDEX

Civilization Theory) by Fukuzawa Yukichi 210
bunkyō seiji 文教政治 (rule through culture and learning) 98
button 佛恩 (Buddha's blessings) 164

C

Chamberlain, B. H. 178, 238, 241–2
Charter Oath (*gokajō no seimon* 五個條の誓文) 204
wisdom (*chi* 智) 39, 41, 122, 125
China 122–3, 125–6, 129, 146–9, 153–4, 158, 162–3, 243, 250
ching 敬 (respect) 43
chinsai 鎮祭 (Pacifying Festival) 205
Chiyo no sumika 千代住處 (The Eternal Abode) by Oka Kumaomi 192
Christianity 10, 18, 21, 29, 47–8, 169, 181–2, 204, 211, 213–6, 221–7, 233, 235–6, 239
Chūai 仲哀 Emperor 30, 85
Chu Hsi 朱熹 Confucianism 8, 16, 88, 98–104
Chuang-tzu 莊子 54, 125, 136
chūkogaku 中古學 (Heian Learning) 82–3
Chūkun aikoku 忠君愛國 (loyalty to the Emperor and love of country 238
Ch'un-ch'iu 春秋 (Spring and Autumn Annals) 103
Chung-yung 中庸 (Doctrine of the Mean) 40
concealed and mysterious (*yūmei* 幽冥) 171, 202, 215, 218
concealed world (*yūkai* 幽界) 22, 55, 167
Compassion (*ji* 慈) 39, 41, 145–6, 193
Confucianism: attacked by Motoori 28; influence on Hirata School, 29; influence on Kitabatake Chikafusa, 38–41; influence on Tokugawa thought, 54; introduction and early influence, 61–9; early influece on Ancient Learning, 79–80; excluded by National Learning, 81, 87; attacked by National Learning, 88–91; (See Chu Hsi Confucianism)

INDEX

Confucian Shinto ··4, 8, 14, 16, 28, 88–9
creativity (*musubi* 產靈) ································18, 20, 24, 55 59, 183, 190, 193 214
Creator Kami (*musubi no kami* 產靈神) ······················195, 211, 214–7

D

dai 臺 (Directorate) ···19–20
daigakkō 大學校 (university) ··19
daigūji 大宮司 (Great Shrine Magistrate) ···································206
daikyō 大敎 (See Great Teaching)
daikyō-in 大敎院 (See Great Teaching Institute)
Daimyōjin 大明神 (Great Illustrious Kami) ·························35–6, 42
dajōkan 太政官 (Council of State) ··204
Dazai Jun (Shundai) 太宰純(春臺) [1680–1747]···············4, 104, 108, 163
Department of Shinto Affairs (*jingikan* 神祇官)···203–5, 212, 222, 233, 237, 239
Dōjō monjin on-kokoroegaki 堂上門人御心得書 (Instructions for Students in the Inner Palace) by Takenouchi Shikibu ···17
dokon 土金 (earth-gold) ···43
Dokugo 獨語 (Solitary Words) by Dazai Jun ································104
Dōmō nyūgakumon 童蒙入學門 (A Child's Introduction to Learning) by Hirata Atsutane ···44
Dual Shinto (*ryōbushinto* 兩部神道) ····························4, 6–8, 26, 38
Dutch Learning (*rangaku* 蘭學) ·································181, 196, 199

E

e 壞 (destructive [kalpa]) ···26
Emishi 蝦夷···63–4
Emperor: Unbroken line of descent, 11, 23, 82, 123, 129, 143, 153: manifest Kami, 15, 61, 145, 222; descendant of Heavenly Kami, 17; in Satō Nobuhiro plan, 19; authority of, 27; loyalty to, 31–2; Heavenly Sun Succession, 113, 126, 143–4
Emperorism (*sonnō shugi* 尊皇主義) ···························89, 169, 211

iv

INDEX

Engishiki 延喜式 112, 236
Engishiki norito kai jo 延喜式祝詞解序 (Preface to "An Understanding of the Shinto Liturgies in the *Engishiki*") by Kamo Mabuchi 121, 124, 130
Ether (*ki* 氣) 99–100, 189

F

Final Age (*mappō* 末法) 26–7, 96
First Tramp in the Mountains (*Uiyamabumi* 初山踏) by Motoori Norinaga 73, 76, 82, 245–6
Founder Shinto (*kyōso shintō* 教祖神道) 5, 10, 16, 21, 29, 45, 209, 234
fu 府 (Bureau) 19–20
fudoki 風土記 (ancient provincial gazetteer) 51, 180
Fujitani Mitsue 富士谷御杖 [1768–1823] 174
Fujiwara Seika 藤原惺窩 [1561–1619] 8, 98
fukko shintō 復古神道 (See Restoration Shinto)
Fukuba Bisei 福羽美靜 [1831–1907] 205, 221–2
Fukuda Gyōkai 福田行誡 [1806–1888] 223
Fukuzawa Yukichi 福澤諭吉 [1834–1901] 210
Fusō 扶桑 Sect 10
Fusō ryakki 扶桑略記 (Abbreviated Record of Ancient Japan) 4
Fu-sui-sō 風水草 (Wind and Water) by Yamazaki Ansai 84

G

gegū shintō 外宮神道 (See Outer Shrine Shinto)
Gengen shū 元元集 (Notes on Origins) by Kitabatake Chikafusa 171
Genji monogatari 源氏物語 (See *Tale of Genji*)
gijidō 議事堂 (Discussion Hall) 19
godō 悟道 (enlightenment) 169
gogyō 五行 (five elements) 84

INDEX

Go-i kō 語意考 (On the Meaning of Words) by Kamo Mabuchi 131
Gonda Naosuke 權田直助 [1809–1887] 174, 190, 192–3
gonge 權化 (incarnation) 39
Great Purification (*ōharae* 大祓) 85, 124, 207, 223
Great Purification liturgy (*ōharae no kotoba* 大祓詞) 30, 59, 70, 83–4, 86, 153, 222
Great Teaching (*daikyō* 大教) 205–6, 208, 219, 233
Great Teaching Institute (*daikyō-in* 大教院) 205–9, 212, 214, 217, 225–7, 233–4
Gukanshō 愚管抄 (Summary of My Humble Views) by Jien 26–7
Gyojū gaigen 馭戎慨言 (Complaint on the Failure to Bridle the Chinese) by Motoori Norinaga 170
gyōki 澆季 (age of attenuation) 96

H

Hachiman 八幡 (Great Boddhisatva) 33, 35–8
Hakatoko 博德 125
hakkō ichiu 八紘一宇 (whole world under one roof) 240
Haruyama no Kasumi-otoko 春山之霞壯夫 69
Hattori Nakatsune 服部中庸 [1757–1824] 181, 196
Hattori Nankaku 服部南郭 [1683–1749] 105, 110, 181, 196
Hayabusa-wake 隼別 Prince 65
Hayashi Razan 林羅山 [1583–1657] 8, 88, 98, 172
Heaven (*ten* 天) 27, 183, 188–9, 191, 194–5, 200, 217
Heavenly Kami (*tenjin* 天神) 17, 21, 167–8, 207, 217
Hihon tamakushige 秘本玉櫛筍 (Secret Book of the Jeweled Comb Box) by Motoori Norinaga 28, 161–2, 170

INDEX

Hirata Atsutane 平田篤胤 [1776—1843]............4, 10, 18, 21, 28–9, 44, 48, 72, 86, 166–9, 174, 180, 182–5, 189–99, 201–29, 241, 243–4
Hirata Kanetane 平田鐵胤 [1799—1880]............203, 209
Hirata School 5, 10, 166, 199, 201, 216–7, 219, 233
Hirata Shinto 9–10, 21, 28–9, 168–9, 203–29, 243
Hitachi fudoki 常陸風土記 (Ancient Gazetteer for the Province of Hitachi) 69
Hitomaro 人麿 116
hōhon hanshi 報本反始 (return to beginnings) 96
honji suijaku 本地垂迹 (See "manifestations of original Buddhas")
honzen no sei 本然の性 (Primary Nature) 99
Hōreki 寶曆 Incident 17
Hori Hidenari 堀秀成 [1819—1887] 201
Hori Keizan 堀景山 [1688—1757] 137
Horikawa 堀河 School 101
Ho-shizume no matsuri 火鎮祭 (Fire-Pacifying Festival) 183
Hyakunin isshu 百人一首 (One Hundred Poems by One Hundred Poets) 111, 137
Hyakunin isshu kaikan shō 百人一首改觀抄 (Notes on a Re-examination of the *Hyakunin isshu*) by Keichū 137
hyaku-ō 百王 (hundred kings) 26–7

I

Ibuki oroshi 氣吹おろし (Wind of Atsutane) by Hirata Atsutane 213
Ichijō Kaneyoshi 一條兼良 [1402—1481] 7, 171, 176–7, 182, 184, 198
I-ching 易經 (Book of Changes) 3–4, 102

INDEX

Ichinobe 市邊 Prince 67
Imbe no Masamichi 忌部正通 7, 171, 176
Imperial Country (*kōkoku* 皇國) 18, 46, 73–5, 139, 144,
                                  203, 207, 233
Imperial Edict (*senmyō* 宣命 or *mikotonori* 勅) ...2, 19, 31–2, 70, 110, 112,
                                  134, 205, 219, 222, 233
Imperial Regalia (*shinki* 神器) 26, 36, 38–41, 187, 230
in 隱 (hidden) 168
India 122, 197–8, 243, 250
inken 隱顯 (hidden and manifest) 168
Inō Hidenori 伊能頴則 200
iryoku 威力 (awesome potency) 2
Ise monogatari 伊勢物語 (See *Tale of Ise*)
Ise Sadatake 伊勢貞丈 [1715–1784] 173
Ise Shintō 伊勢神道 (See Outer Shrine Shinto)
Isonokami sazamegoto 石上私淑言 (Whispered
    Words of the Past) by Motoori Norinaga 28, 138, 170
Itō Hirobumi 伊藤博文 [1841–1909] 228, 235
Itō Jinsai 伊藤仁齋 [1627–1705] 8, 79, 90, 98–102, 104,
                                  108, 132
Itō Togai 伊藤東涯 [1670–1736] 101, 107
Itsu no chiwaki 稜威道別 (Awesome Way-
    Clearing) by Tachibana Moribe 185
Itsu no kuchitsuge 稜威口誥 by Kubo Sueshige 192
Iwakura Tomomi 岩倉具視 [1825–1883] 203, 227, 236
Izanagi 伊邪那岐 14–5, 19, 30, 59, 143,
                                  178, 183, 189, 214, 231
Izanami 伊邪那美 14–5, 19, 57, 143, 152,
                                  178, 183, 188–9, 214, 231
Izumo 出雲 13, 15, 25, 57, 124, 175–7,
                                  185, 188, 191, 206, 209
Izumo fudoki 出雲風土記 (Ancient Gazetteer
    of the Province of Izumo) 69
Izushi-otome 伊豆志袁登賣 69

INDEX

J

japanese Learning (*wagaku* 和學) ··106–7
Japanese spirit (*Nihon seishin* 日本精神) ···············47, 49, 92, 264
Japanism (*Nihon shugi* 日本主義) ·························87–9, 91, 95
ji 慈 (See Compassion)
Jien 慈圓 [1155–1225] ··26
Jikkinshō 十訓抄 (Summary of the Ten Injunctions) ··33–4
Jikkō 實行 Sect ··10
Jimmu 神武 Emperor··26, 203–4, 219–21
jin 仁 (See Benevolence)
Jindai kuketsu 神代口訣 (Oral Traditions of the Age of Kami) by Imbe no Masamichi ·················171, 176
Jindai no maki dokken 神代之卷獨見 (Private Views about the Age of Kami Books) by Ise Sadatake ··173, 176
jingi jimukyoku 神祇事務局 (See Office of Shinto Affairs)
jingiin 神祇院 (Shinto Affairs Chamber) ···············237, 240
jingikan 神祇官 (See Department of Sihnto Affairs)
Jingū 神后 Empress··122, 231
Jingū 神宮 Sect···10
Jinja kyoku 神社局 (Bureau of Shinto Shrines) ················237
jinja shintō 神社神道 (Shrine Shinto) ·····························10, 230
Jinmotsu 神物 (Kami stuff) ··36
Jinnō shōtōki 神皇正統記 (Record of the True Lineage of the Sacred Emperors) by Kitabatake Chikafusa···························26–7, 36, 38–40, 171
Jitō 持統 Empress [646–703] ································115, 124
jō 成 (formative [*kalpa*]) ···26
Jōdo shū 浄土宗 (See Pure Land Sect)
Jōei shikimoku 貞永式目 (Jōei [1232–1233] Code)················34
jōkogaku 上古學 (Nara Learning) ·······························82
Jomei 舒明 Emperor [593–641]································124
jū 住 (existing [*kalpa*])···26

ix

INDEX

jugaku shintō 儒學神道 (See Confucian Shintō)
Jūichi kendai roku hyō 十一兼題錄評 (Criticism of the Elevn Themes) by Sasaki Yūchō 213–4
jukyō shintō 儒教神道 (See Confuctiou Sintō)

K

Kada Arimaro 荷田在滿 [1706–1751] 109
Kada Azumamaro 荷田春滿 [1669–1736] 8–9, 72, 81–2, 84, 86 90,
                                                            106–10, 116–7, 128, 132
Kadono Kawakatsu 葛野河勝..70
Kaempfer, Engelbert [1651–1716] 5
Ka-i kō 歌意考 (On the Spirit of Poetry) by
  Kamo Mabuchi 130
kajiri 呪詛 (imprecation) 155
kalpa (kō 劫 or age) 26
Kami 神 (Japanese deity): definition 2, 55; ancestral 4, 11, 23, 29, 68,
  143, 145, 166; solar, 13, 144–5; creative 19, 143; good and bad, 22–3,
  57–60; essential nature, 23–4; bending and straightening, 24; birth
  of 30, 32; moral ideas concerning 31–6; revelations 43; invoking
  power of 55–7; genealogy, 61; moralization, 68–70; faith in, 125–6;
  diverse types, 151; before Heaven and earth 182, 213; creativity of
  183, 190; in Heaven 188; virtue 207
Kami Body (*shintai* 神體)..34, 38, 41
Kami Country (*shinkoku* 神國)..................21, 37, 89, 238, 242–3
Kamigakari 神懸り (Kami possession) 56
Kamigoto 神事 (worship of Kami) 2, 156, 182
Kami-musubi 神產靈 (Sacred Creating Kami)...18–9, 55, 143, 155, 194,
                                                                 215
Kami no ke 神の氣 (Kami exhalation) 56
Kami no tatari 神の祟 (Kami curses) 56
Kamiyo 神代 (See Age of Kami)
Kamiyo no masagoto 神代正語 (True Words
  of the Age of Kami) by Motoori Norinaga 182
Kamo Mabuchi 賀茂眞淵 [1697–1769]..............9, 43, 54, 82–6, 88, 90,
                                                      95–131, 133–6, 138, 140–2,

INDEX

                          148–9, 152, 158, 160–2, 164, 173, 180

Kamo-ō kashū 賀茂翁家集 [Collected Poems of Kamo] 116, 131

Kamōsho 呵妄書 (Rebuke of Error) by Hirata Atutane 4

kampeisha 官幣社 (shrines supported by national government) 236

kan 官 (Officer) 19

Kannagara 惟神 (being as Kami) 2

Kanji kō jo 冠辭考序 (Preface to Study of Poetic Episthets) by Kamo Mabuchi 111, 130, 133

Kannagara no daidō 惟神の大道 (Great Way of Kami) 205

Karu 輕, Crown Prince 65–6, 85

Karu no Ōiratsume 輕大娘 65–6

Kasuga Shrine 春日神社 35–6

Katari no Omi Imaro 語臣猪麿 69

kataura 肩卜 (scapula divination) 56

Kawamura Hidene 河村秀根 [1723–1792] 2, 68

kegare 穢れ (pollution) 30, 44, 151

kei 敬 (respect) 99

Keichū 契沖 [1640–1701] 8, 71–2, 79–83, 86, 90, 106–8, 111, 116, 128, 132, 137–41, 150, 161, 163, 165, 172–3, 180

ken 賢 (worthy) 125

Ken'en 蘐園 School 104–5

kenkai 顯界 (visible world) 22, 55

Kenkin sengo 獻芹詹語 by Yano Haruichi 203–4

Kenkoku shinbyō 建國神廟 (National Founding Shrine) 239

kenro 顯露 (visible and open) 175–6

Ken'yū-jun kōron 顯幽順考論 (Thought and Theory about the Relationship between

INDEX

the Visible and the Concealed) by Mutobe
Yoshika ··190
Kenzō 顯宗, Emperor································67, 213
keshiki けしき (strange) ·······························58
Ketsuja mondō 決邪問答 (Questions and Answers on Identifying Heresy)·················213
ki 氣 (See Ether)
kihangaku 規範學 (norm study) ···············74–6, 82, 86
Kikkawa Koretari 吉凶惟足 [1616–1694]················8, 172
kikkyō sōsei 吉川相生 (mutual generation of good and evil) ························24–5, 27–8
kishitsu no sei 氣質の性 (Pysical Nature) ···········99
Kitabatake Chikafusa 北畠親房 [1293–1354]·········7, 26, 36–42, 171
kitō 祈禱 (prayer to Kami) ·····················36, 58
kiyoki kokoro 清き心 (pure heart) ············31, 42, 59
Knox, G. W. ······································179
kō 劫 (See *kalpa*)
kobunjigaku 古文辭學 (See Ancient-rhetoric School)
kōchōgaku 皇朝學 (Imperial Learning) ············72
kodō 古道 (See Ancient Way)
kōdō 皇道 (Imperial Way)·······················44
Kōdō sōsho 講道叢書 (Collection of Studies on the Way) ·····························212
Kodō taii 古道大意 (Outline of the Ancient Way) by Hirata Atsutane···············5, 213
kogaku 古學 (See Ancient Learning)
kogaku shintō 古學神道 (See Ancient-Learning Shintō)
Kogaku yō 古學要 (Essentials of Ancient Learning) by Motoori Norinaga ···········196
kogigaku 古義學 (See Ancient-Meaning School)
Kogo shūi 古語拾遺 (Gleanings from Ancient Stories) ·································51, 181
Kōgyoku 皇極, Empress [594–661]··················70
Kojiki 古事記 (Chronicle of Ancient Matters) ···12–5, 24, 28–30, 32, 38, 43, 51–4, 62–70, 73–5,

INDEX

                                       83, 85, 107, 112, 123, 133–6, 140, 142, 149, 150, 162–3, 166–7, 171, 174–9, 181–3, 185, 188, 201, 211–14, 224, 242, 251, 254, 258

Kojiki betsuden 古事記別傳 (Another Commentary on the *Kojiki*) by Ochiai Naobumi 201

Kojiki den 古事記傳 (Commentary on the *Kojiki*) by Motoori Norinaga 12, 72, 134, 142, 150, 173, 181, 185

Kojiki uragaki 古事記裏書 (Notes on the *Kojiki*) by Urabe Kanebumi 170

Kokinshū 古今集 (Anthology of Ancient and Modern Times) 104–5, 111

Kokin yozai shō 古今餘材抄 (Miscellaneous Notes on the *Kokinshū*) by Keichū 137

kokka shintō 國家神道 (State Shintō) 230

kōkoku 皇國 (See Imperial Country)

kōkoku shugi 皇國主義 (Imperial-Country-ism) 11–22, 29, 46–8

kokugaku 國學 (See National Learning)

kokuheisha 國幣社 (shrines supported by provincial governments) 236, 238

Koku-i kō 國意考 (On the Spirit of the Nation) by Kamo Mabuchi 122, 127, 131

kokumi 瘜肉 (skin excrescences) 84–5

Kokushigaku no shiori 國史學の栞 (Guide to the Study of Japanese History) by Konakamura Kiyonori 263

kokutai 國體 (See Nation Body)

Konakamura Kiyonori 小中村清矩 [1821–1895] 264

Konkō 金光 Sect 10, 21

Konoe Tadafusa 近衞忠房 [1838–1873] 205, 212

Korea 60–1, 84–5, 122, 238

Koromo no Ko 衫子 69

xiii

INDEX

kōsei 公正 (fairness) ··37
Koshichō 古史徵 (Evidence of Ancient History)
 by Hirata Atsutane ··181
Koshiden 古史傳 (Commentary on "A Com-
 positition of Ancient History") by Hirata
 Atsutane ···181, 218
Koshi seibun 古史成文 (A Composition of
 Ancient History) by Hirata Atsutane ·········180–82, 212
Kōshō 光勝 Priest ··206
Kōson 光尊 Priest ··206
Kotoshiro-nushi no Kami 事代主神 ····························188
kotodama 言魂 (word spirit) ·····································184
Kōtoku 孝德 Emperor [596–654] ························70, 122
kotoura 琴占 (harp divination) ···································56
kū 空 (empty [*kalpa*]) ···26
kuan 観 (contemplate) ··3
Kubo Sueshige 久保季玆 [1830–1886] ···········174, 190, 192, 217, 219
kukadachi 探湯 (trial by boiling water) ·····················56
Kumaso 熊襲 ···63–4
Kumazawa Banzan 熊澤蕃山 [1619–1681] ···············171
kundoku 訓讀 (reading Chinese characters in
 the Japanese fashion) ···52
Kuni-toko-tachi no Mikoto 國常立尊 ····························7
Kunitsu tsumi 國罪 (earthly *tsumi*) ···························84–5
kuniumi 國生み (birth of land) ···············14–5, 23, 150, 160
kunko chūshaku 訓詁註釋 (exegesis and
 annotation) ··257
Kurozumi 黑住 Sect ··10, 16, 21, 209
Kuzubana 葛花 (Arrowroot Blossoms) by
 Motoori Norinaga ···136, 170
Kwammu 桓武 Emperor [736–805] ····························31
kyōbushō 教部省 (See Ministry of Religion)
kyōdōshoku 教導職 (See Office of Religious Instruction)
kyōkadai no daishi 教化臺の大師 (Upper
 Master of the Directorate of Indoctrination) ············19

xiv

INDEX

kyōmon ron 敎門論 (Discussion of Religious
   Sects) by Nishi Amane 228
kyomu tentan 虛無恬淡 (nothingness and quietism) 125
kyōsei 敎正 (Instructor-Rectifyer) 206
Kyōsho henshū taii 敎書編輯大意 (Important
   Points for Compiling Religious Books) 215
kyōso shintō 敎祖神道 (See Founder Shintō)
kyūji 舊辭 (old stories) 53

L

Lao-tzu (Tao-tê-ching) 老子(道德經) 54, 125–6, 128–9, 135–6
Li-chi 禮記 (Record of Rites) 102
Li P'an-lung 李攀龍 101, 103–4
liturgies (*norito* 祝詞) 9, 30, 51, 56, 111, 113, 124, 181, 183
Love (*ai* 愛) 100, 146
Lun-yü 論語 (See Analects)

M

maga (bent) 58
magatsubi no Kami 禍津日神 (bending Kami) 24, 55, 57, 150
magokoro 眞心 (See Sincere Heart)
majinai 呪 (spell) 56
makai 魔界 (demon world) 192
Maki-bashira 眞木柱 (True-Wood Pillar) by
   Yano Harumichi 216
makura kotoba 枕詞 (poetic epithet) 113
Manabi no agetsurai 學びの論ひ (Discussion of
   Learning) by Kamo Mabuchi 130
mandate of Heaven (*temmei* 天命) 16, 102
manifestations of the original Buddhas
   (*honji suijaku* 本地垂迹) 6–7, 18, 38–9, 167, 208
Man'yō daishōki 萬葉代匠記 (Commentary on
   the *Man'yōshū*) by Keichū 172

INDEX

Man'yō kai tsūshaku narabi ni shakurei jo 萬葉解通釋并釋例序 (Preface to "A General Interpretation to the *Man'yōshū* with Examples") by Kamo Mabuchi 130
Man'yō kō 萬葉考 (Study of *Man'yōshū*) by Kamo Mabuchi 113, 119, 133
Man'yō kō jo 萬葉考序 (Preface to "Study of the *Man'yōshū*") by Kamo Mabuchi 113, 115, 120
Man'yō kō narabi ni bekki jo 萬葉考并別記序 (Preface to "Study of the *Man'yōshū*" and "Supplement to Study of *Man'yōshū*") by Kamo Mabuchi 130
Man'yōshū 萬葉集 (Anthology of a Myriad Word Leaves) 9, 43, 58, 69, 76, 79–82, 88, 104–8, 110–24, 127–8, 133–5, 140–2, 153, 162, 172–3, 254, 258
Man'yōshū monmoku 萬葉集問目 (Questions about the *Man'yōshū*) by Motoori Norinaga 134
mappō 末法 (See Final Age)
Matachi 麻多智 69
mei 冥 (mysterious) 36
meijō shugi 明淨主義 (brightness-purity-ism) 11, 29–48
Meng-tzu 孟子 (See *Book of Mencius*)
mi-utsukushimi 御慈 (divine compassion) 193
Michi no hitokoto 道之一言 (A Word about the Way) by Mutobe Yoshika 195, 201
mikotonori 勅 (See Imperial Edict)
mikunimanabi 皇國學 (Imperial Country Learning) 72–3
Minamoto no Sanetomo 源實朝 [1192–1219] 116
Ministry of Religion (*kyōbushō* 教部省) 205–6, 209–10, 225, 233–4
Ministry of Shintō Affairs (*jingishō* 神祇省) 205, 207, 222, 237
mioya no kami 御祖神 (Imperial ancestral Kami) 142

xvi

INDEX

Misogi 禊 Sect ... 10
Mita Hōkō 三田葆光 ... 223
Mitake 御嶽 Sect ... 10
Miwata Takafusa 三輪田高房 [1823–] ... 218
miyabi 雅 (elegance) ... 115
Mommu 文武 Emperor [683–707] ... 115
mono no aware 物のあわれ (sensibility to things) ... 75, 138, 162
monotheism ... 21, 167, 226
Mori Arinori 森有禮 [1847–1889] ... 224, 225
Mori Terumasa 森暉昌 [1685–1752] ... 108–9
Motoori Norinaga 本居宣長 [1730–1801] ... 4, 9, 12, 17–8, 24, 28, 43, 52, 54, 67–8, 71–6, 82–6, 89–90, 92, 111, 131–70, 173–4, 181–5, 187, 189, 195–6, 198, 212, 214, 216, 241–6, 251, 253, 257–8, 263
Motoori Norinaga 本居宣長 by Muraoka Tsunetsugu ... 77
Motoori Ōhira 本居大平 [1756–1833] ... 196
Murdoch, James A., ... 166
mushi 無私 (unselfishness) ... 37
musubi 産靈 (See creativity)
Mutobe Yoshika 六人部是香 [1798–1863] ... 174, 190–1, 195, 201
Myōtei mondō 妙貞問答 (Dialogue between Myōshū and Yūtei) ... 48

N

Nagoshinoya iko 名越舍遺稿 (Extant Manuscripts of [Gonda] Naosuke) ... 192
Nakamura Masanao 中村正直 [1832–1891] ... 223, 235,
Nan Kojiki den 難古事記傳 (Criticism of *Kojiki den*) by Tachibana Moribe ... 185
Nanri Yūrin 南里有鄰 [1812–1864] ... 48, 168–9

INDEX

naobi 直日 (straightening) 59
naobi no kami 直日神 (straightening Kami) 24, 55
naobi no mitama 直日靈 (Spirit of Straightening) by Motoori Norinaga .... 4 note²⁾, 142, 170
naoki 直 (direct) 115
naru 成る (becoming) 22
Nation Body (*kokutai* 國體) 44, 82, 89, 91, 129, 207, 210, 222, 226–7
National Learning (*kokugaku* 國學) 54, 71–94, 97, 107, 116–7, 128–9, 132, 164–5, 172, 201, 221–2 251–3, 263
ne no kuni 根の國 or *ne no katasu kuni* 根の堅洲國 (root country) 31, 178, 192
Nihongi 日本紀 (Chronicles of Japan) 2–3, 13, 24, 29, 38, 51, 53, 61–70, 73–5, 85, 107, 112, 123, 125, 135–6, 171, 173, 175–7, 181, 182–3, 186, 211–13, 223–4, 242, 254, 258
Nihongi sanso 日本紀纂疏 (Commentaries on the *Nihongi*) by Ichijō Kaneyoshi 7, 171, 176, 182, 184, 198
Nihongi shiki 日本紀私記 (lecture notes on the *Nihongi*) 3
Nihon shiki 日本史記 (Notes on the History of Japan) 171
Niimanabi にひ學び (Primary Learuing) by Mabuchi 115, 130
Ni-ni-gi no Mikoto 邇々藝命 14, 40
ninjō shugi 人情主義 (doctrine of human feeling) 139
Nintoku 仁德 Emperor 61, 64
Nishi Amane 西周 [1829–1897] 228
Nonoguchi Takamasa 野々口隆正 [1792–1871] 174, 190, 196
norito 祝詞 (See liturgies)
Norito kō jo 祝詞考序 (Preface to Study of

INDEX

Shinto Liturgies") by Kamo Mabuchi ········ 84, 111, 124, 130
noroi 詛 (curse) ··· 55, 57–8
noroigoto 詛言 (curse words) ································ 56

O

Ochiai Naoaki 落合直亮 [1852–1934] ·················· 218
Ochiai Naobumi 落合直文 [1840–1891] ··············· 201
Oda Nobunaga 織田信長 [1534–1582] ···················· 97
Office of Religious Instruction (*kyōdōshoku* 教道職) ·· 205–6, 233
Office of Shinto Affairs (*shintō jimukyoku* 神道事務局 or *jingi jimukyoku* 神祇事務局) ··· 203, 208, 217, 218, 219, 233–4
Ogyū Sorai 荻生徂徠 [1666–1728] ········ 8, 79, 88, 90, 101–7, 128–9, 132
ōharae no kotoba 大祓詞 (See Great Purification Liturgy)
Ohoke 意富祁 Prince ·· 67–8
Ōjin 應神, Emperor ······························ 36, 38–9, 69, 221
Oka Kumaomi 岡熊臣 [1783–1851] ············ 174, 190, 192
Ō-kuni-nushi no Kami 大國主神 ········· 13, 155, 167, 184, 188, 193–4, 216–8
Ōkuni Takamasa 大國隆正 [1792–1871] ······ 203, 209, 219, 221
Omi no michi 臣道 (Way of the Subject) by Motoori Norinaga ·· 170
Omoi-kane no Kami 思兼神 (Thought Combining Kami) ·· 55
Ō-na-muchi 大己貴 (Great Kami of Izumo) ······· 57, 175–7, 188
Ōnishi Hajime 大西祝 [1864–1899] ·························· 158
onrai 恩賚 (grace) ·· 193
o-oshiki 雄々しき (manly) ······································· 115
Ōusu 大碓 Prince ·· 63
Outer Shrine Shinto (*gegū shintō* 外宮神道) ········· 7–8, 26, 34, 35, 36
Ōyamamori no Mikoto 大山守命 ······························· 61

P

philology ··································· 76–8, 80, 91–3, 106, 149

xix

INDEX

Plain of High Heaven (*takamagahara* 高天原) ⋯13–5, 23–5, 32, 57, 59, 163, 250, 254–6, 258, 150, 192, 221
Principle (*ri* 理) ⋯⋯⋯99–102, 104, 126
Pure Land Sect (*jōdo shū* 淨土宗) ⋯⋯28, 33, 163–4, 180, 223

R

rangaku 蘭學 (See Dutch Learning)
realism in Shinto ⋯⋯21–9, 46–8, 151
raise 來世 (world to come) ⋯⋯184
rei 禮 (Rites) ⋯⋯102–3
reiki 靈氣 (spirit air) ⋯⋯184
renchoku 廉直 (honest and upright) ⋯⋯34
Restoration Shinto (*fukko shintō* 復古神道) ⋯⋯4, 171–201, 204, 233–4, 241
ri 理 (See Principle)
Ricci, Matteo ⋯⋯10
Right-doing (*gi* 義) ⋯⋯102, 122, 125
Rōshi gudoku 老子愚讀 (Humble Reading of Lao-tzu) by Watanabe Mōan ⋯⋯108
ryōbu shintō 兩部神道 (See Dual Shinto)

S

Sahohiko 佐保彥 prince ⋯⋯62
Sahohime 佐保姬 Princess ⋯⋯62
Saikoku risshi hen 西國立志編 (Biographies of Self-Made Men in Western Countries) Nakamura Masanao's translation of *Seft Help* by Samuel Smile ⋯⋯223
Saimei 齊明 Empress [594–661] ⋯⋯122, 125
saisei ittchi 祭政一致 (See "unity of worship and administration")
Sandaikō 三大考 (Three Great Ideas) by Hattori Nakatsune ⋯⋯181, 196

xx

INDEX

Sanjō bengi 三條辨疑 (Analysis of the Three Principles of Instruction) by Shimaji Mokurai 213
Sanjō engi 三條演義 (Expatiation on the Three Principles of Instruction) by Tanaka Yoritsune 214
sanjō kyōken 三條教憲 (See Three Principles of Instruction)
Sanjō no guben 三條の愚辨 (Humble Appraisal of the Three Principles of Instruction) by Fukuda Gyōkai 223
Sanjō taii 三條大意 (Outline of the Meaning of the three principles of Instruction) by Yano Harumichi 212
Sasaki Yūchō 佐々木祐筆 213–4
Satō Nobuhiro 佐藤信淵 [1769–1850] 18–21, 174, 190–91, 196, 242
Sawada Gennai 澤田源内 42
Sei 聖 (Sage) 125
seichoku 正直 (correctness and uprightness) 32, 34–42
Seigo okudan 勢語臆斷 (Hypotheses about the *Tale of Ise*) by Keichū 137
sempu 宣布 (Imperial Proclamation) 219
Senge Takatomi 千家尊福 [1845–1917] 206, 212, 217–8
sengoku jidai 戰國時代 (Age of Wars) 97
Senkaku 選格 (Selections of Stylistic Forms) by Tachibana Moribe 186
senkai 仙界 (sylph world) 192
senkyō-shi 宣教使 (See Board of Shinto Missionaries)
semmyō 宣命 (See Imperial Edict)
Semmyō monmoku 宣命問目 (Questions about the Ancient Imperial Edicts) by Motoori Norinaga 134
setsumeigaku 説明學 (exposition study) 74–6, 86
Shaku Nihongi 釋日本紀 (Interpretation of the *Nihongi*) by Urabe Kanekata 171

INDEX

shan-hsin 善心 (virtuous heart) ··58
Shasekishū 沙石集 (Collection of Sand and Stone) ··32, 35
Shibun yōryō 紫文要領 (Essentials of Murasaki's Prose) by Motoori Norinaga ······················138, 170
Shih-ching 詩經 (Book of Poetry) ·······················102, 104
Shimaji Mokurai 島地默雷 [1838–1911] ············213, 225–7, 235
shime 注連 (Sacred Rope) ·······························35
Shin Sect (*shinshū* 眞宗) ························208, 223, 225
Shindai kuketsu 神代口訣 (Oral Traditions of the Age of Kami) by Imbe no Masamichi ·····················7
shingaku 心學 (Heart Learning) ························42
Shingaku benkō 神學辨稿 (Definition of Kami Learning) by Sasaki Yūchō ·····················213
Shingon Sect ··79, 108
shinu 死 (death) ·····································22
shinjin 心神 (heart Kami) ·····························36
shinkai 神界 (Kami world) ·····························192
shinki 神器 (See Imperial Regalia)
Shin Kokinshū 新古今集 (New *Kokinshū*) ··············76, 138, 140–1
shinkoku 神國 (See Kami Country)
Shinkō shinshaku 眞誥新釋 (New Interpretations of the True Message) by Nonoguchi Takamasa ····································196
shinkon 心魂 (heart-soul) ·····························183
shinkyō 神鏡 (sacred mirror) ·····························38
Shinkyō setsugen 眞教說源 (Origin of the True Teaching) by Watanabe Ikarimaro ·····················21
Shinkyō yōshi ryakkai 神教要旨略解 (Brief Explanation of the Essentials of Kami Doctrine) by Konoe Tadafusa and Senge Takatomi ··212
shinri 神理 (Kami Principle) ···························168–9
Shinri 神理 Sect ·······································10
Shinshū 神習 Sect ·······································10

xxii

INDEX

shintai 神體 (See Kami Body)
shintenshukyō 眞天主教 (teachings of the true Lord of Heaven) 21
Shintō dokugo 神道獨語 (Monologue on Shinto) by Ise Sadatake 173
shintō jimukyoku 神道事務局 (See Office of Shinto Affairs)
Shintō yōshō 神道要章 (Essentials of Shinto) by Senge Takatomi 218
Shintō yōshō ben 神道要章辨 (Criticism of the *Shintōyōshō*) by Ochiai Naoaki 218
shirobito 白人 (albinism) 84–5
shitsu-choku 質直 (plainness and uprightness) 33
shizen mui 自然無意 (spontanelty and non-activity) 125
Sho-i kō 書意考 (On the Meaning of Japanese Classics) by Kamo Mabuchi 131
shōjō 清淨 (purity) 32, 46
Shoki shikkai 書紀集解 (Collected Annotations on the *Nihongi*) by Kawamura Hidene 2–3
Shoku Nihongi 續日本紀 (Continuation of the *Nihongi*) 4, 31, 110
shōmyō 正命 (correct life) 38
shōshii 正思惟 (correct thinking) 38
shōshōjin 正精進 (correct devotion) 38
Shōtoku 聖德 Prince [573–621] 33, 35, 38–9, 208
Shrine Shinto (*jinja shintō* 神社神道) 209, 230–44
Shu-ching 書經 (Classic of History) 41, 102
Shūsei 修成 Sect 209
Sincere Heart (*magokoro* 眞心) 115, 158–9, 162
Six Classics 102, 104–5
soboku shugi 素朴主義 (doctrine of plainness) 162
sōbyō 宗廟 (ancestral shrines) 37
Sōgakkō kei 創學校啓 (Petition to Establish a School) by Kada Azumamaro 81
sokoku 祖國 (Father Country) 18, 20

INDEX

soko no kuni 底の國 or *sokotsukuni* 底國
  (bottom country) 31, 183
sonnō shugi 尊皇主義 (See Emperorism)
Sorai Learning (*Soraigaku* 徂徠學) 105, 110 117
souls after death 177, 188, 190, 194, 207,
  215, 217–8, 222–3
Sugiura Kuniakira 杉浦國顯 [1678–1740] 108–9
Suiga Shinto 垂加神道 8–9, 14, 16–7, 43, 89,
  163–4
Suinin 垂仁 Emperor 61
suitō hō 垂統法 (method of handing down
  the rule) 18
Sujin 崇神 Emperor 219–21, 231
sumera mikoto 天皇 (all-ruling Emperor) 61
Sun Goddess (Ama-terasu Ō-mi-kami 天照
  大神) 13–6, 19, 23, 25, 27, 30,
  32, 34–5, 37–41, 57, 61,
  73, 143, 151, 157, 160,
  167, 178, 214, 217–8,
  231, 238–9, 242
Susa-no-o no Mikoto 須佐之男命 12–3, 19, 25, 32, 57, 151,
  178, 188
Suzuki Masayuki 鈴木雅之 [1838–1872] 174, 193–4, 200
Suzunoya tōmon roku 鈴屋答問錄 (Suzunoya
  Dialogues) by Motoori Norinaga 170

T

Tachibana Moribe 橘守部 [1781–1849] 174, 185–90, 195, 200
ta-chun 大君 (Earthly Ruler) 16
taikyoku 太極 (Supreme Ultimate) 99
Taisei 大成 Sect 10
Taisha 大社 Sect 10
Taishakyō 大社教 (Great Shrine Teaching) 219
Ta-jikara-o no Kami 手力男神 (Strong-armed
  Male Kami) 55

INDEX

Takamagahara 高天原 (See Plain of High Heaven)
Taka-mi-musubi 高御産靈 (High Sacred Creating Kami) ············18–9, 55, 143, 155, 175, 194, 213–5
takatsu-kami no wazawai 高津神の災 (disasters from Kami on high) ············30, 59
takatsu-tori no wazawai 高津鳥の災 (disasters from birds on high) ············30, 59
Takenouchi Shikibu 竹内式部 [1712–1767]············17
takusen 託宣 (oracle)············56
Tale of Genji (*Genji monogatari* 源氏物語)············76, 80, 111, 251
Tale of Ise (*Ise monogatari* 伊勢物語)············80, 86, 111
Tamaboko hyakushu 玉鉾百首 (One Hundred Poems on the Way) by Motoori Norinaga············28, 43, 142, 150, 170
Tamadasuki 玉襷 (The Jeweled Sash) by Hirata Atsutane············72
Tama katsuma 玉勝間 (Jeweled Bamboo Basket, by Motoori Norinaga············28, 133, 135, 158, 170, 257
Tama kushige 玉櫛笥 (Jeweled Comb Box) by Motoori Norinaga············28, 142, 160–1, 170
Tamamatsu Misao 玉松楳 [1810–1872]············203
Tama no mihashira 靈の眞柱 (True Pillar of the Soul) by Hirata Atsutane············182, 196, 213
Tama no ogushi 玉小櫛 (Small Jeweled Comb) by Motoori Norinaga············28
Tanaka Yoritsune 田中賴庸 [1836–1897]············214, 217
Taoism············3, 100, 102
tariki 他力 (absolute supernatural power)············164, 180
Tatsu no Kimie, Kamo no Mabuchi toi kotae 龍公美賀茂眞淵問答 (Questions and Answers between Tatsu no Kimie and Kamo Mabuchi)············130
Tayasu Munetake 田安宗武 [1715–1771]············109, 133
teiki 帝紀 (annals of the Emperors)············53

xxv

INDEX

Teikoku kempō gige 帝國憲法義解 (Commentaries on the Constitution of the Empire of Japan) by Itō Hirobumi 228, 235
teiren 貞廉 (faithful and honest) 33
temmei 天命 (See mandate of Heaven)
Temmu 天武 Emperor [622–686] 31, 69, 124
tempon 點本 (Japanese readings) 111
Tenchi yōzō kaiku ron 天地鎔造化育論 (On the Creation and Evolution of Heaven and Farth) by Satō Nobuhiro 191
tendō 天道 (See Way of Heaven)
Tenji 天智 Emperor [626–671] 122, 124
tenjin 天神 (See Heavenly kami)
Tenri 天理 Sect 10, 209, 234
tenson kōrin 天孫降臨 (descent to earth of the Heavenly Grandson) 13
Three Principls of Instruction (*sanjō kyōken* 三條教憲) 206, 208–9, 225–6
Togakushi 戸隠 42
Tōka hiden 東家秘傳 (Secret Traditions of an Eastern House) 171
tokoi 詛 (malediction) 55, 58
tokoyo 常世 (See Yonder World)
Tokoyo Nagatane 常世長胤 218
Tokugawa Ienari 德川家齊 [1773–1841] 132
Tokugawa Ieyasu 德川家康 [1542–1616] 108, 127, 160
Tokugawa Tsunayoshi 德川綱吉 [1646–1709] 98, 101
Tokugawa Yoshimune 德川吉宗 [1684–1751] 101, 107, 109, 132
Toyotomi Hideyoshi 豊臣秀吉 [1536–1598] 97
Toyo-uke no Ō-Kami 豊受大神 7
Tsukisakaki 撞賢木 (Sacred Cleyera Tree) by Suzuki Masayuki 193
Tsukushi 筑紫 13–5, 25, 30
tsumi 罪 (abomination) 30–2, 44, 59, 70, 84–5, 152

INDEX

tsutsushimi 慎み (respect) ……………………………………………43
ubusuna 産土 (tutelary) …………………………………………191

U

Uiyamabumi 初山踏 (First Tramp in the Mountains) by Motoori Norinaga ………72–3, 76, 82, 245, 251, 263
uji 氏 (clan) ………………………………………………………60
ukei 誓 (vow to Kami) …………………………………………32, 56
Udai kondō hisaku 宇内混同秘策 (Secret Policy for Merging the Universe) by Satō Nobuhiro…………20
Ugaya-fukiaezu no Mikoto 鸕鷀草葺不合命 ……………………13
umaru 生る (birth) ………………………………………………22
unity of worship and administration (*saiseiittchi* 祭政一致) ……………………………220, 221, 231–3
Unique Shintō (*yuitsu shintō* 唯一神道) ………………………4, 7
Urabe Kanebumi ト部兼文 …………………………………84, 171
Urabe Kanekata ト部兼方 ………………………………………171
uruwashiki kokoro 麗しき心 (fine heart) ………………………58
usu 失す (vanish) …………………………………………………22

V

Vulgar shintō (*zoku shintō* 俗神道) ……………………4, 10, 16, 29

W

wagaku 和學 (Japanese Learning) …………………………106–7
Waki-iratsuko 稚郎子……………………………………………61
Wamyō ruijū sho 倭名類聚抄 (A Japanese Dictionary) …………………………………………………………112
Wang Shih-chen 王元美………………………………101, 103–4
Warongo 和論語 (Japanese Analects) by Sawada Gennai……………………………………………………12, 43
Watanabe Ikarimaro 渡邊重石丸 [1837–1915]…………21, 29, 215
Watanabe Mōan 渡邊蒙庵 [1687– ?]……………………………108
Watarai Nobuyoshi 度會延佳 [1615–1690]………………8, 84, 172

INDEX

Way of Former Kings (*sen-ō no michi* 先王之道) ············102–3, 128
Way of Heaven (*tendō* 天道) ·················4, 100, 105, 123, 125
Wayō shinden 和洋神傳 (Divine Myths in Japan and the West) by Sasaki Yūchō ·············213

Y

Yamaga Sokō 山鹿素行 [1622–1685] ····················88
Yamanoe no Okura 山上憶良 ·······················80
Yamato-e School ·····························46
Yamatogokoro 大和心 (spirit of ancient Japan) ·································44
Yamato-hime no Mikoto 倭姫命 ····················36
Yamato Takeru no Mikoto 日本武尊 ··················63
Yamazaki Ansai 山崎闇斎 [1618–1682] ·········8–9, 16, 47, 84, 89, 98, 172
Yamamuro 山室 ·····························185
Yano Harumichi 矢野玄道 [1823–1887] ·······173, 190–1, 203–4, 212, 215–6
Yao and Shun 堯舜 ·······················102, 123, 129
Yaso no kumade 八十隈手 (Eighty Road-Windings) by Yano Harumichi ··················191–2, 215
Yin and Yang (*inyō* 陰陽) ·····················14, 177
yōkikai 妖氣界 (ghost world) ·····················192
yōmei gaku 陽明學 (Yang-ming School) ···············98, 101
Yomi 豫美 (nether land) ···········15, 23, 30–1, 57, 59, 151, 167, 177–9, 182–5, 189–90, 191–2, 195–6, 200, 215–6, 221
Yomi kōshō 豫美考證 (Study of *Yomi*) ··············214–5
Yonder World (*tokoyo* 常世) ··················23, 59, 70
yoshi 善 (good) ·························22, 58, 155
Yoshida Kanetomo 吉田兼俱 [1435–1511] ·················7
Yoshida Shinto 吉田神道 ·························7
Yoshimi Yukikazu 吉見幸和 [1673–1761] ···············173
yūgen 幽現 (concealed and the revealed) ··············168

INDEX

yuima kyō 維摩經 (Vimalakîrti Sutra) ················33
yuitsu shintō 唯一神道 (See Unique Shinto)
yūkai 幽界 (See concealed world)
yūmei 幽冥 (See concealed and mysterious)
yumeura 夢占 (interpretation of dreams) ················56
Yūryaku 雄略 Emperor ················67–8
yūsokugaku 有職學 (antiquarian study) ················23

Z

zoku shintō 俗神道 (See Vulgar Shintō)
Zoku Shintō taii 俗神道大意 (Outline of Vulgar Shintō) by Hirata Atsutane ················4